Creating Medieval Cairo

Creating Medieval Cairo

Empire, Religion, and Architectural Preservation in Nineteenth-Century Egypt

Paula Sanders

The American University in Cairo Press
Cairo New York

The American University in Cairo Press
113 Sharia Kasr el Aini, Cairo, Egypt
420 Fifth Avenue, New York, NY 10018
www.aucpress.com

Part of Chapter 1 appeared previously as "The Victorian Invention of Medieval Cairo: A Case Study of Medievalism and the Construction of the East," in *Middle East Studies Association Bulletin* 37, no. 2 (December 2003): 179–98. Part of Chapter 4 appeared previously as "The Contest over Context: Fatimid Cairo in the Twentieth Century," in Irene A. Bierman, ed., *Text and Context in Islamic Societies: Sixteenth Giorgio Levi Della Vida Conference Papers* (Reading, UK: Ithaca Press, 2003), 131–54.

Dar el Kutub No. 3131/07
ISBN 978 977 416 095 0

Dar el Kutub Cataloging-in-Publication Data

Sanders, Paula
Creating Medieval Cairo: Empire, Religion, and Architectural Preservation in Nineteenth-Century Egypt / Paula Sanders.—Cairo: The American University in Cairo Press, 2008
p. cm.
ISBN 977 416 095 9
1. Egypt—history—19th century I. Title
962.03

1 2 3 4 5 6 12 11 10 09 08

Designed by Andrea El-Akshar
Printed in Egypt

For Michael

Contents

Illustrations

Unless otherwise indicated, all illustrations are from the author's collection.

Acknowledgments

It is a pleasure to acknowledge the help that made it possible to complete this book. I have benefited from the generosity of many colleagues who contributed in various ways to my research and thinking about this project: Robert Patten, Helena Michie, Thad Logan, and Marty Wiener fielded numerous questions about Victorian culture and history; Carl Caldwell, Carol Quillen, Shirine Hamadeh, Lynne Huffer, Susan Lurie, Helena Michie, Daniel Sherman, Allison Sneider, and Betty Joseph all read chapters at various junctures.

At a very early stage of this project, I was part of a group of scholars discussing nineteenth-century Cairene architectural heritage and history: Irene Bierman, Donald Preziosi, Nezar AlSayyad, Nasser Rabbat, and Nairy Hampikian. Special thanks go to Irene Bierman for organizing this group. I thank my writing group at the National Humanities Center in 2002–2003 for their critiques of parts of the book: Kathryn Burns, Ginger Frost, Grace Hale, Susan Hirsch, Teresita Martinez, Joanne Rappaport, Moshe Sluhovsky, Erin Smith, Faith Smith, and Helen Solterer. The faculty workshop of Rice's Boniuk Center for the Study and Advancement of Religious Tolerance provided an opportunity to present Chapter 2 to colleagues. A conference and graduate workshop organized by Daniel Sherman, director of the Center for 21st Century Studies at the University of Wisconsin, Milwaukee provided a valuable opportunity to meet with colleagues with similar interests. A month spent at the École des Hautes Études en Sciences Sociales in 2001 allowed me to present my work to a truly international community of scholars and to conduct research in Paris. I thank my hosts, Jocelyne Dakhlia and Lucette Valensi, for this invaluable opportunity. My year at the National Humanities Center in 2002–2003 was undoubtedly the happiest of my professional life. I thank all of the NHC staff for the genuinely warm and supportive environment, as well as for concrete assistance in pursuing my research and writing.

My first forays into the study of architectural preservation in Cairo were guided by Alaa El-Habashi, W. Brown Morton III, and Nairy Hampikian. I am more grateful to them than I can properly express, and can only hope that this book will not annoy them too much. I thank Chip Vincent of the American Research Center in Egypt—Egyptian Antiquities Project for providing so many opportunities to visit monuments undergoing conservation. Nicholas Warner was generous with both his expertise and his personal collection of maps and photographs. I am grateful to the entire staff of the American Research Center in Egypt's Cairo office, and especially Mrs. Amira Khattab.

I have been fortunate to receive substantial institutional support for this project. I received fellowship support from the American Research Center in Egypt (1995–1996), the National Humanities Center (2002–2003), and the National Endowment of the Humanities (2003). At Rice, Deans Judith Brown, Gale Stokes, and Gary Wihl provided research support. Three chairs of the History Department—Jack Zammito, Carl Caldwell, and Marty Wiener—provided crucial support at various stages of the project. Rice's Center for the Study of Cultures provided a semester of teaching release during which I began work on Chapter 3.

I am grateful to the staff of the institutions where I conducted research: ICCROM (International Centre for the Study of the Preservation and Restoration of Cultural Property) in Rome; ICOMOS (International Council on Monuments and Sites) in Paris; and the American Academy in Rome for their help and hospitality. I owe special thanks to M. Lesley Wilkins (now of the Harvard Law School Library), former director of the Rare Books and Special Collections Library of the American University in Cairo; Eliza Robertson, Betsy Dain, and Jean

Houston of the National Humanities Center; Francine Arizmendez and Angela Brown of Interlibrary services at Rice University's Fondren Library; Lisa Spiro of Rice's Digital Media Center; Paula Platt and Rachel Zepeda of the Rice History Department.

Jere Bacharach, Tanya Dunlap, Christina Huemer, Michael Maas, Ussama Makdisi, David Nirenberg, Peter Rockwell, Robert Tignor, and Marty Wiener all read the entire manuscript and made invaluable comments. I deeply appreciate their serious and incisive critiques, not all of which I was wise enough to accept. I also thank the anonymous reviewers of the manuscript for their suggestions and corrections.

Many others have supported and encouraged this project over the years and have been cherished conversation partners as I made my way through unfamiliar terrain: Peter Brown, Judy Coffin, Eduardo Douglas, Willy Forbath, Matthias Henze, Werner Kelber, Susan Lurie, Ussama Makdisi, David Nirenberg, István Ormos, Carol Quillen, and Daniel Sherman. Friends and family provided unfailing support: Cary Cavness, Franco and Pina Sgariglia, Ira Gruber, Ken Kennedy, Jane Dailey, Paul Lerner, Shelly and Michael Nemeth, Marilyn Sanders, Peter Adomeit, Marvin and Vicki Sanders, Mike Heymann, Flora Sanders, Sue and Mel Melnick. I owe special thanks to my mother, Lilian Kranitz, whose support I have always been able to take for granted.

It has been pure pleasure to work with my editors, Chip Rossetti and Nadia Naqib, and the production staff of the American University in Cairo Press. Their professionalism is unparalleled in my experience with university presses.

No one has contributed more to this project than Michael Maas. He read every chapter in every incarnation, the bits and pieces that became parts of chapters or didn't, and the entire book in every one of its versions. The perfect combination of editor, friend, and companion, he was brave enough to tell me when I didn't have it right (especially when the chapter was presented with the advance review, "I think I've got it this time") and generous enough to shower me with praise when I did. He bought me ice cream or gelato—depending upon the continent—in both consolation and celebration. Most importantly, he encouraged me to keep rewriting until I actually produced a book that resembled the one that existed in my imagination. For all this, and so much more, I thank him.

Introduction

Frame Tales

The story of conservation in Cairo has been told in different ways. In the conventional version, conservation began in the middle of the nineteenth century, when European engineers, architects, and travelers began to clamor for the rescue of Egypt's dilapidated Arab architecture. The scholars who tell this story focus on the history of the Comité de Conservation des Monuments de l'Art Arabe, the commission founded in 1881 by Khedive Tawfiq and charged with the task of preserving Islamic monuments in Egypt. Another approach treats Egypt as a case study in orientalism, an example of Europeans' imaginative construction of the Orient. In this scenario, the presentation of Egypt's past—whether pharaonic or Islamic—is a thoroughly European enterprise.[1] Donald M. Reid's recent *Whose Pharaohs? Archaeology, Museums, and Egyptian National Identity from Napoleon to World War I* (2002) has changed the direction of our inquiries. Taking nationalism as his framework, he brings Egyptians into the story of conservation for the first time.[2] He also calls on historians to account for the development of the Comité's preservation program and not to take it for granted.[3] Reid's work challenges us to imagine other frameworks in which the history of Cairo and its monuments might be told.

My book builds on all of these approaches, but tells a different story about conservation in Cairo. In my story, what we call Medieval Cairo was created in the nineteenth century. Thus, throughout this book, I use the term 'Medieval Cairo' to refer to this nineteenth-century construct and *not* to Cairo as it was in the Middle Ages.

The first half of this book tells the story of Medieval Cairo in two frames: empire and religion. Chapter 1, "Constructing Medieval Cairo in the Nineteenth Century," follows Reid's attention to politics and culture, but adds two new elements to the story: the Anglo-Indian and Ottoman imperial contexts. While there is considerable discussion in the historical literature of the British quasi-colonial presence in Egypt, the Anglo-Indian context and its implications for the history of Egypt have received little or no attention. Only two brief articles, both published more than a quarter of a century ago, addressed the impact of the British Indian experience for the administration of Egypt. Even Roger Owen's recent biography of Lord Cromer, consul general of Egypt from 1883 to 1907, does not discuss in any detail the impact of Cromer's Anglo-Indian experience on his work in Egypt.[4] Studies of Egypt's Islamic architectural heritage or the emergence of its cultural institutions in the British period do not take the Anglo-Indian experience into account. In short, Egypt has been segregated from the larger history of British imperial practice.

Egypt has also been excluded from the writing of Ottoman history, just as the Ottoman period has often been neglected or minimized in accounts of Egyptian history.[5] Egypt's Ottoman years had a profound impact on its culture, and many features of Egyptian social, cultural, and religious life that have long been considered 'medieval' are actually rooted in Ottoman practices.[6] Even when discussed in works on Egypt's architecture, Ottoman contributions have generally been treated as local phenomena and not as part of the broad culture of competing imperialisms that characterized the later nineteenth century.[7]

Chapter 1 considers how all these elements interacted to shape the way the Comité, the British government in Cairo, European travelers, and Egyptians perceived Arab architecture in Cairo. Building upon the work of Reid and of Alaa El-Habashi, whose unpublished dissertation provides a detailed internal history of the Comité,[8] I explore how different pasts were configured in imperial and local settings, where they overlapped and diverged, and how architecture played a role in them. Just as Reid does not take for granted that preservation should have been the predominant practice in the nineteenth century, I do not take it as given that the old buildings the Comité chose to preserve should have been largely Mamluk or that what emerged as canonical Medieval Cairo should have a Mamluk feel and appearance. One goal of Chapter 1, then, is to account for the identification of the medieval in Cairo with the Mamluk period. To address this problem, I discuss the long history of local conservation under the aegis of *waqf* (pious endowment), as well as Ottoman and Anglo-Indian architectural practice. The Comité's program to survey, record, and preserve old monuments, and the creation of usable historic pasts (to borrow Thomas Metcalf's phrase) expressed through architecture,[9] had preludes in both the Ottoman and British empires. Ottoman preservation took place in Istanbul and the provinces throughout the Tanzimat period (1839–76), and was tied to programs of reform, modernization, and to the official representation of a modern Islamic state. The British constructed national pasts in India partly by means of the work of the Archaeological Survey of India.

My discussion of these imperial contexts of conservation and their interaction with the history of local conservation shows that there is no single or simple cause for the Comité's blindness to Ottoman practices or its disdain for Ottoman architecture. The identification of the medieval in Cairo with Mamluk architecture had many roots. I finish this chapter by arguing that British interest in preserving Arab art is best considered within the broader imperial context of British interests in India.

Chapter 1 also argues that the category 'medieval' had many meanings that were sometimes contradictory. These meanings often served independent Egyptian and Ottoman political agendas that did not present Egypt as backward. But in one arena—that of religion— the meaning of the medieval did reflect asymmetries of power with respect to Europe that construed Egyptians as deficient and largely incapable of change.

The story of architectural preservation has also been isolated from the history of the city's religious life in the nineteenth century. Despite the predominance of religious buildings in the Comité's work, the historiography of preservation has asked few, if any, questions about the character of religious life in Cairo in the later nineteenth century, the role of old religious buildings in local religious life, or the role of architecture in debates and discussions about religion. Why did the Comité exclude contemporary religious practice from their deliberations? What did different Egyptian constituencies have to say about religious architecture and its preservation? Many Egyptian officials and dignitaries were silent on the issue of preservation. What should we make of their silences? Others made policy decisions that frustrated the efforts of the Comité. How should we understand their actions? I address these questions by discussing conservation within the framework of nineteenth-century religious practice.

Chapter 2, "Islam for the Modern World: Medieval Cairo between Egyptian Reformers and British Critics," discusses the ways in which different ideas about Islam and its characteristics as a religion influenced attitudes toward conservation in Cairo. In the late nineteenth century, many Azhar-educated Egyptians, particularly the followers of Muhammad 'Abduh and Rashid Rida, were attempting to create a modern Islam through a wide-ranging program of reform *(islah)*. They believed that funds were better spent on improving mosque personnel than on shoring up old buildings. 'Ali Mubarak, the minister of public works, was willing to tear down old buildings in order to pursue his program of urban modernization. Mubarak's ideas about Islam as a living tradition made the trade-off between antique mosques and wide, modern streets a reasonable one because in his view nothing of importance in contemporary religious life was being sacrificed. While these Egyptians were articulating a vision of a modern Islam, the British—who viewed Islam as stagnant and incapable of reform—were pursuing an aggressive program to conserve Arab architecture that in visual terms represented Islam as medieval.

Chapters 1 and 2 show how reframing the story of conservation allows for a new understanding of Medieval Cairo as a creation of the nineteenth century. Chapters 3 and 4 lay out the questions that arise from this understanding of Medieval Cairo's historically contingent character. Why was this version of Medieval Cairo persuasive in its own time? Why does its persuasive power remain intact more than a century after its creation? What does the success of Medieval Cairo mean for us in the twenty-first century? I address these questions by showing how Medieval Cairo was constructed and maintained through a series of amalgamations that blurred the distinction between old and new. These amalgamations have sustained an unacknowledged colonial legacy that persists in contemporary World Heritage ideology and practice.

Chapter 3, "Cairo of the *Arabian Nights*," weaves together two stories that are ordinarily considered as separate, but which, when told together, highlight the historical contingency central to my account. Looking at the *Arabian Nights* and Medieval Cairo in direct relation to one another sheds light on how they were produced and regarded by readers, viewers, and restorers. I argue in this chapter that Medieval Cairo and the *Arabian Nights* are themselves amalgamations of old and new. Through a close reading of a number of texts and images, I show how these amalgamations were constructed and how they provided fertile interpretive terrain for nineteenth- and twentieth-century European and Egyptian audiences. Chapter 3 demonstrates some of the specific mechanisms through which canonical texts, buildings, or vistas were created at a particular moment and then canonized, erasing the distinctions among their discrete elements.

Chapter 4, "Keeping Cairo Medieval: World Heritage and the Debate over Fatimid Monuments," reveals the nineteenth century's continuing legacy by analyzing one of the most heated controversies over interventions in Medieval Cairo today, namely, the dispute over the Bohra restorations of monuments established in the Fatimid period (969–1171).The Bohras are Ismaili Shi'ites who trace their spiritual lineage to the Fatimids but whose communal roots lie in the Indian subcontinent. Their restorations of Fatimid monuments have been categorically condemned by the World Heritage preservation community, who charge the Bohras with violating international conservation standards. The World Heritage community insists, like its nineteenth-century predecessors, on a medieval appearance and framework for the monuments of Cairo. The Bohra restorations, on the other hand, do not. But this is not merely a contemporary dispute between competing conservation philosophies and practices; it is also a debate over competing notions of historical and cultural authenticity. I argue that these debates can only be understood in the context of the colonially produced relationship between Egypt and India in the nineteenth century.[10] The competing positions that the Bohras and the World Heritage community espouse both belong to the legacy of British colonialism in the East, although they have ended up advocating remarkably different things.[11]

General Background

Egypt in the Nineteenth Century

Egypt was formally a province of the Ottoman Empire throughout the nineteenth century. Its administration had been in the hands, since the Ottoman conquest of 1516–17, of a long series of governors who generally carried out the policies, and acted primarily in the interests of, the central Ottoman government. By the eighteenth century, however, the central Ottoman state was distracted by its wars with European powers, and its effective grip on Egypt had loosened. During the eighteenth century, the Circassian Mamluk beys were therefore able to reassert their influence and exercised effective control over the country. Thus, near the end of the century, Egypt had become largely autonomous.

In 1798 Napoleon invaded Egypt and occupied the country until 1801. The French motivations for the invasion (conventionally referred to as the Expedition) recognized a key fact of Egypt's strategic geographical location: it stood at the intersection of two vast, overlapping commercial networks, constituting the land link between the Mediterranean Sea and the Indian Ocean. The French hoped, by controlling Egypt, to disrupt Britain's communications with India. Napoleon also planned to colonize Egypt and thereby insure a steady supply of grain to France.

The French occupation lasted a mere three years, troubled from its earliest days by a British blockade. In spite of its failure from a military and strategic point of view, it was a success in another respect, the production of the *Description de l'Egypte*, and the consequent rapid development of European knowledge of Egypt and the Orient. The French invasion also had other, unexpected, consequences at the local level. In the aftermath of the occupation, the local religious elites, the *ulama*, saw that the primary advantage of continued Mamluk power—protecting Egypt from foreign invasion—no longer existed. An ambitious Albanian Ottoman official, Muhammad 'Ali (Mehmet 'Ali), gained the trust of the local elites, consolidated his troops, and established himself as an essentially independent ruler of Egypt in 1805. While Egypt continued to be formally a part of the Ottoman Empire until the end of the First World War, it would never again be as firmly tied to the central Ottoman government as it had been in the previous three centuries.

Muhammad 'Ali is credited with introducing the vast reforms that began Egypt on its path to modernization. Most of these reforms were carried out first on his army, but they included also radical changes in education, agricultural policy, industrialization, taxation, and the management and distribution of funds from religious endowments, which had been for close to a millennium the major source of revenues for the construction of what we would call public buildings: mosques, madrasas, Sufi institutions, *kuttab*s (roughly, religious elementary schools), fountains, shrines devoted to saints, and hospitals.

In 1841, Muhammad 'Ali extracted from the Ottoman sultan an edict establishing his dynastic prerogatives as Egypt's governor. Even before this formal recognition of Muhmmad 'Ali's virtual autonomy, he had taken to calling himself by the Persian title *khedive*. In the series of concessions that the Ottoman sultan made to him in this period, the title became official, and Muhammad 'Ali and his successors bore the title until the end of formal Ottoman sovereignty, when Egypt's rulers assumed the title of king, and the house of Muhammad 'Ali continued to reign until the 1952 Revolution.

From the middle of the nineteenth century, the khedives pursued modernizing and, to a certain extent, westernizing policies in the army and among the elites. Many of the most important reforms were economic. Egypt's economy had suffered during the late eighteenth and early nineteenth centuries as the result of drought, a shockingly low population for an agricultural country, widespread corruption among tax collectors resulting in abuse of the peasantry and decreased revenues for the government, and the added expenses of building new state institutions. Along with these changes came also a new emphasis on exporting raw materials, especially cotton, thus creating the need for dramatic changes in Egypt's irrigation system and improvements in transportation. Under both Muhammad 'Ali and his immediate successors, the peasants *(fellahin)* were conscripted through a corvée system that forced them to provide labor for public works projects—especially dredging new canals and building barrages—and often took them far away from their own homes and their crops.

In the 1860s, the American Civil War helped jumpstart Egypt's economy by creating a huge demand for Egyptian cotton in the wake of the Union's blockade of the Confederacy's Atlantic ports. Suddenly, British textile mills had to look elsewhere for raw materials, and they found them in Egypt, where a high-quality variety of long-staple cotton had been cultivated since the reign of Muhammad 'Ali. The sudden increase in demand brought immense amounts of money into Egypt and into the coffers of the khedives.

In 1854, Khedive Sa'id (r. 1854–63) authorized what was to become Egypt's greatest strategic and economic resource: the cutting of a canal through Suez, allowing shipping to move directly from the Mediterranean to the Red Sea, and then on to the Indian Ocean. Such a canal would reduce shipping time and costs dramatically, since sailing around the Cape of Good Hope would no longer be necessary for the sea route to India from Europe. French investors were the major force behind the scheme, which was soundly discouraged by the British, who considered that a canal at Suez would compromise their hitherto unrivaled control of the seas. But the plan went ahead under the direction of the French engineer de Lesseps, and the Suez Canal finally opened in 1869. Khedive Ismail (r. 1863–79) undertook a series of very expensive projects that had as their primary goal the modernization of Egypt on a largely European model. Ismail assumed enormous new debts in order to finance these projects for public works and educational reform as well as his personal, lavish lifestyle. Even the revenues generated by the cotton trade could not keep pace, particularly after the re-establishment of American cotton exports after the end of the Civil War. By the 1870s, he was forced to sell most of his shares in the Canal to European creditors, and Egypt's plunge into economic insecurity and insolvency was underway. As they had earlier in the century in the wake of Ottoman debt, Europe's governments intervened on behalf of Egypt's creditors, imposing a series of draconian fiscal measures that included installing advisors in the Egyptian ministries to supervise the implementation of the mandated economic policy.

Throughout the late 1870s, Egypt struggled to meet its payments on the staggering debt that it had accumulated, but in 1876, Ismail announced the suspension of debt service payments. He was compelled to agree to the formation of the Caisse de la Dette Publique (Public Debt Commission) to funnel money from the Egyptian government to its British, French, Italian, and Austrian creditors.[12] Evelyn Baring (later Lord Cromer) came to Egypt in 1877 as the British representative to the Caisse and spent most of the next few years working in Cairo, caught up in the midst of debates about how much discretion the Egyptian government should have in determining how to use its scarce revenues, how much of any surplus should go to servicing the debt or investing in the development of the country, and a variety of related questions.[13] During these years, Khedive Ismail was deposed by the Ottoman government (under pressure from the European creditors) and his son Tawfiq was installed.

Tawfiq was understandably concerned both to maintain a certain autonomy and to placate his European creditors. But he was a weak ruler, and his regime was troubled by Egypt's astronomical debt (consolidated to roughly £98 million, requiring more than 60 percent of Egypt's revenues to meet the annual payment) and by increasingly disaffected Egyptian elites, who had emerged over the course of the nineteenth century. This largely new indigenous elite had arisen alongside the long-standing Ottoman–Circassian, Turkish-speaking elite, which until the middle of the nineteenth century had a full monopoly on access to positions in the military and civil administrations. By the last quarter of the nineteenth century, there was a small but significant indigenous, Arabic-speaking elite, many of whom were of peasant *(fellah)* origins. In 1881, under pressure from the old Ottoman–Circassian military elite, Khedive Tawfiq proposed a law that would prohibit Egyptians of peasant origin from becoming officers. Colonel Ahmad 'Urabi and a cadre of officers vehemently protested the proposed law. Their protest had more support from indigenous officers and landed notables than the khedive had imagined, and the plan was abandoned. Soon thereafter, 'Urabi's movement—memorialized in the slogan "Egypt for the Egyptians"—picked up steam and a coalition emerged to protest both European intervention in Egypt's financial affairs and the khedive's autocratic powers. These events, and those that followed them, are referred to by historians as the 'Urabi Revolution. In order to prevent a massive uprising, the khedive was forced to appoint 'Urabi as Minister of War in 1882. 'Urabi immediately began to make plans to form a national assembly that would wrest control of Egypt's finances and administration from the hands of Europeans. Tawfiq floundered and had to ask for British assistance. Although there was some debate about whether or not to take military action, the British moved quickly to a position where intervention was necessary in order to protect their strategic and economic interests in the Suez Canal. In June 1882, the British commander of the fleet off the port of Alexandria bombarded the city, and for the next few months, Egypt's major port of entry was blockaded. In September of the same year, the British forces defeated 'Urabi at the Battle of Tell al-Kebir, captured 'Urabi, and occupied the country.

England's military occupation was, in theory, supposed to last only long enough to restore order and to return the khedive to effective power. There were significant disagreements among British officials about the anticipated length and extent of the occupation, and about the advisability of the occupation given its political and economic costs, one of which was England's relationship with the Ottoman Empire. By 1885, Lord Salisbury had concluded that Egypt, rather than the Ottoman Empire, should be the cornerstone of England's policy in the Middle East. Furthermore, he determined that British interests needed to be protected not only against the rising tide of Arab nationalism in the aftermath of the 'Urabi revolt, but also against the possibility of a French occupation.[14] What had begun as a European presence in response to Egypt's fiscal insolvency (which had been created to a very large extent by the European creditors who imposed exorbitant interest rates and a variety of hidden charges and fees) resulted in a military presence that would last until 1956.

The Lessons of India: Fiscal Discipline and the Advancement of 'Oriental' Peoples

By the time the British established their quasi-colonial government in Cairo in 1882, they had been masters over India for well over a century. In India, they had a clearly articulated imperial mission of modernization and a set of developing ideas about what constituted sound colonial governance. The institutions and practices that they experimented with in India also included archaeology, imperial architecture, and preservation.[15]

The major architect of British policy in Egypt for the first twenty years after the occupation was Evelyn Baring, who was Consul General from 1883–1907. Cromer's early career, after his military days, had been spent in India, and he brought to Egypt a set of assumptions about governance and an ideological perspective that were formed in India and in which India never ceased to remain central.[16] Cromer was convinced that the identifiable causes for Egypt's financial problems were to be found in the defects of Ismail as an oriental ruler, and he was equally convinced that the solution to Egypt's problems was in policies that had been proven in India. Like other Anglo-Indian officials, he found striking similarities between India and other British holdings, even the ones that were not formal colonies. The reason for this was not only their entrenched orientalism,[17] but also their propensity to find explanations for historical processes in big theories and the conviction "among Victorian statesmen in the early 1880s of imagining that the problems of government were very much alike everywhere."[18] Cromer's ideas were articulated generally in essays such as "The Government of Subject Races," as well as in the formulation of very specific policies. He believed that the advancement of oriental nations could not be accomplished by transplanting European institutions, which were a product of a specifically European environment, to the East.[19] Colonial administrators believed they had to identify indigenous principles of governance in order to effect reforms; they believed that a single set of laws and policies governed the advancement of all oriental nations.[20]

Advancement, by which the British meant modernization under European tutelage,[21] was rooted first in sound fiscal policy, and in this regard Cromer's program for Egypt was built on a decisively Indian plan: low taxes, free trade, and careful pruning of expenditures.[22] From 1887 to 1894, additional 'fiscal relief' was sought by abolishing the corvée. So fundamental was tax relief to the empire that Cromer often proclaimed "low taxation is the panacea for British rule in India,"[23] and it was also his motto for Egypt. In addition to rigorous fiscal discipline, Cromer also believed (again, based largely on his experiences in India) in the centrality of public works to the overall project of fiscal solvency. In Egypt as in India, large public works projects like railways and irrigation canals were central to the program for advancement.[24]

European Medievalism and Debates over Preservation and Restoration

The nineteenth century was a heydey of preservationism in Europe, where individuals, private societies, and governments undertook the work of conserving and often restoring ancient and medieval buildings as they tried to reclaim a distant and increasingly romanticized past in their progressively industrialized world.[25] From as early as 1837, France had established its Commission of Historic Monuments, whose chief inspector, Prosper Mérimée, had lobbied for it along with Victor Hugo. The French and British engaged in passionate debates about *what* they should preserve and *how* they should preserve it, and their decisions generally fell into the broad categories of interventionist and non-interventionist.[26]

The French embraced restoration as their conventional practice, following the lead of Eugène-Emmanuel Viollet-le-Duc, who described it in this most famous pronouncement: "To restore a building is not to preserve it, to repair, or rebuild it; it is to reinstate it in a condition of completeness which could never have existed at any given time." Architects would determine what this "complete condition" had been (or should have been) by understanding the original context of the building (its time and place). Restoration depended heavily upon stylistic classifications that were, in the nineteenth century, closely connected to racial and linguistic classifications. And restoration was, by definition, modern: "*Le mot et la chose sont modernes*" ('The term and the thing are modern').[27]

Some English architects pursued restoration programs on the model of Viollet-le-Duc, particularly the members of the Cambridge Camden Society, founded in 1839 for the study of ecclesiology and to promote Catholic ritual, proper church building, and knowledgeable restoration. The Society's mouthpiece, *The Ecclesiologist*, announced its principles in the first issue: "We must, whether from existing evidence or from supposition, recover the original scheme of the edifice as conceived by the first builder . . . to revive the original appearance . . . lost by decay, accident or ill-judged alteration . . . ."[28] Viollet-le-Duc's philosophy of restoration, and that of many of his contemporaries and successors, did not stand unchallenged. William Morris and John Ruskin preached the competing philosophy of conservation and formed the Society for the Protection of Ancient Buildings (SPAB), which publicly denounced the work of the restorationists and advocated stabilization of buildings in their current state.[29]

The announcement of the establishment of the SPAB in 1877 characterized restoration as "a strange and most fatal idea, which by its very name implies that it is possible to strip from a building this, that, and the other parts of its history, . . . and then to stay the hand at some arbitrary point, and leave it still historical, living, and even as it once was."[30] By the end of the nineteenth century, the strong profile of the Society, combined with an equally strong measure of British anti-papism, had resolved the issues in England largely in favor of the conservationists, whose position was adopted by the government and seems also to have prevailed abroad.

Morris also roundly criticized Victorian medievalism's penchant for choosing one 'ideal' time and freezing a monument in that moment, arguing instead that one must respect *all* historical changes in buildings. The discussions among those interested in Egypt's Arab art, and the decisions made by various members of the Comité about how to conserve, repair, or restore particular buildings, all echo the ongoing debates in Europe about these matters. In discussions about preservation in Egypt, two major figures, E.T. Rogers and Frank Dillon, espoused a preservation philosophy that was decidedly anti-restoration and very much in keeping with Morris and Ruskin's philosophies of preservation.[31] Dillon aired his views publicly in a letter to *The Times* in 1884: "The Society for the Preservation of Ancient Buildings, to which the [Commission for the

Preservation of Arab Art] is affiliated, has already . . . written to the president of the commission, Mahomed Zeki Pasha, congratulating him upon the work achieved, only venturing to warn him against excess zeal in the matter of restoration—a failing which they freely acknowledge has to be battled with here and elsewhere in Europe."[32]

The Frenchman Arthur Rhoné, on the other hand, argued for adopting some of Viollet-le-Duc's techniques, particularly a commitment to understand local building practices. Rhoné was very disturbed by what he considered to be the negative influence of Italian architects and builders, who dominated much of Cairo's building industry in the latter half of the nineteenth century, and he recoiled at the introduction of an "Italian Gothic style" into Cairene architecture. In making his argument, he pointed to two other structures that were (and remain today) important centers of religious life in Cairo, the mosque of al-Husayn and the mosque of Sayyida Zaynab (Figure 1). He further criticized the work done on other monuments as revealing an ignorance of the historical period in which they were first built.[33] Rhoné's critique of preservation in Cairo in the late nineteenth-century borrowed elements of both Viollet-le-Duc's philosophy of restoration—especially the need to understand fully the context in which a monument had first been built—and Morris's principle that all periods of a building must be respected and represented. The early Comité did not adhere fully to either of those standards. A retrospective on preservation in Cairo published in *The Times* in 1896 gives evidence of these debates when pronouncing a "decided upward course of development" in the Comité's activities: "Under Franz Pasha many useful repairs and temporary proppings were carried out, but few attempts were made at taking an entire monument thoroughly in hand. It was just as well that this was so, for, with all his technical accomplishments and well-proved interest in Saracenic art, Franz Pasha was not happy in his few restorations; witness the unfortunate tomb-mosque of al-Ghuri and the incongruous columns of the mosque of al-Mu'ayyad, on which to comment were unkind. Still, a great deal of useful preservation was begun under his *régime*, and the way was prepared for a more scientific system."[34]

In Cairo, the Comité's survey recorded those monuments deemed suitable for preservation and, within its limited financial resources, it did its best to preserve the original fabric of the monuments. Its resources were so limited that it could often do nothing more than document the monument in its current state with plans, elevations, photographs, and recording of inscriptions. In following this course, the Comité adhered faithfully to its principle of preservation, not restoration. The vast majority of the Comité's work was, in fact, to consolidate monuments to prevent further decay, not to restore.

The Comité's long-time chief architect, Max Herz Bey, was committed also to the principle of preservation. Herz Bey was, in this sense, different from his predecessor, Julius Franz Pasha, the Comité's first chief architect. According to information from his contemporaries, Herz Bey "never employed elements in restoration whose prior existence was not verifiable" and "his method involved discovering the original form and condition of each architectural monument, and restoring only those elements on which reliable data was available."[35] Even so, he was willing to completely restore buildings under certain circumstances, according to Stanley Lane-Poole:

> There is a well-founded prejudice in artistic and archaeological circles against restoration of any and every description; but I believe that an examination of some of the recent restorations carried out by Herz Bey would remove these natural and generally just apprehensions. This architect's principle, as he explained it to me, appears sound and reasonable. It is this. No unique monument (e.g., the mosque of Ibn-Tulun) or monument belonging to an architectural period of which there are very few examples (e.g., the Fatimid Mosques), must on any account be restored; preservation is the only possible treatment for such cases, and nothing more must be done than is absolutely necessary for the stability of the building, and its security from weather and other injury. But when there are numerous mosques of the same period, nearly resembling one another in style, and often even in detail of ornament . . . then a few may safely be selected for complete restoration at all points, so as to present as nearly as possible their original appearance, as when first opened for public worship.[36]

Lane-Poole advocated this principle of preservation in his report to Lord Cromer in 1896, which was appended to the Consul General's annual report to Parliament, as well as translated into French and published in the Comité minutes.[37] This approach was described by Alajos Hauszmann, Herz Bey's former professor in Budapest, as an "archaeological viewpoint."[38] Herz's qualifications, his knowledge of al-Maqrizi's topography ("he knows his Makrizy—that Egyptian Camden—almost by heart") and his "archaeological conscience" ("he refuses to falsify an historical monument, and when he restores it is only after taking great pains to satisfy himself that he is really reproducing the original work") were lauded in the 1896 *Times* article.

All accounts, and the physical evidence itself, support the conclusion that the Comité under Herz Bey's leadership adhered to the principle of conservation as it was understood in the late nineteenth century. A contemporary account by Achille Patricolo, Herz Bey's deputy, numbered at nearly three hundred the monuments that had received the Comité's attention, of which only about twenty had been restored. Recent historical work places the number of preservation projects at 265, including complete restorations of only eleven buildings.[39] According to István Ormos, on the rare occasions when Herz did choose to restore a monument, it was nearly always Mamluk, and "his purpose was to achieve a stylistically pure monument by removing later additions and modifications. These later additions generally dated from Ottoman times and were often in the Imperial Ottoman style, which he regarded as utterly alien to Egypt, referring to it as 'stambouli.'"[40]

A Brief History of Twentieth-century Conservation Practices in Egypt

Herz Bey's personal disdain for, and the Comité's blindness to, the Ottoman did not last. While canonical Medieval Cairo continued to be understood primarily in terms of the Mamluk, the twentieth century saw the emergence of a limited interest in certain buildings of the Ottoman era. In particular, the *sabil*s (fountains) of the Ottoman era were studied and conserved, and the late eighteenth-century style that combined Mamluk and Ottoman elements—called by Doris Behrens-Abouseif the "'Abd al-Rahman Katkhuda style"—was, as we shall see, assimilated into the medieval. Nonetheless, until recent times, the primary focus of conservation activities remained the Mamluk medieval, a situation echoed in the historiography of Egypt. In addition, conservation efforts were generally focused on individual monuments.

In the 1930s, M. Edmond Pauty argued that the prime historic monument of Cairo is the old city itself in its entirety.[41] This was the first expression of an approach to saving Medieval Cairo and its monuments that would ultimately be expressed in the phrase 'area conservation.' But the resources of the Comité in those years remained relatively limited, as they always had been, and no comprehensive plan was put into place. The work of the Comité continued until 1952, when its foreign members were expelled and its activities ceased. The last proceedings in French (the official language of the Comité) were published in 1953. A summary volume in Arabic covering the years 1954–61 later appeared.[42] It is clear that during the Nasser years, there was little official interest in conserving medieval architecture, which is not surprising given Nasser's view of the Mamluks as invaders. In 1971, the body was renamed "The Egyptian Antiquities Organization" (EAO) and in 1994, its name was changed once again to the "Supreme Council of Antiquities" (SCA). The SCA is part of the Ministry of Culture, as was the EAO.

In the 1970s, the majority of preservation work was undertaken by foreign missions attached to national archaeological institutes in Egypt. Conservation projects were carried out by the French, Germans, Poles, Danes, and Italians.[43] While some of these projects undertook preservation of a number of monuments in an urban area (for example, those of the German Mission), the activities were geared largely to the preservation of single monuments. The situation changed in the aftermath of an international seminar hosted by the German Institute for Archaeology and the EAO in 1978. This seminar led to the successful nomination of Islamic Cairo for inclusion on the World Heritage list (see Chapter 4). In spite of growing interest in the preservation of Cairo's architectural heritage, sustained and intensive efforts occurred only in the aftermath of the 1992 earthquake. The available funding and philosophy of conservation activities in Egypt since that time have changed considerably. Urban conservation now predominates and a major focus of conservation efforts is its impact on the social and economic life of neighborhoods. Large-scale efforts supported by international organizations like UNESCO, ICOMOS, the Aga Khan Award, and the Aga Khan Trust for Culture are transforming the character of conservation and restoration activities.[44] Many aspects of conservation in Cairo have changed, but some of its underlying assumptions have remained intact. In the chapters that follow, we shall investigate those assumptions and discuss the various contexts that produced and have sustained them over a period of more than a century.

1

Constructing Medieval Cairo in the Nineteenth Century

Egypt in the nineteenth century stood at the crossroads of two great empires, the British and the Ottoman, and it also had a long history of indigenous architectural and cultural practices. I argue below that these varied parts came together under the Comité to produce a version of the city that was canonized as authentically medieval, and look at how all the elements of these overlapping imperial spheres came together in the late nineteenth century to produce what came to be referred to as Medieval Cairo.

This chapter is made up of two large sections. In the first, I show how the idea of preserving Arab art emerged from a number of different impulses and practices, both European and Egyptian. These different impulses and settings were superimposed upon one another, and so it is not always easy to disentangle them. For the sake of clarity, however, I treat British imperial and Ottoman Egyptian practices separately. Next I show how the medieval in Cairo came to be identified so closely with Mamluk architecture. Just as Donald Reid reminds us that it is preservation, and not neglect, that calls for explanation, I argue that the strongly Mamluk character of Medieval Cairo requires investigation and explanation. Understanding how Medieval Cairo was constructed as an essentially Mamluk city allows me to address the issue I raise in the second section: the different meanings that this 'medieval' city had when it was in the process of being constructed and canonized. The second section of this chapter, then, discusses why and how Medieval Cairo could signify so many different things to so many different people.

Creating a Mamluk Medieval in Cairo

Architectural Preservation as Imperial Practice: The Archaeological Survey of India

The British had been in India for nearly a century before the government assumed responsibility for recording and preserving its antiquities. In January 1862, the Governor General lamented "the neglect with which the greater portion of the architectural remains, and of the traces of by-gone civilization have been treated, though many of these . . . are full of beauty and interest." He hastened to add that he did not mean by "neglect" the failure to restore or preserve them, a task which was beyond the resources of the government. He meant, rather, the duty "of investigating and placing on record, for the instruction of future generations, many particulars that might still be rescued from oblivion, and throw light upon the early history of England's great dependency; a history which, as time moves on, as the country becomes more easily accessible, and traversable, and as Englishmen are led to give more thought to India than such as barely suffices to hold it and govern it, will assuredly occupy, more and more, the attention of the intelligent and enquiring classes in European countries."[1]

The motivation for the Archaeological Survey of India (ASI) was not knowledge of India's antiquities for their own sake, but rather the duty to place them on record, as described by the Governor General, for the instruction of future generations—not future Indian generations, but future British generations.[2] The Archaeological Survey was placed under the direction of Major Alexander Cunningham, who honored the charge to search for remains of great antiquity or historical interest by following in the footsteps of Alexander the Great and the Chinese Buddhist pilgrim Huen Tsiang. His quest took him to places that claimed the attention of a British public fascinated by the search for origins and convinced that these sites represented the high point of ancient India's civilization.[3] The survey was, as Thomas Metcalf argues, part of the colonial administration's "larger project of defining the enduring elements of India's society . . . to order its past, and its present." As Metcalf further notes, "The British were determined not only to recover India's past, as part of the larger Victorian fascination with the ancient world, but to order this past into a coherent narrative that extended up to the present. In so doing, the British could, or so they imagined, create a secure and usable past in India for themselves."[4]

Conservation was not initially part of the Archaeological Survey's charge, although two years later the Survey was empowered to "prevent injury and preserve buildings remarkable for their antiquity, or for their historical and architectural value."[5] Motivated by concerns over the pilfering of objects from architectural sites,[6] British officials proposed the creation of a central department that would preserve antiquities in their original context. The Survey was suspended in 1865 and reestablished in 1871, this time with "professedly scientific objectives."[7] Now, Cunningham was to undertake a systematic survey of the entire country and describe "all architectural and other remains that are remarkable either for their antiquity, or their beauty, or their historical interest."[8] These decayed monuments called out for Britain's protection and "testified to Britain's self-proclaimed role as guardian of India's past."[9] Britain's role as guardian of India's past, sovereign of India's present, and shaper of her future was expressed not only in archaeological and conservation activities, but also in the development of Indo-Saracenic forms for British imperial architecture in India.[10] The Archaeological Survey and Anglo-Indian administrators saw in Muslim architecture the remnants of the Muslims as an invading force, a foreign presence that prefigured their own conquest and their role as both guardians of the past (a past largely of their own invention) and agents of change.[11]

Classifying and recording India's architecture was a primary element in the production of knowledge about India's past. Architecture, it was believed, provided the most reliable data about India's history, its religions and social groups, and the relations among its various communities.[12] In order to read these buildings properly, it was necessary to ascertain the 'original context' of monuments, a kind of inquiry that went hand-in-hand with the work of oriental philologists, who were constructing (in their view, reconstructing) from texts a systematic knowledge of India's past. In his opening address to the Aryan section of the Second International Congress of Orientalists (London, 1874), Professor Max Müller insisted that it was the orientalists who were restoring corrupted versions of religion to their pure forms. He praised the Indian government for its "readiness" to assist "every enterprise tending to throw light on the literature, the religion, the laws and customs, the arts and manufactures of that ancient Oriental Empire . . . . There are two surveys carried on at the present moment in India, a Literary and an Archaeological Survey."[13] Müller's point was a simple, but important, one. The work of the Literary Survey and the publication of ancient texts was revealing to natives the "folly of their way." He asserted triumphally, "Thus the religion, the literature, the whole character of the people of India is becoming more and more Indo-European," and congratulated his fellow orientalists on "the new life which we have imparted to their ancient history."[14]

The work of orientalists and archaeologists gained increasing importance under Lord Curzon, viceroy from 1898–1905, who was tireless in his attention to the conservation of India's architectural heritage.[15] Under his watchful eye, monuments were returned to their "original function," but it was the British who determined what that would be. If it were to be religious worship, the history of the site as told by orientalists, not its current ritual use by natives, would determine what was appropriate. Not surprisingly, the British frequently found themselves at odds with the local population over the question of the appropriate use for a given site. Although the government often deferred to the locals in order to avoid open conflict, the British clearly believed that original (as determined by the British) practice was authentic and ought to carry the day.[16] Whenever possible, however, they resisted acknowledging the legitimacy of contemporary local religious traditions, a fact that clearly played a part—as we shall see in Chapter 2—in the Comité's understanding of Mamluk architecture as the authentic representation of Islam.

Preserving Arab Art in Cairo as an Adjunct to British Imperialism in India

European interest in preserving Arab art arose out of more than one source. As Ussama Makdisi has discussed, two different phases of European romanticism generated the desire to preserve pre-modernities in the Orient: one sought to preserve a premodern East as a response to European modernization and its attendant traumas; the other sought to preserve a premodern East in response to an independent Ottoman modernization.[17] 'Arab art' in the sense of architecture had been introduced to the literate European public from the 1830s to the 1870s through the works of Pascal Coste, Jules Bourgoin, Prisse d'Avennes, and Owen Jones.[18] These artists, architects, and draftsmen reveled in the beauty of Arab art, though their high opinion was not shared by all. Some observers deemed the architecture "ornamental enough . . . yet . . . coarsely so."[19] The mid-century judgment of Richard Francis Burton offers not only a critique, but a diagnosis of the origins of the ills of Saracenic architecture: it is a "plagiarism from the Byzantine, and it was reiterated in the Gothic . . . ," the result of what he called an "architectural lawlessness" and "disregard for symmetry" that he attributed to "an imperfect 'amalgamation and enrichment.'" On the whole, however, European travelers were admiring of Arab art, and they began to show interest in preserving its artifacts during the heydey of European preservationism, especially in the second half of the nineteenth century.

The first suggestion that Arab art (in the sense of artifacts) should be preserved had come in 1869, when two European architects in the department of pious endowments *(awqaf)*, Auguste Salzmann and Julius Franz, suggested to Khedive Ismail that he establish a museum for objects of Arab art in the mosque of al-Zahir Baybars, north of the walls of what is today referred to as Fatimid Cairo.[20] Ismail did, in fact, issue such a decree, but nothing was done and little discussion of Arab art seems to have taken place until several years later, when the British Consul at Cairo, E.T. Rogers, added his voice to the chorus. He did not make his case directly to the khedive, but put forward a motion before the Archaeological Section at the Second International Congress of Orientalists (1874) calling for the establishment of a committee "for the preservation and restoration of monuments of Oriental art and architecture, and for duly recording those monuments which are decaying and which cannot be restored."[21]

This is the same meeting at which Professor Max Müller had opened the Aryan section with his encomium to the Literary and Archaeological Surveys in India. By 1874, when the International Congress was held, the Archaeological Survey of India was well underway. Staffed by experts who had already completed a significant portion of the business of recording, describing, classifying, and documenting the vast architectural heritage (Hindu, Buddhist, and Muslim) of India, the ASI was by then an official instrument of the Indian government. The suggestion at this same meeting by the British consul that a similar program be put into place in Egypt was no coincidence.

Stanley Lane-Poole's account of the motion brought before the Archaeological Section, and his analysis of the problem, make the connection between India and Egypt explicit: "The system and growth of Arab architecture, the art in which the Arabs achieved most success, are subjects with regard to which we are utterly in the dark. And our ignorance is most complete where our knowledge should begin; we do indeed know something, just a little, about Indian and Moresque architecture, both of which are exaggerated or even debased forms of the Arab; but of the mother of both of these, of Arab architecture itself as seen in Egypt, we know absolutely nothing."[22] It is important, then, to know Arab architecture because it is the authentic form, the genealogical parent, of other better-known but debased forms of Arab art.

Lane-Poole goes further in characterizing the knowledge that Europeans have (or, rather, lack), when he says, "Of course we look at the mosques with conventional admiration. But this is not *knowing* . We do not really *know* anything about the development of Arab architecture" (italics in original).[23] Lane-Poole's distinction between "conventional admiration" and "knowing" is significant in a colonial context, for "knowing" is the systematic ordering that characterized the colonial enterprise itself. In India, this systematic ordering of the past through architecture was already being carried out in the work of the Archaeological Survey of India, which Thomas Metcalf argues lay at the heart of the project of ordering India's past into a usable history for the British.[24]

Nothing came of the 1874 motion, however, no doubt because it coincided with the years in which the khedive was attempting unsuccessfully to satisfy his creditors. In 1881, however, he responded positively to the suggestion that a commission to preserve Arab antiquities should be formed. There were many reasons why he should respond positively to this suggestion, but his interest in maintaining the good will of the European supervisors in his government, and British approval of the proposal, must certainly have played a role in his decision. Only weeks after the formation of the Comité, the 'Urabi revolution shook the foundations of Egypt's government and the British military occupation began. In this larger political context, the preservation of Arab heritage came to be understood as a responsibility of Egypt's British stewards, a view shared by the general public as well as those in government.

How could the preservation of Arab art be understood to meet the strict criteria for fiscal discipline that the advancement program, the realities of Egypt's insolvency, and the general responsibilities of government demanded? Given Cromer's aggressive debt reduction strategies, there would be no expenditure that could not be justified, in some important way, as part of the fiscal management that was fundamental to the British objective of modernizing Egypt. In the study and preservation of antiquities, as in other areas of administration, Cromer drew on British experience in India, where the Archaeological Survey constituted one imperial prelude to the Comité in Egypt.[25]

The British were frank about their position as the primary consumers and producers of knowledge about ancient and medieval Egypt. In archaeology, in museums, in architecture, the ancient and medieval Egyptian past was preserved, classified, and presented primarily for the benefit of Europeans, not Egyptians. In 1883, Lord Dufferin—British ambassador to the Sublime Porte in Constantinople and Her Majesty's Envoy Extraordinary to Egypt—wrote to the Earl of Granville proposing an antiquities police force, addressing the question of the propriety of the expenditure: "Although not belonging to the category of political questions, there is no subject in which the literary, scientific, and artistic world of Europe is more interested than that of the antiquities of Egypt, whether mediaeval or pre-historic."[26] Lord Granville acknowledged that "the extra expenses entailed by these measures should be defrayed to a certain extent by those Europeans in whose interest they have been conceived."[27] Lord Dufferin's proposal was welcomed by the British public, too. The unnamed author of an article in *The Times* wrote approvingly, "Among the minor questions which Lord Dufferin has wisely included in his general revision of Egyptian affairs, the protection of the monuments of Cairo deservedly holds a prominent position."[28] Egyptians themselves knew where they stood in relation to their own past, as a correspondent to the Anglophone *The Egyptian Gazette* who identified himself only as "An old Egyptian" complained, "Rightly or wrongly, the Museum staff is paid for in the interest of Europeans and not of native Egyptians . . . ."[29] But antiquities really were a political question, just as they had been in India. The work of the Comité was underfunded for the first years of its existence, but as soon as the financial situation permitted, its budget was increased. From 1896 onward, Baring's annual *Report on the Finances, Administration, and Condition of Egypt, and the Progress of Reforms*, included sections on archaeological excavations, museums, and the preservation of Arab and Coptic monuments.[30]

Creating a Mamluk Medieval Cairo

The process of surveying, recording, conserving, and restoring—that is, the construction of Medieval Cairo—produced a version of the 'medieval' city that was overwhelmingly identified with Mamluk architecture. But why is this the version of Medieval Cairo that came into being? Here, I explore the reasons for the fundamentally Mamluk appearance of the medieval city that emerged. I argue that the identification of Medieval Cairo with Mamluk architecture was the product of interactions among British imperial, Ottoman imperial, and local Egyptian histories and practices in which, often for quite different reasons, the Mamluk was privileged.

I begin by discussing how the Comité understood Cairo as it encountered the city in the late nineteenth century. Throughout, I focus on the Comité's actions and reactions because, comprised of a diverse group of men—French, Austro-Hungarian, British, and Egyptian—it represents a cross-section of those who were concerned with the preservation of Arab art in the period, and its members represent the range of views that were under discussion at the time. At the same time, the Comité was larger than its membership: it was an official organization of the Egyptian government, and so its activities must be considered within all the contexts that were shaping fiscal and governmental policy within Egypt during the British occupation.

After discussing the Comité's views of Cairo, I discuss the historical circumstances that produced their understandings, misunderstandings, and blindnesses. Some of these factors are rooted in more general European views of the East, and of Cairo in particular, but others are clearly a function of histories—some local, some imperial—that were inaccessible to the members of the Comité. These histories and contributing factors are superimposed upon one another and they are not easy for us to perceive even at the distance of more than a century. For the sake of clarity, I treat the different elements (British, Ottoman, local) separately, but I remind readers that they were all interacting, and that the extent to which we can disentangle them now is at least partly the result of historical distance.

Cairo as Received and Understood by the Comité

When the Comité began its work in Cairo, there were over four hundred buildings dating largely from the Middle Ages still standing in various states of disrepair and dilapidation. Beginning in the 1870s, Europeans interested in the preservation of Arab art had diagnosed the causes and proposed remedies for the dilapidation that they saw. At the 1874 Oriental Congress, the destruction of Cairo's monuments (described as "Oriental") was laid at the feet of European tourists:

> The principal subject which occupied the attention of the Archaeological section of the Oriental Congress on Friday, the eighteenth, was a motion proposed by Mr. E.T. Rogers, late H.B.M. Consul at Cairo, and seconded by Mr. Stanley Lane Poole, "That this section nominate a committee of gentlemen, with power to add to their number, for the preservation and restoration of monuments of Oriental art and architecture, and for duly recording those monuments which are decaying and which cannot be restored." Brugsch Bey endeavoured, but not very successfully, to show that European travellers were

> most to blame in the matter of the destruction of the monuments, and drew a humorous picture of the defacement of the buildings, by English names scrawled over them with no great reference to calligraphic effect, and proposed that in order to put a stop to these acts of vandalism a list of culprits should be published annually, containing the names of all those travellers who had endeavoured to obtain a sorry immortality by thus defacing the monuments. Professor Ebers, of Leipzig, proposed that a system of watchmen should be organised for the protection of the monuments. After this the motion was carried almost unanimously; but its form was slightly modified by being referred to the consideration of the Council of the Congress, with the recommendation of the section, instead of being acted upon by the section itself.[31]

Others, including Stanley Lane-Poole and Gabriel Charmes, were more inclined to place the blame for the destruction of the medieval urban fabric on Khedive Ismail's penchant for European-style villas or long centuries of neglect by the Ottomans. Certainly, by the time the Comité was actually established in 1881, the sense that it was the Ottomans and Egyptians who were largely responsible for the decay of Cairo's architectural heritage was the predominant line of thinking, adding to the list of Ottoman/Egyptian failures yet another item that justified the interventions of Europeans, who were deemed better suited in all respects to preserve and study the Arab heritage of Egypt than her own residents, a situation consistent with the policy of exclusion in Egyptology as well.[32]

But the state of Cairo's Arab monuments was not primarily the result of any one of these factors. These structures were built and maintained over more than five centuries largely through the institution of *waqf* (pious endowment or trust).[33] By the fourteenth century, the accumulation of institutions founded through *waqf* made Cairo the most important religious, political, and cultural center in the Islamic world, and determined to a very large extent the architectural and urban character of late medieval Cairo. Largely because of the abundance of *waqf* institutions, the North African scholar Ibn Khaldun called her *Umm al-Dunya* ('the mother of the world').[34] When the Ottomans conquered Egypt, nearly one-half of the buildings and monuments in Cairo and its environs were *waqf* institutions.[35]

However, Europeans did not understand this long local history of the establishment, maintenance, and even the progressive disrepair of monuments in its own terms. Although the members of the Comité knew that the monuments had been built and maintained through the institution of *waqf*, they had little understanding of how this legal, social, and economic institution had actually functioned over the course of more than five centuries in Egypt.[36] As a correspondent to *The Times* put it in 1883, "The pious zeal or personal vanity which prompted their erection evidently died with their founders, and subsequent generations preferred building new monuments in their own honour to preserving those which were erected in honour of their ancestors. It is the way with all Eastern architectural ambition."[37] Local Egyptian chroniclers, however, saw things differently; although they generally had little good to say about the Ottomans, they still praised Ottoman zeal for the protection of *waqf*. Why were the judgments of Europeans so completely out of step with the understanding of Egyptian historians on this issue? In the following section, I discuss the history of *waqf* preservation during the Ottoman period and explain why these preservation strategies were not recognized by the Comité and its official supporters in the Anglo-Egyptian government.

The Role of Waqf in Preserving Architecture during the Ottoman Period

The preservation of Cairo's built environment was a central feature of Ottoman administration of the Egyptian province, in keeping with a political culture that held the creation and protection of *waqfs* both as a sign of piety and a central responsibility of Islamic rulers. Throughout the Ottoman period, Mamluk *waqfs* were transferred, reendowed, or otherwise adapted to changed circumstances. These changes were not always carried out strictly in accordance with the requirements of Islamic law, but they were nonetheless conventional practice. For the Ottomans, the continued support of existing *waqfs* was part of a program to 'ottomanize' Mamluk endowments and thereby foster at least minimal loyalty from the Egyptian *ulama*, whose support was indispensable to maintaining Ottoman legitimacy.

Many buildings fell into disuse or disrepair and were illegally exchanged for more lucrative properties, a practice known as *istibdal*. While *istibdal* could be used to protect the interests of the endowment, it was also subject to abuse for personal gain.[38] A *waqf* could also be leased to a new tenant, who would presumably restore or rebuild the property, a practice known as *khuluw*.[39] These leases (sometimes for periods of up to a century) often were the only way to keep a foundation going at all in the absence of liquid assets.[40] While *istibdal* and *khuluw* might be used to sustain a failing endowment, both practices were highly suspect. The historian Doris Behrens-Abouseif refers to these practices collectively as Ottomanization, though we might also call them, in today's parlance, 'adaptive reuse.'[41]

Protecting *waqfs* and preventing their illegal exploitation remained one of the most serious concerns of jurists and rulers alike. The Ottoman conqueror of Egypt, Selim I (r. 1512–1520), justified his invasion partly on the grounds of *waqf* abuse: he claimed that the chief judge of the corrupt Mamluk Sultan al-Ghuri had told a visiting Ottoman official (ostensibly a pilgrim) that appropriating the land on which al-Azhar stands for a private dwelling would be permissible through *istibdal*. Just weeks after his arrival in Cairo, Sultan Selim ordered a new cadastral survey, along with a survey of *waqfs* and military land grants. The old Mamluk officials allegedly concealed the old registers, but eventually the Ottomans got the information they wanted. The law code Selim promulgated in Egypt, the *Qanunama* (from the Persian, *Kanunname*), prohibited outright the practice of *istibdal*, and he took measures to protect even the *waqfs* of the defeated Mamluk sultan.[42]

During the first two Ottoman centuries in Egypt, *waqf* abuses were handled by the Islamic courts on a case-by-case basis. In the eighteenth century, Egyptian governments attempted to correct these abuses more systematically, but it was difficult to do so because the terms established in *waqf* endowment deeds often gave considerable discretion to their trustees *(nazirs)*. By the nineteenth century, systemic *waqf* reform was underway, along with Muhammad 'Ali's other wide-ranging reforms of the military, the administration, land tenure, and taxation. In the fall of 1812,

Muhammad 'Ali abolished the *iltizam* system of tax-farming and confiscated *waqf* lands. In spite of the mass confiscation, the *waqf* system did not come to an end. Landowners created new *waqfs* throughout the nineteenth century for many of the same reasons they had done so in previous centuries: to consolidate family wealth and influence, to prevent confiscation of personal property, and to care for female family members.[43] Nineteenth-century *waqf* reforms from Muhammad 'Ali to the British occupation removed abusive trustees and established a central department of *waqfs*.[44]

Throughout its long history, the *waqf* as an institution had dual purposes: it legitimately served the financial self-interest of the endowers as well as the greater interests of the community. Before the reforms of Muhammad 'Ali and his successors, these purposes were not deemed to be mutually exclusive, although critics recognized that they were in tension with one another and sought to prevent and redress abuses that arose from conflicts of interest. It was only in the nineteenth and twentieth centuries that a different sensibility altogether determined that the institution of *waqf* itself was irreconcilable with the public interest.[45] The reasons for this new sensibility are complicated, but its impact is easily described. As a local preservation tradition, there was no collective responsibility for maintaining what we would consider to be public institutions. Each existed on its own, and in the classical *waqf* system, the strict prohibition on distributing revenues generated for one *waqf* to another meant that some endowments inevitably fell into ruin for lack of funding while others enjoyed surpluses. There was, in theory, no decision to be made about whether to conserve or repair one foundation as opposed to another. Each stood on its own, with its own source of revenue, trustees, beneficiaries, use, and function, and none was privileged in any systematic way over another. All of this would change in the later nineteenth century as the *waqf* institution became a branch of government responsible *collectively* for the mosques and other religious institutions of Cairo, working from 1881 through the Comité de Conservation des Monuments de l'Art Arabe.

By the end of the nineteenth century, the irreconcilability of traditional *waqf* organization and the interest in preserving large numbers of monuments had entered the wider public discourse. An unnamed correspondent for *The Times* had this to say about *waqf* in Egypt:

> The present system of attaching certain trusts to certain mosques, &c., will be found to be based upon no sound documentary evidence; the separate endowments have become hopelessly mixed; and the whole trusts will have to be lumped together and administered to the best advantage of the religious foundations as a whole. Pious founders' intentions, even if ascertainable (which is extremely doubtful) must be overruled, and the money applied not chiefly to well-preserved mosques which do not need it, but to their decaying neighbours which have lost their endowments by the successive confiscations and peculations of Sovereigns and trustees. There must no longer be the excuse that a monument (like the mosque of El-Maridani) cannot be preserved because it has no "Wakf," whilst a wealthy, unhistorical, inartistic mosque hard by squanders its surplus . . . . It is sincerely to be hoped that the present step towards a better administration may result in the settlement of an adequate annual grant to the *Comité de Conservation des Monuments de l'Art Arabe*, and that this Commission may be given a perfectly free hand in the application of its funds.[46]

It is not true, however, that the intentions of the founders were unknown. All *waqf*s had an endowment deed written at the time of their foundation. These deeds (called *waqfiya*, or *hujjat waqf*) contained detailed information about the properties of the endowment as well as the stipulations attached to the revenues. The deeds were, in principle, to be taken out on a yearly basis and read publicly in the presence of a judge in order to ensure that their conditions were being fully met. They were also examined in the event of disputes or court cases. Did these deeds survive into the nineteenth century? Certainly, many did not. But hundreds of these documents *did* survive and were housed in three different archives at the turn of the twentieth century. Why, then, do they not seem to have been known to or consulted by officials who were engaged in the conservation of monuments? The documents were housed mainly in court archives where they were consulted for legal matters in the event of dispute.[47] The *waqf* documents that historians and architectural historians now consider to be among our most important sources for the history of monuments were not considered, in the nineteenth or early twentieth centuries, to be sources for historical information. Even at the time of the foundation of the 'Abdin archives in the twentieth century, these documents were not recognized as containing information of *historical* value.[48]

By the middle and late nineteenth-century *waqf* revenues were in fact being used for purposes other than those designated by their founders. They were not always (or even frequently) used to support other foundations. To what purposes had the surplus revenues of *waqfs* been devoted? In the era of Khedive Ismail, *waqf* revenues were redirected by 'Ali Mubarak to support the network of schools he established as head of the ministry of schools *(diwan al-madaris)*. He was, at the same time, the head of the ministry of *awqaf*.[49] The revenues had been directed toward new schools that incorporated many of the educational reforms to which Mubarak and other modernizers were committed, including improved pedagogical methods and the introduction of secular subjects like history and geography into the curriculum. Many of these innovations, including the redirection of *waqf* revenues, were enshrined as government policy in the 1867 Edict of 10 Rajab. This extensive set of principles and policies addressed explicitly the issue of using *waqf* revenues for the schools. Article Ten of the proposed edict had gone so far as to propose giving the ministry of schools authority to redirect *waqf* revenues to the schools. This provision was not accepted by the Privy Council, which instead stated that the ministry of *awqaf* should retain direct authority over all *waqfs*, but that it should direct all surplus revenues to the fulfillment of the educational mandate of the ministry of schools.[50] The separation of authority was essentially moot, however, as Mubarak was head of both ministries at the time, and it was not uncommon in succeeding years for a single person to hold positions of authority in multiple departments or ministries.

In addition to the impact of the *waqf* on the absolute availability of revenues, there were also local preservation traditions dictated by the system of *waqf* that the Comité did not understand. Once established, a *waqf* could not simply be abandoned, and its funds had to be disbursed in the manner stipulated in the foundation deed. *Waqf* revenues were used first for repairs and only then to fulfill the other conditions of the endowment, and Mamluk *waqfs* employed an architect or carpenter to ensure routine maintenance. The priority assigned to repairs and the employment of architects and carpenters were practices that the Ottomans continued to honor for *waqfs* established in the Mamluk era.[51] Contrary to the unnamed *Times* correspondent's claim in 1883, Ottoman officials in Egypt were more inclined to restore older Mamluk sites, especially shrines, than to construct large-scale buildings of their own.

The Comité saw the Mamluk buildings but not the Ottoman interventions that had preserved them; similarly, Europeans did not perceive (or, if they saw them, did not value) new Ottoman contributions to the landscape. The Comité's relative blindness to the Ottoman architectural legacy was partly the result of the character of Ottoman building projects in Cairo. New Ottoman construction of the sixteenth and seventeenth centuries was likely to follow a Mamluk plan that was popular in the later period, that is, building smaller structures adapted to oddly sized and shaped plots and lacking a courtyard.[52] Even in the early nineteenth century, new structures in Cairo were likely to have a "predominantly Mamluk vocabulary modified with limited Ottoman features."[53] Ottoman officials in Egypt also followed a different path from those in either Istanbul or the other large provincial cities of the empire: they did not concentrate their projects in a central area, but rather built according to more local needs.[54] Generally, Ottoman patrons in Cairo founded urban and commercial foundations that served their neighborhood rather than the large-scale Sufi convents and madrasas that had characterized the building programs of Mamluk amirs. Ottoman pashas, unlike Mamluk sultans, were generally more concerned with urban maintenance than with growth, also distinguishing their activities in Cairo from the rest of the Ottoman Empire. The predominance of the neighborhood in Ottoman urban management and preservation practice remained consistent throughout the period, and these were the concerns that directed the activities of amirs and aghas.[55]

Ottoman amirs invested their resources in the expansion of their households, not in the establishment of large-scale urban institutions;[56] they tended to support existing religious institutions rather than found new ones;[57] and they found different outlets for the expression of their piety. For example, supporting the pilgrimage *(hajj)* and being the Commander of the Pilgrimage *(amir al-hajj)* was a preferred form of piety under the Ottomans in the sixteenth and seventeenth centuries. The pilgrimage remained an important focus for public piety throughout the period under consideration, and state sponsorship of the *mahmal*—the caravan transporting the embroidered tapestry sent from Cairo to cover the Ka'ba at the time of the annual pilgrimage—was an important symbol of authority (Figure 2). Only in the eighteenth century did amirs once again display piety by sponsoring some large-scale monuments and rebuilding shrines.

In addition, the urban policies of the French and of Muhammad 'Ali did much to undermine the integrity of the neighborhoods that had concerned the Ottoman amirs. The French had ordered the destruction of the gates that protected Cairo's quarters. Muhammad 'Ali ordered the cutting of wide boulevards through the city, hoping to improve the air quality in the narrow, twisting lanes that were believed to give rise to foul vapors that caused disease and crime. These measures, each of which had a logic of its own, incrementally erased the logic of old neighborhoods.[58] Combined with the Comité's own myopia regarding large-scale monuments of the Mamluk period, the impact of these erasures was to render the Comité effectively blind to the underlying sense and structure of neighborhoods. As I shall discuss in Chapter 2, their inability to see the coherence of the neighborhood and its local institutions and practices was also a factor in their blindness to the vibrancy of contemporary religious life, one that facilitated their view of Islam as a medieval religion.

By the mid-nineteenth century, a majority of Cairo's remaining (albeit increasingly dilapidated) monuments—most of them restored in some fashion during the Ottoman period—dated to the Mamluk era. In reality, Ottoman Cairo was remarkably similar to the Mamluk city.[59] The Comité's perception of the essentially Mamluk (and thus, to their mind, medieval) character of Cairo was not, then, simply an imaginative construct of Europeans, but was the outcome of the cumulative practices of the preceding centuries that converged with the predispositions and practices of the Comité.

The Historiography of Ottoman Decline and the Comité's Work

The Comité's early decisions about what buildings to list, how to classify them and represent their histories, and finally how (or whether) to preserve them were often shaped by an ignorance of local traditions and by misunderstandings of both Mamluk and Ottoman history.[60] These understandings and misunderstandings of local history, and the decisions based upon them, were both culturally constructed and politically charged. Dominated by English, French, and Austro-Hungarian engineers and architects, the Comité was decidedly anti-Ottoman. The larger world in which the Comité's European members had been educated and shaped politically requires us to question the claim of its founding documents that decisions to list certain monuments or to make particular restoration decisions were guided only by the buildings' aesthetic or historic value.[61] Such judgments, while framed in aesthetic or historical terms, were not neutral in the cultural and political world of late nineteenth-century Europeans, all of whom had come of age at a time when the Ottoman Empire was a world power with which they had to reckon.

The disdain for things Ottoman was also a function of the European historiography of the Ottoman Empire. Until recently, European scholarship still characterized the seventeenth and eighteenth centuries as a period of relentless decline. This general judgment about the state of the Ottoman Empire in the aftermath of the golden age of Suleiman the Magnificent extended also to Egypt, an Ottoman province from 1517 onward. European historians were convinced that Egypt had enjoyed something akin to a golden Mamluk age in contrast to a declining and profligate Ottoman period, although they assigned the responsibility for decline differently.[62] For example, in the absence of any real evidence, historians assumed that the population of Mamluk Cairo was larger than that of Ottoman Cairo, a conclusion that André Raymond characterizes as "haphazard" and attributes to nothing more than the "feeling" that historians had that the Mamluk period was more positive.[63] The stereotype does not hold, however, for the population of Ottoman Egypt increased even in the face of internal problems at least until 1770. Decline came later.[64] Similarly, the conventional wisdom that Egypt's economy was in a state of decline is contradicted by the steady increase in the price of agricultural goods throughout the eighteenth century,[65] as well as the steady stream of foreign merchants who settled there.[66] Cairo's economic growth is also indisputable. The central commercial district *(qasaba)* increased in size by nearly 50 percent and the number of caravanserais *(wakalas)* grew nearly sixfold, from fifty-eight in the mid-fifteenth century to 360 in Ottoman times.[67]

Working from the assumption of Ottoman decadence and decline, Europeans took the state of Cairo's buildings as yet another symptom of Ottoman neglect. That they did not acknowledge Ottoman contributions to preserving the fabric of the city is evident in Arthur Rhoné's comment in 1881 that "the city of Cairo was still intact, at least in the sense that its monuments continued to fall quietly into ruin following the eternal way of the Orient; at least nothing was attempted in the way of works called 'improvement' and 'restoration.'"[68] Some particularly astute observers, like Amelia Edwards, deplored the "ravages" of the previous two decades of Haussmannizing, more than Rhoné's "eternal way of the Orient" in accounting for the loss of architectural fabric by the time the Comité had come into existence.[69] Most, however, shared the opinion of the anonymous correspondent for *The Times*, who wrote in 1883, "It is certain that the present deplorable condition of most of the mosques presupposes centuries of neglect and indifference." There was also the question of contemporary Egyptian taste, especially as it was expressed in the nearly ubiquitous practice of painting alternating courses of red and white on buildings (Figure 3) (called *badigeon* by the French), which was soundly and frequently condemned by the Comité.[70]

Local preservation practices had produced a city with scores of old buildings that remained functional, but which were in varying states of dilapidation that Europeans took as evidence of neglect. For example, the Ibn Tulun Mosque was used in the nineteenth century as an asylum for the poor and its arcades were bricked in to create living spaces (Figure 4).[71] Europeans also commented negatively on the dilapidation or disappearance of ornamental and decorative elements on old buildings, taking this, too, as evidence of general neglect. Here, again, they did not know the history of local preservation practices. In maintaining buildings, priority was given to structural integrity and the continued functioning of the building; when funds were scarce, decorative elements like marble or copper were stripped and sold (Cairo had a thriving used-building-materials market) in order to raise funds for needed structural repairs.[72] But European ignorance of local traditions was also filtered through a relatively new lens that had only recently been ground in the old cities of Europe: the view that the preservation of old architecture was a positive value in itself. In this milieu, preserving old architecture meant, for many Europeans, the maintenance and restoration of symmetrical, coherent, and rational systems of *ornamentation*. European criticisms of dilapidation, then, emerged from misunderstandings that resulted both from an ignorance of local tradition and from an emerging sensibility that shaped Europeans' views of their own old cities.

The members of the Comité did not have a deep historical view of how the city or its neighborhoods had changed over long periods of time, what motivated the decisions that produced particular configurations at particular times, or what principles and assumptions lay behind Cairo's local traditions, preservation practices, and adaptive changes. Egyptians over the course of time had asked and answered such questions. Egypt, and particularly Cairo, had a long-standing tradition of topographical writing dating back to the Middle Ages. The topographers Ibn Duqmaq (b. ca. 1349) and Taqi al-Din al-Maqrizi (1364–1442) were as meticulous in documenting Cairo's ruins as they were her great mosques and madrasas. These ruins did not, as we might be tempted to assume, characterize only poorer neighborhoods; they were a common feature of the Cairo landscape in nearly every part of town. Dilapidation was part and parcel of the long-term urban history of Cairo in ways that remain little studied and poorly understood by historians of the city. Eleventh- and twelfth-century Judeo-Arabic documents often mention ruins,[73] especially when describing properties, where the ruins are noted as bordering buildings and where they are often given as gifts—'fixer-uppers'— to be rebuilt by their recipients.[74] 'Ali Mubarak, the minister of public works during the period the Comité was doing its work, wrote a new topography of Cairo modeled on al-Maqrizi's topography that provided detailed information on the history of buildings, the changes they had undergone over time, the changes in their neighborhoods, and material and functional changes.[75] His own diagnosis of the cause for much of Cairo's dilapidation laid responsibility with the failures of proper governance during the Ottoman period, which he contrasted with the restoration of splendor under Muhammad 'Ali.[76] Ironically, then, the views of 'Ali Mubarak, one of the most controversial figures of the classic Comité narrative, appear to converge with European views of Ottoman culpability for bringing Mamluk Cairo to ruin. Unlike Europeans, however, he was fully aware of, and documented with precision, Ottoman contributions to the preservation of Cairo's monuments.[77]

Mamluk and Neo-Mamluk Architecture in Late Ottoman Egypt

The Comité's penchant for the Mamluk did not reflect only anti-Ottomanism or ignorance of local history and tradition: Egyptians had also developed their own attraction to Mamluk architecture. Incipient Egyptian nationalisms—in the context of both European and Ottoman imperialism—contributed to new views of the Mamluk as a local Egyptian art form. As the architectural historian Nasser Rabbat has demonstrated, an interest in Mamluk and neo-Mamluk architecture was part of a new symbolics of power in later nineteenth century Egypt as Muhammad 'Ali's descendants (who comprised the ruling family of Egypt until the 1952 revolution) sought to express political independence from the Ottoman empire through the patronage of neo-Mamluk architectural projects. Their interest in neo-Mamluk architecture represented a retreat from the architectural policy of Muhammad 'Ali, who had styled himself as an Ottoman and preferred to dissociate himself from the Mamluk legacy in all respects, including architecture.[78]

Muhammad 'Ali's grand mosque (Figure 5)—built on the grounds of the former stronghold of Mamluk power, the Citadel—broke completely with Cairene architectural tradition in turning away from Mamluk structural and decorative themes toward a classical Ottoman imperial form.[79] While relying upon classical Ottoman imperial architecture, the mosque (typically called by European travelers 'the Alabaster Mosque' because of the large amount of alabaster facing on the structure) also incorporated a number of European elements that had become popular in Istanbul during the eighteenth century, eventually resulting in a style that came to be known as 'Ottoman Baroque.'[80] The use of Ottoman imperial motifs in Muhammad 'Ali's mosque both lent legitimacy to his rule (he was, technically, the Ottoman governor) and subverted Ottoman imperial authority. His foundation inscription acknowledged Ottoman political suzerainty, but his two minarets—normally used only by Ottoman sultans or members of the royal family—usurped an explicitly imperial prerogative.[81]

Later in the nineteenth century, when Muhammad 'Ali's descendants asserted their independence from the Ottoman Empire, they in turn dissociated themselves not only from the Turco-Circassian elite but also from Ottoman architectural style. Neo-Mamluk architecture became a marker of a specifically Egyptian, non-Ottoman political and cultural identity. Where Muhammad 'Ali opted for a modern Ottoman design over a neo-Mamluk one in mid-century, his descendant Khedive 'Abbas Hilmi II (r. 1892–1914) chose a neo-Mamluk design to complete the mosque of al-Rifa'i at the turn of the twentieth century. In 1869, Khushyar Hanem, the mother of Khedive Ismail (r. 1863–79), commissioned the Egyptian architect Husayn Fahmi Pasha to draw up the plans and entrusted the construction to her chief eunuch, Khalil Aga. The project was plagued by problems from the beginning, including cost overruns and the khedive's unhappiness over suggested changes. After Ismail's abdication in 1880 and Khushyar's death in 1885, construction was abandoned until 1905, when Khedive 'Abbas Hilmi II commissioned a new design from Max Herz Bey, the Austrian chief architect of the Comité. Herz Bey modified the original plan according to a new, neo-Mamluk design that echoed closely the Mamluk mosque of Sultan Hasan across the street, complete with Mamluk minarets and dome (Figure 6), and a variety of other neo-Mamluk decorative elements on its façade.[82] Indeed, Herz Bey's laudatory description of Mamluk architecture in his guide to the Museum of Arab Art might well describe in general terms the façade he designed for the Rifa'i Mosque:

> The manner in which the façades are planned shows a rational and progressive development of elements bequeathed by preceding periods. Large surfaces are furrowed at intervals by a system of lofty shallow niches forming on the walls an arrangement of recesses in which are inserted windows in

> double rows. Each niche ends in a horizontal cornice formed by several beds of stalactites. The doorway is modelled on the same principle, except that in this case the niche is much larger and deeper. The consequence of this arrangement is to give a much richer and ampler development to the use of stalactites.[83]

Many new constructions in late nineteenth and early twentieth century Cairo were built in the neo-Mamluk style, including the khedivial library (Figure 7), the *awqaf* ministry, and the city of Heliopolis.

How the Mamluks Became Egyptian: An Ottoman Imperial Story

A variety of factors converged to produce the Mamluk orientation of the Comité, and one of those factors was the stark contrast that European Comité members saw between Egyptians as Arabs and Ottomans as Turks, manifesting itself very obviously in the invention and dominance of the category 'Arab art.' When Europeans began to refer to Mamluk art as 'Arab art,' they were echoing (no doubt unwittingly) an eighteenth- and nineteenth-century Ottoman imperial point of view with respect to the Circassian elite, one that figured them as 'Egyptian' rather than 'Turkish.' This 'Egyptianization' of the Mamluks began in the Middle Ages, but continued throughout the nineteenth century. In what follows, I lay out this long process in order to help explain why the Turkishness of the Mamluks was largely invisible to Europeans, what that invisibility meant for both European and Egyptian representations of the Egyptian past, and why Mamluk architecture was understood as and came to be synonymous with the category 'Arab art.'

By the time the British began to visit Egypt, it had been under the rule of Turks (of one kind or another) for more than half a millennium. The *longue durée* of the relationship between Arabs and Turks began in the ninth century, when the Abbasid caliph al-Mu'tasim began to import Turkic slave soldiers (sing. *mamluk*, pl. *mamalik*) in large numbers. Subsequently, for more than a thousand years, the rulers of the central Islamic lands were largely of Turkic origin. The Mamluk regime in Egypt was the most elaborate and highly developed expression of the *mamluk* institution in pre-modern Islamic societies. Over the course of two and a half centuries, the military Mamluk institution thrived as first Kipjaks and later Circassians were imported in large numbers as slave soldiers, educated in the barracks, manumitted, and assimilated into the complex networks of patronage that provided continuity in Egyptian political life. Staunch Sunnis, they characterized themselves as defenders of the faith, legitimized in part by their role as hosts to the vestiges of the Abbasid caliphate, which was reconstituted in Cairo (by a distant branch of the family) after the Mongol conquest of Baghdad in 1258.

The subject Arab population of Egypt was ambivalent about its overlords: on the one hand, they were alien rulers of a savage nature and on the other, they were the defenders of the lands of Islam, having turned back the Mongols at ʿAyn Jalut in 1260 and thus rescued Syria and probably Egypt from Mongol rule.[84] Although the Turks are a diverse group of Central Asians, the Arabs perceived them as a homogeneous ethnic group and called them *al-turk* or *al-atrak* regardless of their specific origins.[85] The ninth-century belles-lettrist al-Jahiz attributed to them (in addition to their military prowess) natural intelligence, religious feeling, independence, and versatility. He called them *aʿrab al-ʿajam* ('Bedouins among the non-Arabs'), thus ascribing to them the most valued qualities of the nomadic ancestors of the Arabs. By the fourteenth century, after a history that included assuming religious and political power in the Abbasid caliphate, expelling the Crusaders, and defeating the Mongols at ʿAyn Jalut, the North African Ibn Khaldun extolled the Turks, but his unequivocally positive view of the Turks was the exception, not the rule. Other scholars, particularly those with more experience in the East, the *mashriq*, were ambivalent, appreciative of the soldierly skills that had defeated the enemies of Islam, but wary of a world in which power had devolved to foreigners.[86] Willing to cede to the Turkish Mamluks an exclusive expertise and control over the military, the religious and scholarly elite *(ulama)* jealously defended their own prerogatives as guardians of the religious sciences and culture.

Less than a decade before the Mongol sack of Baghdad in 1258, one group of Mamluks in Cairo had risen to power, unseated the last of the Ayyubid princes, and established rule in Egypt. These Turkish slave-soldiers constituted a military and political elite with some remarkable features: power was concentrated in the hands of those Turks who had come to Egypt as slaves. A complex system of mutual loyalties and obligations (both horizontal and vertical, and with competing loyalties in constant tension with one another) among slaves, freed slaves, masters, and former masters provided the building blocks that maintained the continuity of political life.

Throughout their long centuries of rule in Egypt, the Mamluks insisted on a Turkish identity that distinguished them from the local Egyptian subject population. They referred to their ruling elite not as a *mamluk* state, but as *dawlat al-atrak* ('the regime of the Turks' and, during the Circassian period from 1382–1517, as both the 'regime of the Turks' and the 'regime of the Circassians' *(dawlat al-jarakisa)*. As Ulrich Haarmann and Thomas Philipp observe, "[t]he reproduction of the ruling class by recruitment from abroad prevented its assimilation into the local population and fostered a group consciousness and loyalty among the members of this elite."[87] Their own progeny, called the *awlad al-nas*, were at first excluded from the military and therefore from the halls of political power. By the mid-fourteenth century, however, the *awlad al-nas* were beginning to play significant roles in the military, serving even as high-ranking amirs and holding top offices. Their newly found access to power was the result of policies instituted by Sultan Hasan, himself a second-generation member of the *awlad al-nas*.[88]

The golden days for the sons of Mamluks did not last. Under the Circassian regime, the status of the *awlad al-nas* once again declined. Whereas sons of Mamluks had been major fief-holders in the first Turkish period, they largely ceased to be so under the Circassians. In their place, the so-called rank-and-file Mamluks rose to prominence throughout the fifteenth century.[89] In the later Mamluk period, the sons of Mamluks often turned to scholarship since they could not follow their fathers into military service. Now viewing the Mamluks and their progeny as competitors, the judgments of the *ulama* became even harsher. The population, however, had a more generous attitude toward the Mamluks, preferring the "injustice of the Turks rather than the righteousness of the Arabs" *(zulm al-turk wa-la 'adl al-'arab)*.[90] The popular bias in favor of the Turks did not last, and anti-Turkish sentiment began to take hold in the

Egyptian guilds from the late sixteenth century onward. In keeping with the earlier lack of discrimination of one Turkish group from another, the negative judgments were applied to all who could somehow be described as Turk.[91]

The Ottoman conquest provided the incentive for new distinctions to be made among different sorts of Turks. Whereas Arab chroniclers during the Mamluk sultanate typically referred to the Circassians as *atrak*, both literary and documentary sources of the Ottoman period maintained the ethnic distinctions among Circassians, Turks, and Arabs.[92] The Arab chronicler of the Ottoman invasion, Ibn Iyas (himself one of the *awlad al-nas*), also made a distinction between the Mamluk elite, referring to them as *atrak*, and the Ottomans, whom he called Rumis *(arwam)*, Turcomans *(tarakima)*, or Ottomans *('athamina)*.[93]

The Ottoman period brought about another series of transformations that included the reemergence of the Mamluks as a military and political force in the seventeenth and eighteenth centuries. In an atmosphere of deep antagonism between Mamluks and Ottoman soldiers in Egypt, there were pleas for brotherhood in the name of Islam and obedience in the name of the Ottoman sultan, who implored his co-religionists in the aftermath of the 1524 Mamluk revolt, "Let us not call one another Turkoman or Circassian. We are all the sultan's servants and brothers in Islam."[94] In other words, while ethnic distinctions continued to be recognized among Ottomans and Circassians in particular, brotherhood in Islam was supposed to supersede such identities. Circassians were considered as cousins to the Turks and were thought to share the militaristic qualities that had traditionally been ascribed to Turks by Muslims in the Middle Ages.[95] By the eighteenth century, however, it is increasingly difficult to distinguish Mamluks from Egyptians in the sources, as they married into the local population, became Arabic speakers, and assumed Arabic names.[96] Indeed, the earlier Turcophone Mamluks had maintained Arabic as their language of administration.[97] The difficulties that scholars have in identifying Mamluks may not have been shared by contemporaries, however, given the differences in costume and appearance between Ottoman soldiers and Mamluks: Ottomans were clean-shaven, Circassians bearded, and Ottomans wore costumes that differed in important details from those of the Circassians.[98]

Whatever their actual origins, Mamluks of the later period maintained their strongest identity with Egypt itself. What scholars refer to as 'neo-Mamluk' political culture "consisted mainly of a strong Egyptian identity as contrasted with a more general Ottoman or Turkish one. This consciousness had at least a latent hostility toward the Ottomans . . . ."[99] The most important strain of anti-Ottomanism in the seventeenth and eighteenth centuries did not emanate from the indigenous Arab population, but rather from the Turkish-speaking Mamluks.[100] In other words, by the eighteenth century, the Mamluks had, without a doubt, developed a local identity.

The two most important components of this local identity were Mamluk religious orthodoxy and the predominance of the Mamluk household as the basic unit of society.[101] As Michael Winter points out, the wider context for these developments was the "'localization' of the elites in Egypt and the other provinces,"[102] a process that was facilitated in large part by Ottoman policy. Continued Ottoman reliance on Mamluk military power, the use of Mamluk amirs as administrators (especially in the countryside), and the conscious articulation of a policy of continuity with the Qalawunid dynasty, all helped to preserve the demographic presence of the Mamluks and to create an identity that was, like earlier Mamluk identity, self-conscious, but unlike earlier Mamluk identity, tied very much to Egypt.[103]

Early in the Ottoman period, the Mamluks were still identified by labels associated exclusively with Turks. Arab chroniclers typically called them 'Turks,' while Turkish chroniclers typically referred to them as 'Circassian.' Following an interlude in which it is difficult to determine the ethnic meaning of labels, by the early nineteenth century, the Mamluks once again were a clearly identifiable group. By that time, they were ordinarily referred to as *jins al-mamalik* ('the Mamluk race') and were identified by the terms *misriya*, *misirliya*, or *misriyun*, that is, Egyptians. Their identification with place was firmly embedded in both the vocabulary and, apparently, the consciousness of their contemporaries.[104] The Mamluks had become Egyptian.

Meanings of the Medieval in Egypt

The medieval and other pasts were not created only by Europeans and, even then, not only in relationship to the East. Ottomans and Egyptians also engaged in various projects of creating usable pasts that were deployed in the service of creating difference, of creating new and distinct presents, and of creating and maintaining political authority. In all of these endeavors, architecture was intimately connected with a sense of history and was consciously used to represent particular pasts. Medieval Cairo could be and was interpreted in different ways. Some meanings of the medieval worked to create a temporal distance between East and West, helping to construct Egypt, in particular, as distinct and inferior to the British West in ways that are linked to orientalism. Some, working as an extension of European medievalism, linked West to East while allowing for differentiation without subordination. Still others, for example, Ottoman medievalism, worked to establish the Ottoman imperial past as distinct and superior to the Mamluk medieval, at the same time configuring an ideal Ottoman medieval past from which a modern imperial architecture could be recovered and embellished. Finally, whatever it might have been called, an Egyptian medieval signified by Mamluk architecture came also to represent a national Egyptian past.

Terminology of the Medieval

The period between the seventh and the sixteenth centuries in Egypt did not become classified as 'medieval' until the latter part of the nineteenth century, when the terms 'medieval' and 'Middle Ages' first appear in English scholarly and popular writing on Egypt. As a classification, 'medieval' was first used in relation to art and seems to have stood primarily as a way of distinguishing Islamic monuments from pharaonic. It was used by writers whose primary interest was in Christian or ancient Egypt. A.J. Butler noted as an aside in an article entitled "Ancient Monuments in Egypt" (1881) the fact that "the condition of mediaeval monuments is also receiving attention."[105] Just two years later, Amelia Edwards (a major figure in nineteenth-century Egyptology) lauded the "mediaeval Arab architecture" of Cairo, and an unsigned article referred synonymously to the "medieval architecture of Cairo" and Cairo's "Arab monuments."[106] The Rev. F.A. Walker expressed his regret that so much money should be spent building the new Rifaʿi mosque rather than restoring the "noble specimen of mediaeval art" (the mosque of Sultan Hasan) right across the street.[107] In the preface to his *Art of the Saracens in Egypt* (1886), Stanley Lane-Poole explained why he preferred the term 'Saracenic' to either 'Arab' or 'Mohammedan' in describing the subject of his book. It was because the term, which implied "the two ideas of Oriental and mediaeval, exactly fulfils the conditions of a general term for the art with which we are concerned."[108] The term apparently was beginning to acquire some currency with Anglophone Egyptians. The writer of a letter to *The Egyptian Gazette* who signed himself simply as "An old Egyptian" reproached the director of the Bulaq museum, Gaston Maspero, for its poor organization. Among his complaints, he noted, "In the same case, without a syllable of explanation, is placed a mediaeval Arabic mug, No. 27321."[109] And it had even infiltrated the political sphere: in the letter to Lord Granville proposing new Codes to protect antiquities, Lord Dufferin noted the need to protect "pre-historic" [pharaonic] as well as "Arabian mediaeval art and architecture."[110] By the 1890s, then, the term 'medieval' had taken its place alongside 'Arab/Arabian,' 'Saracenic,' and 'Mohammedan' in describing the art and architecture of Islamic Egypt.

The gradual introduction of a new term seems to have gone unnoticed, or at least, not to have occasioned any comment from those most concerned with the subject. A.J. Butler's review of Stanley Lane-Poole's *Art of the Saracens in Egypt* scrutinizes every term but 'medieval,' which he uses himself to describe the book's subject as "Egyptian mediaeval art." Butler notes:

> The question at the root of the whole matter is, Was there ever an Arab art? Mr. Lane-Poole says decisively, 'The artists in this style were seldom Arabs, and many of them were Christians.' He, therefore, rejects the terms 'Arab' and 'Mohammedan' and substitutes 'saracenic'; yet adds immediately that 'saracen' was 'the universal designation of *Muslims* in the Middle Ages,' to whatever part of the eastern world they belonged. Yet if 'saracen' is synonymous with 'Muslim,' we fail to see the distinction between 'saracen' and

> 'Mohammedan.' The very word 'saracen' therefore commits the author to a theory which he himself helps to prove untenable" (italics in original).

There follows an even longer discussion of the significance of the terminology, but Butler never questions Lane-Poole's use of the 'medieval.'[111]

Throughout the 1890s, 'medieval' continued as a classification of art and architecture,[112] but it also became an adjective used to describe the city of Cairo itself. Whereas in the 1880s, writers had referred to the medieval art, architecture, or monuments of Cairo, they now began to speak of 'medieval Cairo.' The frontispiece to Stanley Lane-Poole's edition of Edward William Lane's *Cairo Fifty Years Ago* (1896) was a map entitled "Plan of Medieval Cairo," an attraction announced also on the book's title page, although Lane himself had never used the word 'medieval' with respect to Cairo in any of his writings.[113] What is most striking is Lane-Poole's almost casual use of 'medieval,' which reviewers of the book repeated without comment.[114]

In fact, the usage was entirely new. Whether in official documents, scholarly works, travel books, or more popular publications, Cairo had been simply 'Cairo.' It had largely ceased to be even the 'Grand Cairo' of earlier centuries. Throughout the 1880s, articles appeared with titles like "Monuments of Arab Art in Cairo,"[115] "The Architecture of Cairo,"[116] "The Commission for the Preservation of the Monuments of Cairo,"[117] and letters discussed the "Arab monuments of Cairo."[118] Beginning early in the 1890s, however, the city itself—not merely its monuments—was figured as medieval. In *Cairo: Sketches of its History, Monuments, and Social Life* (1892), Stanley Lane-Poole announced as his purpose to give a "general view of the historical, archaeological, and social aspects of *mediaeval* and modern Cairo."[119] An article in *The Times* (1896) assessing the efforts of the Comité was entitled "The Preservation of Medieval Cairo."[120] One critic observed, "It is curious that the part of mediaeval Cairo that has been, perhaps, most neglected by the archaeologists is the famous citadel . . . ."[121] Another criticized Sir William Muir's *The Mameluke or Slave Dynasty of Egypt* on the grounds that for such a study to be successful, "the writer must be at home in mediaeval Cairo," a standard which Muir failed to meet.[122]

By the late 1890s, not only did 'medieval' serve as a classification for art and a descriptor of the city of Cairo, but the 'Middle Ages' now constituted a discrete historical era in Egyptian history. The medieval was broadening to include the East, as we can see clearly from the comment of the anonymous review, published in *The Athenaeum* on 19 July 1890, of F.F. Arbuthnot's *Arabic Authors: A Manual of Arabian History and Literature*, which makes serious criticisms of the volume while noting that "it will be of service in drawing the attention of students to that vast treasure-house of Arabic literature which is at last beginning to take its rightful place among the authoritative sources for mediaeval history and civilization."[123]

This new periodization was enshrined by the Baedeker guide in the fourth edition, published in 1898.[124] In the third edition (1895), the "Outline of the History of Egypt" was presented in a chronological table organized dynastically under the following rubrics: Primaeval Monarchy, Middle Monarchy, Hyksos Period, New Empire, Persian Domination, Period of the Ptolemies, Roman Period, Byzantines, Mohammedan Period, French Occupation, and Muhammad 'Ali and his successors. The 'Mohammedan Period' began with the conquest of Egypt in 640 and ended with Murad Bey and Ibrahim Bey (the last date mentioned is 1773). In 1898, the dynasties that had been the primary categories of the third edition were now subsumed under three broad historical eras: Ancient History, the Middle Ages, and Modern History. The Middle Ages began with the Mohammedan period (now understood as only the earliest period of Islamic rule over Egypt), and was broken down further under the subsequent dynasties. But the introduction of the historical era 'Middle Ages' was not the only change. In the 1898 edition, the Middle Ages ends with the Ottoman conquest of Egypt; what is called in both the third and fourth editions the "Turkish Domination after 1517" is, in the fourth (1898) edition, a part of Modern History. Although the narrative itself remains the same, the implications are different: a firm boundary had been drawn between the Ottomans and the Mamluks, between modern and medieval.[125]

It is no coincidence that one of the first historians to adopt and popularize the notion that the period from 640–1517 constituted an Egyptian Middle Ages was Stanley Lane-Poole, great-nephew of Edward William Lane and brother of Reginald Lane-Poole, the distinguished historian of medieval Europe and founding editor of *The English Historical Review*.[126] Stanley employed the category in *A History of Egypt in the Middle Ages* (1901), published as volume six of the Methuen & Co. series, *History of Egypt*, and *The Story of Cairo* (1902), published in J. M. Dent & Co.'s Mediaeval Towns series.[127] In *The Story of Cairo*, Lane-Poole makes it clear that the medieval is not merely an arbitrary division of time, but is also an attribute: "Cairo is in the fullest sense a mediaeval city. It had no existence before the Middle Ages; its vigorous life as a separate Metropolis almost coincides with the arbitrary millennium of the middle period of history; and it still retains to this day much of its mediaeval character and aspect."[128]

Lane-Poole also used the term 'medieval' to describe the period of Muslim rule in India:

> The Mediaeval Period of Indian history, though it does not exactly correspond with the Middle Age of Europe, is not less clearly defined. It begins when the immemorial systems, rule, and customs of Ancient India were invaded, subdued, and modified by a succession of foreign conquerors who imposed a new rule and introduced an exotic creed, strange languages and a foreign art. These conquerors were Muslims, and with the arrival of the Turks under Mahmud the Iconoclast at the beginning of the eleventh century, India entered upon her Middle Age . . . .The Period ends when one of the last of these rulers, oppressed by the revival of Hindu ascendency, placed himself under English protection, and Modern India came into being.[129]

Meanings of the Medieval in Cairo

Many observers who came to Egypt sought to recapture a past that no longer existed in Europe, one for which they had developed a distinct nostalgia. As Ussama Makdisi has shown in another context, this represented one strain of romanticism that sought to find in the East a simpler life untainted by rampant industrialism. As Stanley Lane-Poole put it, "The blessed conservatism of the East has happily maintained much of the old city in its beautiful ruinous unprogressive disorder."[130] In old Cairo they found the dark, winding streets and the old buildings that no longer existed in London and a host of other industrialized English cities. One meaning of the 'medieval' in Cairo, then, was simply 'not modern.'

The "unprogressive disorder" that Lane-Poole relished was in some respects an artifact of nineteenth-century city planning. As Timothy Mitchell has shown, the "disorder" of Cairo became visible as Egyptian urban space was reorganized by radiating boulevards, wide streets, and a clear center.[131] Cairo was actually becoming a modern city through a process that, while inspired by European urban modernization, was nonetheless progressing independently.[132] In a manner reminiscent of another strain of romanticism inspired by resistance to independent modernization in the East, Khedive Ismail's new city—with its paved streets, wide boulevards, and bland façades—was judged a pale and pathetic imitation of a European city and compared unfavorably to the veracity and authenticity of the medieval city. Ismailiya (now modern downtown Cairo) was considered to lack any sort of authenticity, and was relegated to being either utterly inauthentic or inferior imitation. Eustace Reynolds-Ball deemed the "hausmannising tendencies of Ismail" to have barely scratched the surface of the city. In fact, he equated both Muhammad 'Ali's and Ismail's attempts to Europeanize the city as mere vulgarization.[133] Egypt might rank high on the list of tourist attractions because of its antiquities, but viewed "as a community or modern state, the Egypt of to-day holds a very low rank among semi-civilised countries."[134] This was, of course, a well-rehearsed argument; European travelers displayed a similar disdain for the newer architectures of the Ottoman Empire, and in particular the self-consciously modern architecture of the Tanzimat.[135] If modernization were to occur in the East then it was to be entirely on the terms of Europeans.[136] In this environment, the 'medieval' signaled not only 'not modern,' and in that sense, 'authentic,' but also 'not capable of becoming modern on its own.' This sense of the medieval was clear in Stanley Lane-Poole's assessment of the trauma that Europeanization caused to what he understood to be a decidedly medieval city: "The introduction of a bastard European style, the laying out of new streets, and the broadening of old ones, during the past fifty years, are responsible for more havoc among the monuments of Saracenic art than the centuries of former neglect. The street fights of the Mamlûk Beys and Turkish Pashas did less damage to the mosques of Cairo than the futile attempt to Europeanize a medieval Eastern city."[137]

These meanings, however, did not exclude what may seem to be a contradictory and even surprising meaning: the national. This sense of what constituted an authentic national art depended, in fact, upon the accumulation of other meanings, in particular the rejection of an indigenous modern in favor of the medieval. Lane-Poole encouraged English and American tourists to visit the museum and to avail themselves of the opportunity to study the "exquisite national art of medieval Egypt." Similar sentiments are echoed in an unsigned article published in *The Athenaeum* in 1889, condemning a proposed new street in Cairo that would run from the bottom of the Muski near the Mixed Tribunals to Bab al-Nasr. As the author decries the proposed modern street, with the attendant destruction of ancient monuments, he at the same time acknowledges the need for the new thoroughfare. His primary goal is to prevent the erection of "tenements so mean and abject, so irredeemably vulgar and trumpery—scarecrows beyond even the conception of the most unscrupulous jerry builder of a London suburb" as had been built along Clot Bey and Muhammad 'Ali Boulevards. He proposes, instead, that interested architectural societies should lobby the authorities at Cairo to avoid buildings in "the Turkish style of the last century, whose ornamentation is tawdry and mechanical, and would never rise above stolid mediocrity" and to return "to the true national art, that of the Memlook Sultans."[138]

However, this 'national' did not imply an independent nation-state, a situation not unusual in imperial contexts. One of its most important meanings marked Egypt as distinct from the Ottoman Empire. Throughout the 1880s and 1890s, the British debated the question of England's occupation of Egypt, its primary goals, and its limits. England's policy in the Middle East had traditionally been centered on the Ottoman Empire, a configuration that would change in the aftermath of England's occupation of Egypt in 1882, a move that significantly weakened Ottoman prestige. Throughout the 1880s, the Salisbury government sought to negotiate a settlement on the Egyptian question with the Ottomans in order to preserve the traditional power arrangements.[139]

If England were to stay in Egypt, then Cairo would inevitably displace Constantinople as the center of English Middle Eastern policy. And so 'medieval' could, like 'Arab,' also mean 'not Ottoman.' The 'national' meaning of the medieval could be posed, then, against 'Ottoman.' This equivalence of 'national' and 'medieval' as 'not Ottoman' is clearly visible both in explicitly political and artistic assessments of what constitutes 'Egyptianness.' In a letter to Foreign Minister Salisbury in February, 1892, Lord Cromer wrote of the new khedive Abbas II, who had just acceded to the throne, "I see that the young Khedive is going to be very Egyptian, by which I mean, not so much anti-European—and certainly not anti-English—as anti-Turk, anti-Syrian etc . . . ."[140] This notion of Egyptian as 'not Ottoman' was already evident at an earlier period, and remained significant in both popular and scholarly writings. When an anonymous reviewer of Stanley Lane-Poole's *Art of the Saracens in Egypt* referred to the "mosques and palaces of mediaeval Egypt before the advent of the Turks," he meant, of course, not the Mamluks but the Ottomans.[141]

The Mamluk medieval signified 'not Ottoman' for Egyptians and Ottomans, too. In the Tanzimat period, Ottoman preservation in Istanbul and in the provinces was tied directly to programs of reform and modernization, as well as to the representation of a modern Islamic state. As Ahmet Ersoy notes in his brilliant dissertation on Ottoman architectural revival,[142] Ottoman intellectuals and architects wrote about their own architecture and its meaning in the *Usul-i Mi'mari Osmani* ('The Fundamentals of Ottoman Architecture'), published in 1873 by the Ottoman government as "an official manifesto for the new directions taken in the architecture of the Abdülaziz era."[143] The *Usul*, largely the work of Marie de Launay, was published in French (the primary language of the text), German, and Turkish.[144] While influenced by European writings on architecture, it was deeply informed, also, by new traditions of Ottoman historical writing, which were part of the general project of "historicizing an Ottoman identity" and "rendering a more tangible and convincing vision of the remote past."[145] Ottoman architecture was presented as part of a linear path of civilizational progress of an increasingly sophisticated and aesthetically desirable style with roots in multiple cultures (Arabic, Eastern [meaning Persian], and Greek).[146]

The *Usul* also identified a specific 'medieval' period in Ottoman architecture that was epitomized by Bursa's Green Mosque. Built in the first quarter of the fifteenth century by Sultan Mehmet I, it was hailed as a decisive moment in the creation of a distinctively Ottoman architecture that both synthesized and moved beyond the earlier Saracenic (Arab), Eastern, and Byzantine styles.[147] It was part of an Ottoman romantic medievalism that glorified the syncretism of the early Ottoman dynasty and presented it as model for the emerging modern Ottoman imperial state.[148]

As part of this new history of progressive style, a classical period and canon, corresponding to the era of the great Ottoman builder Sinan, was also defined. Thus the heydey of Ottoman imperial culture, the era of Suleiman (called 'The Magnificent' by Europeans and 'Kanuni' ['The Lawgiver'] by Ottomans), was enshrined in the *Usul* as the apex of Ottoman architecture, in terms that were shaped by European aesthetics of the classical. The authors of the *Usul* did not hesitate to reify (rather than challenge) European aesthetics and to appropriate those very standards to establish an Ottoman canon that was distinct from the monolithic category of the oriental and that also met the aesthetic standards of western art.[149]

With this canon in place, the Ottoman Empire began to represent itself through its distinctive architecture in World's Fairs beginning in the 1860s.[150] In 1862, the Ottoman government accepted the invitation to the London exhibit only after learning that three of its provinces—Egypt, Serbia, and Tunisia—had already accepted invitations. Such independent exhibits were a direct challenge to the authority of the Ottoman state and could not go unanswered.[151] Of these challenges to Ottoman authority, the most important and potentially damaging was that from Egypt, which received nearly an equal amount of display space as the Ottoman imperial exhibit.[152] The Sublime Porte's exposition commission recognized the importance of making a powerful statement: "Many states, in particular the provinces of Egypt and Tunisia along with other lands that are within the imperial territories, are spending generous sums for building and decorating [their own sections in the exposition]. Accordingly, it is a requisite of the proper course of affairs that the buildings and displays to be exhibited by the sublime state eclipse those of the mentioned lands in firmness, elegance and beauty."[153] Thus, even Egypt's early self-representations in Europe provoked controversy and tension within an Ottoman imperial context.

The task of providing an official version of Egypt's history and architecture was undertaken at the time of the Paris Exposition of 1867, in a volume written by Charles Edmond, adorned by a frontispiece with a woodcut of the khedive, and introduced by a brief history of Khedive Ismail's reign.[154] Edmond, like most of his nineteenth-century contemporaries, believed that architecture was a fundamental way to read the character of a people.[155] The buildings that he thought properly represented Egypt's past were located within each of three different historical eras corresponding to a distinct architectural style: ancient, medieval, and modern. The medieval period is deemed by Edmond to have given birth to the Islamic architecture that won fame in the West. The volume has a strictly chronological organization, but significantly, the long years of Ottoman rule are not mentioned explicitly at all. The volume also boasts woodcuts of buildings representing each of the three eras: an Egyptian temple (between pp. 20–21), a khedivial residence, the "Selamlick" [an obviously Ottoman term used to describe a Mamluk era structure] (between pp. 129–30) (Figure 8), and a caravanserai (*wakala*, Fr. *okel*) complete with mashrabiyas (between pp. 202–203). The visual representation of Egypt's historic past was confined, then, to the ancient and the Mamluk medieval, clearly and definitively dissociating Egypt from the Ottoman context at the same time that Ottoman imperial authority bypassed the Mamluk era in architectural representations of the empire's past.

Some fourteen years after the publication of the *Usul*, Muhammad Effendi 'Arif, an architecture instructor at Egypt's Khedivial School of Engineering, published his own treatise on architecture, *Khulasat al-afkar fi fann al-mi'mar* (1887), providing a history of Arab architecture as well as a technical manual of architectural theory and construction techniques.[156] 'Arif's publication, the first of its kind in Egypt, should certainly be understood in the context of the *Usul* as well as the standard works by European architects on Arab architecture. His chronology of Arab architecture resembles in its broad outlines that of the European architects whom he mentions by name (and in the most laudatory terms): Jules Bourgoin, Pascal Coste, and Julius Franz Pasha. 'Arif takes issue, however, with Viollet-le-Duc's statements in his introduction to Bourgoin's volume on Arab art, and explicitly responds to his critique of Arab architecture.[157] 'Arif insists on the continuous civilization of the Arabs, dating from the time of the Flood, and the status of Arab civilization as the root from which all other civilizations borrowed. Furthermore, he states, "They (the Arabs) are the root of the art of engineering and building, just as they are the root in courage, honor, trustworthiness, faith, and the noble traits *(makarim al-akhlaq)* and no one except an ignorant person or someone feigning ignorance would deny that."[158] 'Arif showers praise on Franz Pasha, whom he credits not only with revitalizing the ancient monuments of Arab art and building the mosque of Sayyida Zaynab, but also with reviving the Arab crafts, particularly architecture, thereby revitalizing the "souls that had nearly died of hunger from neglect of these Arab crafts."[159] While framed in terms of European intervention, the emphasis on crafts reflected both a growing Egyptian preoccupation and a broader Ottoman concern with traditional crafts as a crucial component of the historic roots of national identities, a concern that also echoed European romanticism's lauding of the manual crafts in the face of rampant industrialization.[160]

We have already seen how the khedivial family and many Egyptians in the late nineteenth century embraced both neo-Mamluk architecture and the conservation project. The efflorescence of the neo-Mamluk, whether in religious architecture (as in the case of the Rifa'i Mosque), the Khedivial Library, or the commercial and residential architecture of the planned suburb of Heliopolis, marked a distinctively non-Ottoman urban architecture.[161] In embracing the neo-Mamluk, Egyptians as well as Europeans explicitly rejected both classical Ottoman architectural forms and the Late Tanzimat era Ottoman architecture that was popular in the Ottoman metropole. This embrace of the Mamluk medieval was part and parcel of the emergence of a national identity expressed in a local Egyptian nationalism that was rooted in Islam without acknowledging the sovereignty of the Ottoman sultan (who also claimed the title 'caliph').[162] But not all Egyptians understood their 'Egyptianness' in terms of anti-Ottomanism. The 'Urabists, their sympathizers, and many others embraced an Ottomanist Islamic identity, and paid homage to the Ottoman sultan-caliph as an essential component of their emerging national self-definition. Both Egyptian and European Mamluk medievalism registered anti-Ottomanism in imperial and local contexts.

Conclusion

We have seen in this chapter how three superimposed sets of ideas and practices in overlapping imperial and local spheres interacted to produce and canonize Medieval Cairo as a largely Mamluk city. We have also seen that this version of a medieval city had multiple meanings, sometimes in tension with one another; that these meanings of the medieval did not always distance and subordinate Egypt to the West; and that they might serve independent Egyptian and Ottoman political agendas. The fluidity of these meanings of the medieval made them available for a multiplicity of imperial and non-imperial purposes. But in one respect—religion—the meaning of the medieval remained squarely within the dynamics of power and worked to construct Egypt and Egyptians as deficient and stagnant. In the next chapter, I show how the Comité's construction of Medieval Cairo visually represented Islam as 'medieval' in the sense of 'incapable of becoming modern on its own' at the very time when reformist Muslims in Egypt and the rest of the Ottoman Empire were pursuing a clear program of Islamic modernization.[163]

2

Islam for the Modern World

Medieval Cairo between Egyptian Reformers and British Critics

Introduction

In Chapter 1, I considered the Mamluk orientation of Medieval Cairo and the different meanings that 'medieval' could have in the context of overlapping imperial and local settings: 'not modern,' 'not capable of becoming modern on its own,' but also 'not Ottoman' and 'national.' I argued that some of these meanings of the medieval were fluid and shifting, that contradictory meanings could coexist without being mutually exclusive, and that the medieval did not always reflect asymmetries of power along an East–West axis. Finally, I concluded with an assertion, namely, that Mamluk Medieval Cairo consistently signified the superiority of the West in one important respect, that of religion. This chapter builds the case that the Comité's construction of Medieval Cairo visually represented Islam as 'medieval' in the sense of its being deficient, stagnant, and incompatible with modernity at the very time when reformist Muslims in Egypt and the rest of the Ottoman Empire were articulating a clear vision of a reformed Islam that was compatible with, and embedded in, modernity.[1]

Curiously, religious contexts per se have received little attention in telling the story of the construction of Medieval Cairo. In spite of the predominance of religious buildings in the Comité's activities, the historiography of preservation has said little, if anything at all, about the character of religious life in Cairo in the later nineteenth century, the role of old religious buildings in local religious life, or the role of architecture in debates and discussions about religion.

I will address these issues—and provide a history of the religious contexts that are so important—by considering the intense discussions and debates over religious institutions, including religious architecture, in which some of Egypt's foremost exponents of religious and social reform expressed sharp differences with the Comité and other voices of European and Egyptian culture. Most educated Egyptians recognized that Egypt sat on the brink of a new world. Indeed, most Egyptians had already experienced or were aware of the drastic changes in their own society that had been introduced by Muhammad 'Ali in the early nineteenth century. Most members of the religious elite believed that educational reform was needed. Some of these debates were cast in terms of reform, progress, and modernization, but not all of them offered the same diagnoses of Egyptian society's ills or the same remedies.

In the sections that follow, I focus first on the voices of two Egyptian reformers who participated, in very different ways, in these debates: Muhammad 'Abduh (1849–1905) and 'Ali Mubarak (1823–93). Their primary concerns were different—'Abduh's was social, educational, and religious reform, Mubarak's was the modernization of the city of Cairo—but from these different vantage points, each confronted the relationship between religion and architecture. I then discuss two European voices, represented by the Comité and Lord Cromer. The Comité largely ignored contemporary religious practice in its deliberations and other European perspectives were equally blind; Cromer, a strong and active supporter of architectural conservation as practiced by the Comité, was also a powerful voice against religious reform and expressed clearly the view that Islam was incapable of reform.

At the heart of these debates were fundamentally different ideas about Islam and the possibilities for Islam as a religion in the modern world, ideas that also found expression in decisions over the fate of old and new buildings in Medieval Cairo as it was being constructed in the late nineteenth century. 'Abduh and Mubarak worked from the assumption that Islam could be reformed in ways that were both faithful to its essential truths and fully compatible with modernity. Their modernizing activities were not isolated, for such programs were also fundamental to Ottoman imperial policy in the nineteenth century.[2] Europeans largely rejected their premise of the possibility of reform, and while such a position was not explicitly stated by the European members who dominated the activities of the Comité, it clearly informed their activities.

In Egypt, Azhar-educated Egyptian reformists, particularly under the leadership of Muhammad 'Abduh, were advocating the creation of an Islam for the modern world through a wide-ranging program of reform *(islah)*. At this moment, when Ottoman and Egyptian reformists were articulating a thoroughly modern Islam, and when Egyptian officials like 'Ali Mubarak were informed by a rich sense of what constituted a vibrant religious practice, Europeans continued to insist that Islam was a medieval religion with no possibility of real reform or advancement. This political, cultural, and social judgment was expressed in official policy, in writing, and visually in the creation of Medieval Cairo by both Europeans and Egyptians through the preservation program of the Comité. In a late-Ottoman imperial context, where religion and religious institutions were configured as markers of modernity, the Comité's preservation program in Egypt appropriated religious symbols and institutions as markers of the medieval. European preservation's insistence on privileging the medieval undercut the Ottoman program at the same time that it undercut indigenous Egyptian efforts to reform Islam. Those ideas about Islam as a medieval religion found one expression in the Comité's architectural program, which rejected two Muslim modernities, one Ottoman, the other Egyptian, in favor of a Mamluk medieval. In this way, they were not only creating and canonizing Medieval Cairo, but also insisting on a medieval and not a modern Islam.

Muhammad 'Abduh's Islah for Mosques: Architectural Preservation and Religious Reform

Muhammad 'Abduh (ca. 1849–1905), the great Egyptian Muslim reformer, was one of the most important voices of the nineteenth century calling for social and religious reform. An Azhar-educated intellectual who was a judge in the People's Courts, he laid out a program of repair for mosques as part of his broad program of religious reform. His general program entailed reforming administrative and financial organization and employing personnel who were qualified to carry out the religious mandate of places of worship: better *khatib*s (the men who deliver the address at Friday prayer), better imams, and better wages so that current mosque personnel—whom he referred to as "lazy ignoramuses," willing to work for a few piasters—could be replaced with qualified religious officials. The repair of material structures, particularly large monuments, was not his priority, nor was this kind of repair or preservation deemed necessary or even desirable by many, who believed that the money allocated to physical preservation of old mosques could be better spent.

'Abduh was well aware of the activities of the Comité, and he was resolutely critical of their work. The Comité's preservation program was intended, as 'Abduh observed, largely for a foreign audience. These are the complaints of a reformer who wanted mosques to function as houses of worship, not as tourist attractions or museums. He further charged that the Comité's repairs were superficial, limited to the material structure and to irrelevant material elements at that, and used funds that could be better spent to achieve true reform by improving wages in order to hire better personnel. 'Abduh's reform program for mosques was, in fact, a restoration program but one with entirely different—even contradictory—goals from those of the Comité. Unlike the Comité program of restoration, in which conserved mosques were not ordinarily conceived as sites of religious worship (except, perhaps, in an incidental way), 'Abduh's reform program was intended specifically to make mosques appropriate places of religious activity for the local population. This is a concern about which the Comité is silent, for their primary concern was not to restore mosques as functioning religious institutions for the local Muslim community.[3]

'Abduh's specific proposals for the reorganization and improvement of mosques were part of his comprehensive program of social and religious reform. In a piece published in June 1904, 'Abduh laid out the program he had long advocated for mosque reform, one that addressed explicitly religious questions. His program was founded upon raising the wages of imams, *khatib*s, and muezzins in order to make sure that qualified men were officiating in mosques. 'Abduh lamented the state of religious officials in his age. Most of the imams, he complained, "are ignorant even of the laws of ritual purity and prayer and most of the *khatib*s make errors on the minbar, even [when reciting] verses of the Qur'an . . . ."[4] 'Abduh further complained about dishonesty and lies in exhortatory sermons *(wa'z)* and "manufactured nonsense." "Is it not amazing *(min al-'aja'ib)*," 'Abduh asks, "that a Muslim who persists in these disapproved acts *(munkarat)*, one who seeks to continue them, rather than desisting from them in the name of religion—that such a person should nonetheless be one of the *ulama* of the Muslims?"[5]

From 'Abduh's point of view, one of the basic obstacles to reforming Islam was the generally low quality of education at all levels. Students were required to memorize dictated text, without attention to interpretation or analysis of its meaning. This emphasis on memory was in keeping with long-standing pedagogy in Islamic education.[6] Since Muslim children across the Islamic Empire spoke different vernaculars and even different dialects of Arabic, students often had no understanding of what they were memorizing.[7]

A true reform of Islam required a ruthless peeling away of the nonessential accretions of the centuries and radical reform of the educational system. In place of the blind, uncritical adherence to tradition and the obsolete educational methods that emphasized rote memory, 'Abduh advocated new methods. His insistence was not only a result of exposure to Western pedagogical methods that had been introduced recently into European education, but grew also out of his own unhappy experiences as a schoolboy: "I spent a year and a half without understanding a single thing, because of the harmful character of the method of instruction; for the teachers were accustomed to use technical terms of grammar or jurisprudence which we did not understand, nor did they take any pains to explain their meaning to those who did not know it."[8] So frustrated was he by these experiences that he ran away more than once before his attitude toward learning was irrevocably altered by the inspirational uncle who introduced him to mysticism. In his autobiography, 'Abduh notes that the same futile pedagogical methods were still in use at al-Azhar. Such methods he considered not only ineffectual, but harmful, for they produce adults who only suppose that they understand the subject matter and who are "thereafter . . . inflicted upon the people and become a calamity upon the public."[9] These were no doubt the "lazy ignoramuses" whom 'Abduh would try to extirpate from the mosques through his reforms.

'Abduh wanted not only to change the pedagogical methods in use, but also to introduce new subjects for study. 'Abduh and the reformists recommended the introduction of western science and techniques. At the level of higher education, the curriculum had remained constant for some centuries, focusing on the so-called 'transmitted sciences' (also called the 'traditional' sciences): theology, Qur'anic interpretation, traditions of the Prophet's life *(hadith)*, jurisprudence, and the roots of law. Once those were mastered, advanced students would move on to the study of Arabic grammar and syntax, prosody, rhetoric, logic, technical terminology of the Science of Traditions, and astronomy, subjects that were considered to be an aid to understanding the transmitted sciences.[10] His comprehensive reform program, especially for higher education, encountered resistance from fellow Egyptian *ulama* as well as from British officials. His fellow *ulama* had a wide range of views about how to improve education and to reverse the state of religious decline that many Egyptian intellectuals and politicians diagnosed, even as they disagreed about the proper remedies for it. Many *ulama* who were not reformists, for example, were nonetheless committed to the project of improving higher education, although they disagreed about how to go about it.

The reorganization of Muslim teaching, especially in the Azhar, was to be accomplished in large part by reorganization of the mosques and the *waqf*s. But these goals could not be accomplished as long as the scarce resources available in the *waqf*s were being misdirected toward unneeded and irrelevant material repairs in mosques that would be frequented by tourists.

Old Actor, New Story: 'Ali Mubarak's Islam and Preservation

'Ali Mubarak's place in the story of religion and preservation is different. He did not advocate, as did 'Abduh, a comprehensive program of religious reform, but he was nonetheless both a reformer and a modernizer. As Minister of Public Works under Khedive Ismail, he was largely responsible for introducing the hallmarks of modern urbanization in Cairo. It is he who planned and executed the new district of Ismailiya in response to Ismail's order to make him a "Paris by the Nile." He cut major arteries through the city, planned and built straight and wide streets that wheeled vehicles could traverse, and in the process, appropriated and destroyed numerous old buildings. In the classic story of the Comité, 'Ali Mubarak appears as a protagonist for modernizers and as a dubious figure—possibly a villain—in the story of conservation. This narrative pits conservationists against modernizers and 'traditional' Egyptians against Europeans, framing the story as a turf battle between the ministry of public works, modernizers, and the Comité.

Biographical treatments of 'Ali Mubarak and critical assessments of his great topography, *al-Khitat al-tawfiqiya al-jadida*, treat him primarily as a modernizer. But just as we have seen how nineteenth-century religious life and practice as a context for preservation brings new actors like Muhammad 'Abduh into our story, so does this context allow us to tell a new story about an old actor and the unspoken assumptions behind his decisions.[11] Michael Reimer points out the tensions and contradictions in 'Ali Mubarak's discussion of al-Azhar that resonate with the concerns expressed by the reformists. Mubarak saw al-Azhar, Egypt's greatest educational and religious institution, as a highly problematic one that opposed the study of the modern sciences like history, geography, and philosophy.

'Ali Mubarak's alter ego and protagonist in his fictional account of an Egyptian student in Paris in the nineteenth century, *'Alam al-din*, expounds upon the ill effects of the pedagogical methods of Azharis: "When I became a student in al-Azhar, I found the movement (of its members) very minimal. They sit for long periods reading and they have no time for entertainment. For the sake of attaining knowledge, I did like them, and was static all the time, although I knew that that was a bad habit, especially for one's health, for the floor was cold and the covers on it thin. . . . This way, I developed all kinds of ailments.'"[12] This echoes, with a slightly different focus, 'Abduh's critique of pedagogy. Reimer concludes from both the *Khitat* and *'Alam al-din* that Mubarak considers the Azharis to "demonstrate by their conduct and appearance a contempt for the kind of religion compatible with modern civilization."[13]

But what understanding of religion underlies Mubarak's critique of the Azharis? And what do these assumptions about religion have to do with his role in the remaking of Cairo? Placing 'Ali Mubarak in the story of Medieval Cairo is not as simple as we once thought if we consider him in the context of religious life. 'Ali Mubarak was dismayed by the deterioration of al-Azhar materially and institutionally, and he considered the pedagogical methods of al-Azhar to be counterproductive in a modernizing nation. In this respect, he was in good company. But 'Ali Mubarak also had a broad notion of what constituted religious life in the city, one that went beyond critiques of pedagogical methods or objects of study—both issues embedded in a notion of religion and education as being centered on textual traditions. His writings about al-Azhar understandably receive considerable scholarly attention, but 'Ali Mubarak also wrote in detail about what scholars commonly call "popular religious practice." His topography pays ample attention to old mosques, following al-Maqrizi in his effort to record the history of all sites still in existence, but also records faithfully the full range of religious life in the city of Cairo. In so doing, he enters into the broader conversation and debates about the character of Islam as a religion, and he treats Islam as he understood and experienced it, as the living religious tradition of Egypt.

'Ali Mubarak insists that al-Azhar must be replaced because it is too resistant to change, but he never suggests that the practices at local shrines—to which many reformers, including Muhammad 'Abduh, objected—should be prohibited or abandoned (although he does mention the reactions of some Azhari officials to these practices). On the contrary, he attests to the efficacy of such practices. After listing the tomb of Sayyida Nafisa as one of the four places well known in Egypt for the answering of supplications (to God), he explains that Egyptians who have been struck by calamity or death or catastrophe still go to one of these places in order to make supplications to God, who answers the prayers of those who are suffering from these tribulations.[14] In descriptions of other sites, 'Ali Mubarak gives equally detailed accounts of the founding of shrines, the biographies of saints, and the practices associated with them, including a lengthy account of the history and practices at the mosque–tomb of Sayyida Zaynab, who is arguably Egypt's most revered saint.[15]

Here, Mubarak enters indirectly into one of the most heated debates about religious life that occupied the attention of nineteenth-century *ulama*: the legitimacy of Egypt's cult of saints, a feature of Egyptian religious life for many centuries. This collection of practices—including celebration of their *mawlid*s (birth or death anniversaries), visits to saints' tombs in the cemeteries of Cairo, and pleas for their intercession—was widely observed as well as roundly criticized. The notion that saints could perform miracles was often a source of concern.[16] The question of intercession *(shafa'a)* was especially contentious. In classical Muslim thought, intercession was largely discussed in the theology of the eschaton. Many classical Muslim theologians found ample evidence in the Qur'an and *hadith* that the Prophet would intercede on behalf of his community on the Day of Judgment, but there was considerable debate over the question of the intercession of saints. Large numbers of Sunni Muslims subscribed to the belief that saints (and the Prophet) could and did intercede for them on a variety of issues. Visits to saints' tombs and supplications for a variety of needs in this world (not the next world and not the eschaton) were a widespread form of popular piety. Egypt was particularly rich in saints' tombs, and the practice of *ziyara*, or visits to saints' tombs, was so widespread that guidebooks were produced in the Middle Ages for pilgrims.[17]

In spite of the controversies among scholars over these practices, many *ulama* participated in ritual activities associated with the saints. An eighteenth-century Azhar shaykh built a boat to transport pilgrims to the *mawlid* of one of Egypt's most celebrated saints, al-Sayyid al-Badawi, in the Delta city of Tanta.[18] When al-Azhar's *ulama* wanted to protest the unusual appointment of a Hanafi to the office of Shaykh al-Azhar (a position over which the Shafi'is held a monopoly), they spent the night at the tomb of al-Shafi'i.[19] This move made perfect sense in Egypt, where religious institutions were fully integrated into social and political life, and where dead saints were believed by many to have the capacity to intervene actively in the affairs of the living.

The Causes of Stagnation: Lord Cromer on Egyptian Religion and Education

Lord Cromer believed that Egypt, like the rest of the East, was mired in stagnation.[20] There was a fundamental flaw in the oriental character that was irremediable of its own accord; Islam was a 'medieval' religion, meaning one that was obscurantist and freighted with superstition, and was therefore an insurmountable obstacle to progress.[21] British critics were especially disdainful of Egyptian religious practices, which they dismissed as empty ritual, including in the category everything from Muslim postures in prayer to the habit of swaying back and forth while reciting the Qur'an.[22]

The Muslim reformist position noted the same flaws—magical and religious superstition chief among them—but attributed them to a different source. The problem with such practices and ideas was not that they were 'medieval,' for the term did not exist in Arabic usage or thought, but rather that such customs constituted innovation *(bid'a)*. Most importantly, the reformist diagnosis of the ills of Muslim society was decidedly anti-essentialist. The problem with Muslim societies was not the result of any essential flaw in Islam, but was the consequence of corrupting innovations *(bid'a)* that had been introduced over many centuries.[23] As the Islamic modernist Muhammad Rashid Rida (1865–1935) lamented, "We wore out our pens and our voices through writing and repeating that the misfortunes of the Muslims cannot be blamed on their religion, but rather on the innovations that they have introduced into it . . . ."[24] If such destructive innovations could be rooted out, Muslims could advance like anyone else.

For Rida and his reformist colleagues, the problem was innovations introduced over the course of centuries by Muslims themselves. For Cromer, the source of the problems lay primarily in what he considered to be essential features of Islam. Even for the British, however, the causes of stagnation were multiple and they could not all be ascribed to Islam itself.

The British considered the rote memorization of the sacred text to be a definitive sign of Egyptian backwardness. In addition to Islam's essential flaws, Cromer also blamed Muslim exposure to the wrong sorts of Europeans, and he urged his readers to exercise "Christian charity" in making "every possible allowance for the moral and intellectual shortcomings of the Egyptians," some of which, he was forced to admit, were "due to association with European civilisation in a debased form."[25]

Cromer's assessment of Eastern Christianity also defaults to geographical and racial difference when religious difference does not serve his purposes:

> The Christianity of the Copt has been as conservative as the Islamism of the Moslem. 'The Eastern Church,' Dean Stanley says, 'was, like the East, stationary and immutable; the Western,

like the West, progressive and flexible.' . . . It is true that the Coptic Christian has remained stagnant, but there is this notable difference between the stagnation of the Moslem and that of the Copt. The Moslem stands in everything on the ancient ways because he is a Moslem, because the customs which are interwoven with his religion, forbid him to change. . . . The Copt, on the other hand has remained immutable, or nearly so, not because he is a Copt, but because he is an Oriental, and because his religion, which admits of progress, has been surrounded by associations antagonistic to progress.[26]

In other words, the Muslim is immutable because Islam is medieval; the Eastern Christian is immutable because he is oriental.

Cromer admits here that broader cultural and political contexts do, in fact, make a difference and do, in reality, override raw ideology. And here, Cromer points to a crucial difference between Muslims in Egypt and Muslims in India: "In India, the Moslems have to a certain extent become Braminised. In spite of the unbending tenets of their creed, custom and association have been too strong for them. The Hindoos, being in a majority of five to one have copied nothing from the Moslems. The Moslems, on the other hand, have insensibly assimilated certain Hindoo ideas, notably the idea of caste."[27] Cromer's assessment was that "Egyptian Moslems are . . . in the transitionary phase through which their co-religionists in India have already passed."[28] Whereas the "more subtle and assimilative Hindoo everywhere got the better of the slow-moving Moslem," the latter had now caught up. In other words, a 'superior' cultural and moral milieu might eventually have the desired civilizing effect.

While noting important differences between Egypt and India, Cromer nonetheless believed that the lessons of India should be studied by all who held positions in the East. In a footnote, he recommended Sir Alfred Lyall's treatment of the question of the ultimate effect on public and private morality of Europeanization: "Every European who occupies a high position in the East should study Sir Alfred Lyall's works. They display a profound knowledge of Eastern habits of thought, and a remarkable grasp of the difficulties underlying the treatment of Eastern problems."[29] European civilization, said Cromer, destroys one religion without substituting another. On the question of whether European civilization could be decoupled from Christianity, Cromer concluded that the question could be answered only by future generations.[30]

British Remedies for Stagnation

The British considered the rote memorization of the sacred text to be a definitive sign of Egyptian backwardness, conveniently sidestepping the reality that only a few decades earlier, British education itself had consisted largely of Christian indoctrination.[31] British educators had not abandoned doctrinal education for moral inculcation until the advent of the Lancaster movement, the brainchild of Quaker moralist Joseph Lancaster (d. 1838), which preached that students should be taught to derive the moral lessons from Scripture, not simply to recite the text.[32]

One expression of this insistence on moral education through classical texts had already found its way into the debates between orientalists and Anglicists in India. Orientalists held steadfastly to the belief that properly and systematically establishing the textual tradition of oriental peoples was an essential part of the Britiain's colonial mission and of educating the indigenous population in their classical traditions. Popular religious practices and beliefs were, it was hoped, to be banished in favor of the classical text.[33] This belief in the value of a reliably established sacred text seems not to have extended, however, to the Qur'an. There was another important difference between Hindu classical texts and Muslim classical texts: it was European orientalists who had constructed what they considered to be the Hindu classical textual tradition, whereas Muslims in Egypt and other parts of the Islamic world had a long-standing textual tradition of their own upon which to draw. 'Classical' Islam, unlike 'classical' Hinduism, was not brought into being by the British colonial regime.

Proper education on a British model was, therefore, desirable, but the possible contribution of the Islamic reformists was not. The exasperation and disapproval of British observers and policymakers at rote memorization, the rejection of modern science, and resistance to independent analysis—flaws that many Egyptians had already noted—did not lead the government to embrace the reforms that Muhammad 'Abduh and his allies were advocating. The British project of reforming education was seen as being entirely separate from the project of religious reform, unlike the Ottoman and Egyptian reform movements, which saw educational reform and religious reform as being intimately connected. The connection between religious reform and educational reform was ignored at best and sabotaged at worst.

In India, the situation had been different. Since it was a practical impossibility to teach Christian doctrine in Indian schools, these were officially secular, using instead of Christian texts the classics of English literature (understood and interpreted, of course, in a thoroughly Protestant framework and believed to express Protestant moral virtues). The goal was the same, the inculcation of essentially Christian morals, although the medium was different.[34] Education in India, then, was remarkably unlike education in England, where not only had explicit Christian doctrine been abandoned by the late nineteenth century, but even the English language had been displaced by the Latin and Greek classics as the focus of the curriculum.

Muhammad 'Abduh's Remedy for Stagnation: Return to First Principles

Muhammad 'Abduh held firmly to his belief that Islam was inherently adaptable to contemporary conditions, and he held equally fast to his conviction that the path to adaptability was in a return to Islam in its original form. The foundational tenet of *islah*, then, was the principle of return *(ruju')* to first principles. In 'Abduh's view, an Islam stripped down to its absolute essentials would be the catalyst for a general religious awakening among Muslims.[35] The objective of enlightened reform was the "correction of the articles of belief and the removal of the mistakes which have crept into them through misunderstanding of the basic texts of the religion, in order that, when once the beliefs have been made free of harmful innovations, the activities of Muslims may, as a result, be made free from disorder and confusion, the conditions of the individual Muslims may be improved, their understanding enlightened by the true sciences, both religious and secular, and wholesome traits of character developed."[36] Many of these problems had come into being because the system of religious law had become so unwieldy and complicated that only an educated person could understand or derive from it an understanding of what true Islam really was.

The program of reform to address these ills was very broad: the aim of *islah* was the total reform of Muslim life. Chief among the explicitly religious goals was to restore prayer to its original form and to abolish practices that had no foundation in the traditional sources of authority for Muslims, Qur'an and sunna.[37] Such practices (the cult of the saints, invoking the dead, publicly reciting the Qur'an over tombs, celebrating *mawlids*, the activities of the brotherhoods in general) only seemed to be religious and were, in fact, innovations. Reformers also urged the unity of the Community of Believers (including a plea to overcome the split between Sunnis and Shi'ites), the education of Muslim men and women in hygiene and domestic economy, the virtues of saving, and the awakening of intellectual curiosity, so Muslims would study modern science and foreign languages. They supported the development of youth programs like scouting, artistic and cultural activities, and associations of young Muslims. These all represented attempts to bring into the world a generation of new Muslim men.[38]

While embracing the traditions of the Prophet and the earliest pious scholars, reformers rejected mindless imitation and mindless submission. They called, instead, for "active fidelity" *(ittiba')*,[39] which constituted an attempt for authenticity. The rejection of blind imitation *(taqlid)* was a rejection of all that, in the eyes of the reformists, was part and parcel of the innovations that had produced the stagnation of the Muslims; to *taqlid* was attributed the blame not only for Islam's cultural stagnation, but also for the passive submission of its masses to the *ulama* and the shaykhs of the brotherhoods.[40] The reformists thus repudiated all Muslim groups and ideas that they believed were guilty of obscurantism, in particular the brotherhoods. Their ideology emphasized the importance of change in the present, invoking Qur'an 8:54, "God does not change what is in a people until they change what is in themselves."

'Abduh's methodology distinguished between foundational and non-foundational religious tenets and practices, and allowed him to develop a nuanced response to one of the central religious beliefs of the brotherhoods, that is, the existence of saints' miracles. There was a long and contentious history of discussion about this issue among Muslim theologians. That the prophets can perform miracles was beyond doubt and, indeed, a fundamental tenet of faith. The supposed miracles of saints, however, were not foundational according to 'Abduh. He gave Muslims broad discretion in determining whether or not they accepted the possibility of miracles on the part of saints. Given the central importance of the cult of saints in the religious practice of most Egyptian Muslims of 'Abduh's time, his nuanced position on this issue is of considerable importance, for while he does not deny the possibility of saints' miracles, he states clearly that there is no obligation to accept them: "[T]rue Muslims of all shades and sects are unanimous that there is no obligation to believe in any such miracles on the part of a 'saint' since the rise of Islam. It is permissible for every Muslim, by communal consensus, to deny the occurrence of any 'miracle' whatever from any saint, whoever he be. Such denial in no way contravenes anything in the fundamentals of Islam and in no way deviates from authentic tradition." 'Abduh caps his argument with highly resonant language, declaring that "it is in no sense an aberration from 'the straight path'."[41]

'Ali Mubarak's Remedy: The Transformative Power of Knowledge

'Ali Mubarak's ideas about stagnation and its possible remedies were well known to his contemporaries, especially those who attended the renowned salons that he held regularly at his home. According to a contemporary account, he would discuss "the backwardness of the East and the reasons for it, and the progress of the West and the reasons for that."[42] His remedy, most clearly articulated in his fictional *'Alam al-din*, focuses on education and does not address issues of religious practice or observance. Here, Mubarak imagines a conversation between the shaykh and his travel companion, a British orientalist, on the question of religion. Through their conversation, Mubarak's shaykh (clearly voicing Mubarak's own ideas) develops two central convictions about Islam in the modern world. First, he explains to the orientalist that nothing in Islam prohibits the acquisition, use, or advancement of any useful sciences, be they religious or secular.[43] Second, he proposes that all civilized societies have progressed through a primitive period of barbarism to reach their current advanced level, and they have done so largely through the "expansion of the domain of knowledge." Mubarak's shaykh considers borrowing technical knowledge, information, and concepts from other cultures to have been a fundamental element in the transformation of Europe over time. He assigns a particularly large role to borrowings from the East, beginning with the Crusades, which for him are significant primarily as the time when Europeans observed eastern cultures and carried the lessons learned from them back home. This newly acquired knowledge stimulated Europe's advance and, ultimately, her domination in world politics.

The orientalist's critique of Europe's culture at the time of her ignorance (which Mubarak renders with the evocative Arabic term *jahiliya*) resembles nineteenth-century European critiques of Islam: "[They] used to busy themselves only with books of religion, and were forbidden to look into any other, of whatever sort. If anyone used to speak in contradiction to what was said by the priests in the churches and if news of that reached them, he would be exposed to all manner of abuse."[44] For Mubarak's shaykh, as for British Protestants, the priesthood and priests constitute a major obstacle to progress. This obstacle, as Mubarak easily shows, is not present in Islamic societies, which have neither priests nor rules forbidding the pursuit of secular knowledge. Indeed, this diagnosis plays a central role in Mubarak's case for the essential compatibility of Islam and modernity. Arabs were once among the most learned men in the world, mastered all the sciences and trades, and were responsible for the revival of these sciences and trades in Europe. It is the Arabs who preserved all of the ancient sciences, which would otherwise never have been recovered by Europeans. After a lengthy exposition on the role of the *ulama* in preserving ancient science, the shaykh concludes: "All the learned men of Europe ought to grant willingly to the Arabs progress in merit and knowledge, even though before the appearance of Islam no name nor word had been heard of the Arabs—for what is attributed to the Arabs is attributed to the people of Islam. Therefore, it was Islam which was the wellspring of civilization and knowledge, since knowledge and civilization did not appear in the European countries until a thousand years after the appearance of Islam . . . ."[45]

The orientalist concurs, and the relationship between him and the shaykh advances to a new level of trust and affection, one in which the possibility of discussing Christianity and Islam in relation to one another now exists, without fear of denigrating Islam. The two characters have achieved a level of mutual respect that allows them to discuss religion in the abstract. How, then, does the shaykh account for the state in which Islamic society finds itself in relation to Europe? It is not, as he emphatically explains to his son, the result of any flaw in Islamic society or in Islamic belief and doctrine. Quite the contrary, there is abundant evidence that Islamic civilization, which flourished for many centuries, has the capacity for advancement. Religion alone, in any case, would not present a fundamental obstacle to advancement: Christianity is fundamentally flawed and yet has become civilized.[46]

There are other reasons for the presence or absence of a capacity for transformation. In the case of Christian Europe, one of the most important obstacles to progress is the papacy. It is the desire of learned men in Europe to preserve the papacy and its authority that accounts for the persistence of misunderstandings about the true nature of Islam as well as other problems in the West. And yet, the shaykh insists, Europe managed to triumph over barbarism and achieve civilization, in spite of its flawed Christian theology, the papacy, and the clergy. The real obstacle to progress is a society's unwillingness to acquire new knowledge and to borrow from other cultures.[47]

It is this unwillingness of the *ulama* to pursue new branches of knowledge that accounts for the stagnation of Muslim society. He identifies the cause of the East's loss of power in relation to the West:

> When the study of history left its schools, its people lost the knowledge of the conduct of its past generations, who were the cause of its power, its greatness, strength, and capability. Since the community has no power unless the people have power, and the power of the people is not perfected except through knowledge, the abandonment of the science of history and the rest of the fields of knowledge is among the factors which weakened the power of the *milla* and caused the loss of its renown, and put it in captivity to others who oppressed and humiliated it.[48]

Further, he asserts that while earlier generations of Muslims wrote their own history, later generations ceded the writing of history to Islam's adversaries.

In his chapter "*al-Salaf wa-l-khalaf fi-l-islam*" ('early and late generations in Islam'), the shaykh pursues his analysis of the process of decline in Islamic society. The root cause is, for him, not innovation *(bid'a)*, as it is for Muhammad 'Abduh, but a combination of bad governance by rulers who do not have the best interests of their community at heart and a loss of intellectual curiosity among the *ulama*, whose position within Islamic society was as central as that of the ruler.[49] Where Muhammad 'Abduh locates the decline of Islamic society within a broad framework of general dissolution caused by *bid'a*, 'Ali Mubarak introduces historical specificity. The "new Islamic civilization," characterized by profligate rulers who sought only to satisfy their own unsavory desires, came into existence during the Abbasid era, and particularly during the caliphate of al-Ma'mun (r. 813–833 CE). Mubarak assigns special importance in the dissolution of Islamic civilization to the introduction of *mamluks*, slave-soldiers of Turkish origins who rose to dominate the military and, eventually, to appropriate the prerogatives of the caliphate itself:

> The Mamluks thus came to be the possessors of authority, which meant that authority rested no longer with its rightful holders, and that fools had been set to rule over the affairs of the honorable . . . . The might of the Mamluks increased until they encroached upon the caliphate itself, and that brought about its abolition. Islamic authority was dispersed, and the revealed laws were despised . . . . Islamic civilization was fashioned into something different from its original likeness. Its origin had been based upon knowledge and justice, which were the greatest foundations of religion. But the civilization which took its place was based upon injustice and oppression, and on the subjugation of the worshippers. In the first civilization, groups associated together within the *umma* by consent and choice, to receive the benefits which were common to all, great or lowly . . . . But in the second civilization . . . mutual hatred grew among them, and there came to be two distinct

parts to the *umma*: the ruler, and those who were ruled over. The former was favored with advantages and high ranks, and the satisfaction of goals and appetites, while the latter were driven along the road of humiliation and subjugation. Gradually divested of the advantages of honor, the ruled came to be virtually equivalent to the dumb beast, whose owner deals freely with it, and which has no power of choice. No one doubts that that is the greatest cause of the retrogression. What a difference there is between a time in which the religious ceremonies are celebrated, and in which eyes are enlightened, and the sciences and knowledge are increasing, and a time in which the laws are ineffective, the people of Islam loathe each other, and the fields of knowledge are extinguished, and nothing remains of the laws except the formalities.[50]

British Responses to Islamic Reform: "Demoslemized Moslems" and "Invertebrate Europeans"

'Ali Mubarak's optimism in the conversation he invented between his reformist shaykh and the British orientalist was not borne out in reality by a similarly respectful view of Islamic reform on the part of the British government.[51] The British attitude toward Islamic religious reform was as ambivalent and contradictory as it was toward other kinds of 'progress.' Cromer concluded that the reformists could satisfy neither conservative Muslims nor Europeans: "They are too much tainted with a suspicion of heterodoxy to carry far along with them the staunch conservative Moslem. On the other hand, they are often not sufficiently Europeanised to attract the sympathy of the Egyptian mimic of European ways. They are inferior to the strictly orthodox Moslem in respect to their Mohammedanism, and inferior to the ultra-Europeanised Egyptian in respect of their Europeanisation."[52]

Cromer preferred "conservative Moslem thought," and because he could not imagine any real progress that was rooted in Muslim religious reform, he easily assimilated reformist Muslims to a more familiar category of derision: French Catholicism. These "Gallicised Egyptians," as he called them, were drawn to French civilization for all the wrong reasons: the French are friendlier and easier to imitate. The intellectually inferior Egyptians preferred "the rather superficial brilliancy of the Frenchman to the plodding, unattractive industry of the Englishman or the German."[53] "Gallicised Egyptians" were problematic in part because the "agents for the accomplishment of this object [of learning the French language] have been mainly Catholic priests."[54]

Cromer's analysis of the "Gallicised Egyptian" fits perfectly with a British identity through the mid-nineteenth century that was centrally tied to Protestantism. Protestantism was only one of the most important characteristics of British national identity—the others being Christianity more broadly, prosperity, civilization, and liberty—but it was the axis around which the others revolved.[55] Although the centrality of Protestantism to British identity was increasingly contested at home in the second half of the nineteenth century, its echoes were nonetheless evident in many different areas. For example, elementary-school teaching still emphasized a national identity that was tied to Protestantism.[56] School subjects like geography and history demonstrated how closely tied religion, politics, and patriotism were. The praiseworthy national character of the British was invariably tied to its Protestant character, while others like the Irish and various orientals were deemed barbaric and cruel (thus justifying the empire).

Later in the century, when other varieties of Christianity as well as agnosticism had come more into play, Protestant Christianity was seen as the essential component of civilization. Anti-papism reached its peak at mid-century, even as Roman Catholics came to participate in British national and imperial endeavors in increasing numbers. Furthermore, Protestantism itself was undergoing important changes in the face of challenges from within and without. Anglicans had to contend with challenges from agnostics, from Catholics, and from other Christian sects like evangelical Methodists, but they also faced challenges within the Anglican Church, as the Anglo-Catholic wing of the Church of England grew.[57]

Cromer's remark lamenting the role of French Catholic priests in the education of the Egyptians sat squarely at the intersection of British views of French Catholics with orientalism, and it takes on added significance in light of the reduced emphasis on the opposition between Protestant Britain and Catholic France in favor of that between Christian civilization and uncivilized colony.[58] Britain's most important Others, French Catholics, were edged out marginally by oriental Others in the mid-nineteenth century and later. Indeed, it appears that France as 'Other' was easily and conveniently assimilated to the oriental Other. For example, Cromer described the Armenian Prime Minister, Tigrane Pasha, as "Franco-Byzantine, that is to say, the foundation was Byzantine, whilst the superstructure was French. He was, intellectually speaking, the direct descendant of those orientals who, in the early days of Christianity, engaged in endless disputes over barren and almost incomprehensible points of theology. . . . when some broad question of principle was at stake, Tigrane Pasha would split hairs over a minor issue, which was almost incomprehensible, or which was at all events devoid of importance to the non-Byzantine mind."[59] In one respect, from the point of view of the British, the assimilation of the French Catholic and the Muslim had already occurred in the alarming French–Turkish alliance of the Crimean War.

The British were both attracted to and repelled by Muslim reform. Similar reactions to Muslim reform were found in both India and Egypt. In India, these contradictory attitudes were articulated at a relatively early stage by W.W. Hunter in *The Indian Mussalmans* (1871), who admonished the Indian government to support Muslim education that tempered the "bitter doctrines of their own medieval Law . . . with the sober and genial knowledge of the West."[60] Western education would make Muslims "less fanatical," but it would also make them "less sincere" and "less earnest." They would become, in other words, much like their Christian contemporaries who "doubted their faith but still wished to believe."[61] Lord Cromer quoted an English clergymen who expressed a similar sentiment, saying "God is present to Mohammedans in a sense in which He is rarely present to us amidst the hurry and confusion of the West."[62]

For all of their eagerness to transform Egypt, Cromer and most of his contemporaries remained suspicious of indigenous Muslim reform and of the short-term results of Europe's "civilizing" influence on Egypt. Egyptian society was, in Cromer's view, in a "state of flux," neither fully Egyptian nor fully European. In perhaps his most devastating judgment—one imbued with a mixture of both orientalism and medievalism—of the perils of change, Cromer declared that reform had brought into existence a group of people that were "at the same time, demoslemized Moslems and invertebrate Europeans."[63]

"Reformed Islam Is Islam No Longer"

Cromer's suspicion and rejection of the reformist doctrine was probably based largely on a misunderstanding of its central positions, but it was equally rooted in a late nineteenth-century British view of religion. One might expect a man like Cromer to have embraced the reformists' ideals and their criticisms of contemporary Muslim thought and custom as it was espoused and practiced by the Azhar traditionalists, particularly in its scholasticism and slavish adherence to the orthodox schools *(taqlid)*. But, then, as Cromer said, it would not be religion. He pronounced definitively to his readers something that "should never be forgotten," namely, "that Islam cannot be reformed; that is to say, reformed Islam is Islam no longer; it is something else; we cannot as yet tell what it will eventually be."[64]

The finality of this devastating judgment—that Islam was incapable of reform—raises the important question of what Cromer and his contemporaries were able to recognize as religion given their broader views (and not just their views of the religions of the East). Victorians were as ambivalent about religious reform at home as they were about religious reform abroad. They both desired it and feared its consequences. They yearned for times of simpler faith while itching at the same time to be rid of what they considered to be 'medieval' religion's shadowy and superstitious underpinnings. At home, they shared the conviction that the less educated among them enjoyed a more sincere and earnest faith than the more educated,[65] who were coming to dominate the middle classes. Abroad, their views of eastern religion and their worries about religious reform reflected the same assumptions about the character of faith.[66] In both India and Egypt, the British denounced (Metcalf's word) Muslim reformers, believing they could produce only a pale imitation of their true faith which, while deficient compared to Christianity, was preferable to its debased forms. If exposure to western (read: Christian) education did not result in outright conversion to Christianity, its "reforming" effects were perhaps best avoided.

Fig. 1. Mosque of Sayyida Zaynab. Early 1900s.

Fig. 2. Procession of the *mahmal*, the litter carrying the embroidered cover for the Ka'ba sent to Mecca annually. Early 1900s.

Fig. 3. Red-and-white stripe overpainting, referred to as *badigeon* in French and *ablaq* in Arabic. Late 1800s.

Fig. 4. Ibn Tulun Mosque, showing arcades bricked in to form dwelling spaces. Ca. 1870.

Fig. 5. Mosque of Muhammad ʻAli, the Citadel, and Bab al-Wazir cemetery. Early 1900s.

Fig. 6. Mosques of Sultan Hasan (14th c.), left, and Rifa'i (19th–20th c.); view from the Citadel.

Fig. 7. Khedivial Library (now Museum of Islamic Art), built in neo-Mamluk style and opened in 1903.

Fig. 8. Selamlick at the Exposition Universelle à Paris, 1867, built to represent the medieval period of Egyptian history.

Fig. 9. Lord Curzon's lamp, modeled on a Mamluk-era mosque lamp in Cairo, installed in the Taj Mahal, Agra, India. Ca. 1906.

Fig. 10. Douglas Sladen's *Oriental Cairo*, juxtaposing modern cart and chapter "Oriental Cairo."

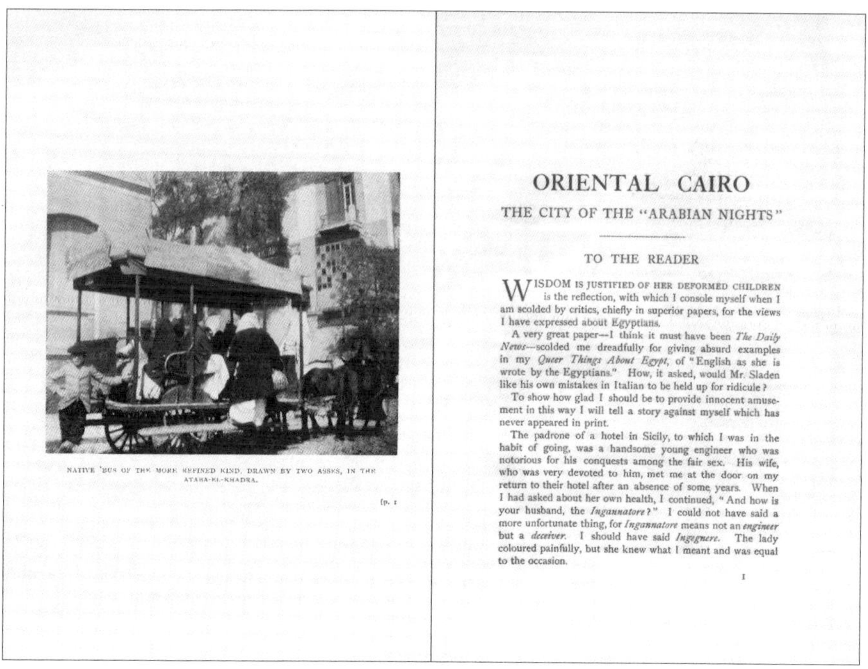

NATIVE 'BUS OF THE MORE REFINED KIND, DRAWN BY TWO ASSES, IN THE ATABA-EL-KHADRA.

[p. 1

ORIENTAL CAIRO

THE CITY OF THE "ARABIAN NIGHTS"

TO THE READER

WISDOM IS JUSTIFIED OF HER DEFORMED CHILDREN is the reflection, with which I console myself when I am scolded by critics, chiefly in superior papers, for the views I have expressed about Egyptians.

A very great paper—I think it must have been *The Daily News*—scolded me dreadfully for giving absurd examples in my *Queer Things About Egypt*, of "English as she is wrote by the Egyptians." How, it asked, would Mr. Sladen like his own mistakes in Italian to be held up for ridicule?

To show how glad I should be to provide innocent amusement in this way I will tell a story against myself which has never appeared in print.

The padrone of a hotel in Sicily, to which I was in the habit of going, was a handsome young engineer who was notorious for his conquests among the fair sex. His wife, who was very devoted to him, met me at the door on my return to their hotel after an absence of some years. When I had asked about her own health, I continued, "And how is your husband, the *Ingannatore*?" I could not have said a more unfortunate thing, for *Ingannatore* means not an *engineer* but a *deceiver*. I should have said *Ingegnere*. The lady coloured painfully, but she knew what I meant and was equal to the occasion.

1

Fig. 11. Napoleonic cart in front of Mamluk tombs.

A STORY-TELLER RECITING FROM THE "ARABIAN NIGHTS."

In the background are the ramparts of the Citadel.

Fig. 12. "A storyteller reciting from the 'Arabian Nights'," Douglas Sladen's *Oriental Cairo.*

THE SÛK-EN-NAHASSIN.

The most beautiful, romantic, and mediæval street in Cairo, with the most exquisite street fountain in Cairo at its end. Left and right are *meshrebiya*-latticed Oriels. In front are a forage-seller and a bread-seller.

Fig. 13. *Sabil-kuttab* of 'Abd al-Rahman Katkhuda in the Suq al-Nahhasin, 1911.

Fig. 14. Reproduction of *sabil-kuttab* of 'Abd al-Rahman Katkhuda at World's Columbian Exposition, Chicago, 1893.

Fig. 15.
Cairo 'medieval'
skyline, 1996.

Fig. 16. Mosque
of al-Hakim,
after restoration
by Bohras, 1996.

Fig. 17. Onion
market in front
of mosque of
al-Hakim, 1996.

Fig. 18. Arcades of Ibn Tulun Mosque, showing smaller minaret (no longer standing), 1918.

Fig. 19. Arcades of mosque of al-Hakim, 1918.

Fig. 20. Complex of al-Salih Najm al-Din Ayyub, showing tomb and minaret. The sabil is from a later period and was built by Khusrow Pasha.

Fig. 21. Southern minaret of mosque of al-Hakim, 1918.

Fig. 23. Northwest wall of mosque of al-Hakim, showing tomb of Qurqumas before its removal.

Fig. 22. "Ruined Mosque of al-Hakim," line drawing, 1903.

Fig. 24. Mosque of al-Salih Tala'i' before demolition of Ottoman minaret, 1918.

Fig. 25. Mosque of al-Salih Tala'i' after Comité's restoration, photograph looking down from Bab Zuwayla, 1995.

Fig. 27. Al-Lu'lu'a after Bohra restoration, 1996.

Fig. 26. Al-Hakim minaret (left intact) and arcades (after restoration by Bohras), 1995.

Fig. 28. Tomb of Sayyida Ruqayya, internal view of metal grille installed by Bohras, 1996.

Fig. 29. Reproduction of al-Aqmar Mosque bevel at tomb of Sayyida Ruqayya after restoration, 1996.

Fig. 30. Bevel of al-Aqmar Mosque, 1995.

Fig. 31. Bohra Mosque in Houston, Texas, 1999.

Fig. 32. Al-Juyushi Mosque before restoration, 1903.

Fig. 33. Al-Juyushi Mosque after Bohra restoration, 1996.

Fig. 34. Al-Aqmar Mosque before restoration, 1901.

Fig. 35. Al-Aqmar Mosque after Bohra restoration, 1996.

Fig. 36. Stylized reproduction of restored al-Aqmar façade used as set for celebration of Sultan Burhan al-Din's eightieth birthday, Bombay, India, 1991.

What was not at work for the British was an opposition of secularism and religiosity. Secularization was not a desideratum, for late Victorian Britons still believed that religion was central to civilization and to progress. What they wanted was religion adapted to modernity, and from their point of view the only religion that could do that was Christianity, and most particularly, Protestantism. It comes as no surprise, then, that Cromer was no more eager to have "de-Moslemized Egyptians" in the government than were many conservative Muslims. But his attitude remained on this issue, as so many others, inconsistent. He lamented that the appointment of Riaz Pasha as Prime Minister was necessary because of the limited options available. Cromer's discussion of the political decisions at the time of Mustafa Fahmy's dismissal was similarly bound up in his emphasis on the priority of religious credentials. In spite of his later change of opinion, Riaz Pasha had seemed a reasonable candidate for Prime Minister at the time:

> I thought that the wisest thing to do was not to run strongly counter to the Mohammedan movement, which the recent behaviour of the Khedive had evoked, but rather to attempt to guide it. The choice of guides, however, was very limited. The Gallicised Egyptian would carry no weight with the Mohammedans. Amongst the turbaned classes, not one could be found of sufficient education and experience to be raised to the rank of Minister. A retrograde Pasha of the thorough-going Turkish school was out of the question. He would have quarrelled with every European official in the country, whilst, at the same time, he would not have commanded the sympathies of the natives. Practically, if the experiment of guiding the Mohammedan movement was to be tried, the choice was limited to Riaz Pasha. He was less European than the Gallicised Egyptian or the Armenian. He was, as I hoped and believed, less Mohammedan than his Moslem followers.[67]

For Cromer, becoming religious and acting fanatically went hand in hand:

> Riaz Pasha has, I understand, lately become very religious, and would thus be predisposed to act in a fanatic and anti-European spirit. From having before felt a strong aversion for Riaz Pasha, the Khedive may now, perhaps, be attracted by his arbitrary character, and the two may unite against England. In this case trouble will follow. The Khedive was visited yesterday by a large number of natives. Although this demonstration was in part prearranged, and although the Khedive has gained no real popularity, but very little is wanted to place him in the position of an anti-foreign and anti-Christian Egyptian patriot. The portion of the press which represents ultra-Mohammedan feeling has assumed a very violent and mischievous tone.[68]

Cromer speculated on the meaning of the term 'Egyptian,' asking, "Did not the Khedive, and those who surrounded him, rather confound the terms khedivial and Egyptian, which, in fact, were far from being synonymous?"[69] Sir Arthur Hardinge wrote to Cromer:

> The Palace tone is what the Khedive calls 'Egyptian.' Though the sympathies of most of the Beys and Pashas of the household are, from tastes and education, rather French than English, they are not in favour of French political aspirations in Egypt. Like Tigrane Pasha they fancy that they are able to rule without foreign assistance of any kind, and they are ambitious of place and power for themselves and their protégés and dependants. Of the feelings of the great body of the Egyptian people, or of any class of it outside the official, I suspect they know and care very little. They are mostly lax Mohammedans, with very free-thinking notions about religion.[70]

Neither conservative Muslims nor "free-thinking" Muslims were suitable for government service.

Cromer's view of Islam was as negative as his assessment of the character of the oriental "race,"[71] and his writings display a slippage between religion and race in a manner typical of late nineteenth and early twentieth century British thinking. Cromer's ideas about Egypt and Islam are laid out in successive chapters entitled "Dwellers in Egypt," "The Moslems," and "The Christians," but elements of race-based and religion-based arguments are found in all three. Like most nineteenth-century British, Cromer believed in the essential irrationality of the oriental mind and he saw the evidence for his convictions in institutional practice, religious practice, and even in street plans: "The European is a close reasoner . . . he is a natural logician, albeit he may not have studied logic; he loves symmetry in all things. . . . The mind of the Oriental, on the other hand, like his picturesque streets, is eminently wanting in symmetry."[72] The conclusion he drew from this evidence of irrationality was that Islam could not remain Islam and become modern in the sense of becoming 'civilized.' He stated bluntly: "Although there are many highly-educated gentlemen who profess the Moslem religion, it has yet to be proved that Islam can assimilate civilisation without succumbing in the process."[73] Or, as he put it succinctly, "Reformed Islam is Islam no longer."

Conclusion: Monuments, Islam, and Preservation in Different Registers

What, then, are we to make of these views on religion in relation to the question of the preservation of Arab monuments in Cairo? Muhammad 'Abduh had little to say about the preservation of antique mosques except that the funds devoted to the Comité's project could be better spent elsewhere. 'Ali Mubarak, on the other hand, was not reluctant to tear down old mosques and was on many occasions at odds with the Comité in its earliest days. What did he think the implications of these demolitions were? Did he think it was necessary to preserve every vestige of the architecture that Europeans were beginning to call 'medieval'? Clearly not, for, as we have seen, Mubarak did not see a contradiction between his role as an urban modernizer and as a Muslim in the modern world. To paraphrase Donald Reid's perceptive critique of the concerns of historians, for 'Ali Mubarak, it was conservation that needed to be justified, not its absence.[74]

How are we to understand 'Ali Mubarak's view of conservation? For him, the state of the monuments did not indicate any essential flaw in

Egyptian culture and society, nor were the monuments markers on a one-way road of decline. Mubarak saw the changed state of buildings as part of the ebb and flow of "the change of dynasties and upheavals of time, which have sometimes brought increase and sometimes decline, sometimes fluorescence and sometimes decay."[75] Europeans, on the other hand, viewed the state of these monuments as an indictment of Egyptian culture, as a sign of its unreadiness for nationhood and self-rule. If Egyptians would not see to their own monuments, if they could not recognize their aesthetic and historical importance by keeping them in good repair, then wiser Europeans—civilized people in a position to appreciate the importance of preserving the past—would do it for them.

But what could preservation mean in the context of different assumptions about religion? To be sure, when many of these structures had been built, they were monumental, and some of them were even meant to be monuments to their founders. But as such, their monumentality was vested in what they could communicate about the authority, power, and legitimacy of their founders. In the Middle Ages, such monuments were fully integrated into the religious, social, and economic life of the city and its quarters, and many of them played particular roles in specific neighborhoods. Over time, they were reappropriated, rededicated, and reinvested with new meanings in a variety of ways: some by the way they were used, some by the incomes they brought into neighborhoods, some by the reappropriation of the site to build upon its legitimating aura and symbolic meaning to serve new masters. Many such sites were thick with symbolic meaning that was reconfigured and reappropriated over several centuries of use and reuse. Also over time, some sites fell by the wayside. Their symbolic gravity lightened for one reason or another or they fell out of the rhythms of ritual life in a neighborhood or a quarter. Sometimes it was deliberate: a ruler died and his successor sponsored buildings of his own; a courtier or wealthy patron fell into disfavor and so did the sites associated with him, often to be reabsorbed in a different form and under a new patron's shadow; a new mosque or madrasa or zawiya was built and, for one reason or another, people were simply more attracted to it. Whatever the fate of these buildings, what they all had in common in the Mamluk and Ottoman periods was an organic connection to the city and to a neighborhood that either persisted or could be successfully reconfigured within a new set of local relationships or a connection to an identifiable group of people. To be successful, such reconfigurations had to have meanings that grew out of ties in the present.

The Comité's preservation program, however, operated under different assumptions and with different goals. The Comité was committed to preserving these buildings materially by restoring them to an 'authentic' and original form. They remade them exclusively as monuments of the past. Unlike Mamluk and Ottoman restorers (all of whom were individuals doing work in their own names), who redefined and reappropriated sites in ways that were meaningful within the logic of local political, religious, social, and economic life, the Comité's architects reconfigured these sites in ways that broke their ties to the present for Egyptians even as they configured these sites in relation to European tourists as representations of a continuous medieval.

'Ali Mubarak's intention as he describes it in the Introduction to his *Khitat* was to introduce these places in a different way to his audience. His Arabic *Khitat* was quite obviously intended for a literate Egyptian public that did not understand its *athar*. The Arabic term, which might loosely be translated as 'monuments' or 'antiquities,' actually has a much broader sense. As Michael Reimer points out, it "may mean memorable works, things or 'effects' of any kind . . . anything which is historically significant, which has left an impression in written works or upon the memory, or . . . upon the landscape."[76]

For 'Ali Mubarak, even more than the fifteenth-century topographer and historian al-Maqrizi, the *Khitat* was a *lieu de mémoire* (site of memory).[77] Indeed, Mubarak seems unique among nineteenth-century thinkers, both Egyptian and European, in contemplating the role of architecture in society. His emphasis is not the history of the building or site for its own sake, but rather for the moral lessons that these sites—and most of all his narrative about them—can convey to his audience.[78] Mubarak complains that his fellow Egyptians cannot interpret or explain the dynastic changes and upheavals, nor "guide us aright in understanding the country's notable monuments. We look upon these works but do not know the circumstances of their creation, we wander through them but do not know who made them. . . . How many the mounds that were once towering buildings, the ravines that were once splendid gardens, the tombs that lie hidden along the narrow lanes and the shrines scattered about in the open country, which the common people are wont to misidentify. . . . How many the mosques which are ascribed to men who did not build them . . . ." Mubarak exhorts his readers: "[It] is our duty to know these things, for it is not fitting for us to remain in ignorance of our country or to neglect the monuments of our ancestors. They are a moral lesson to the reflective mind, a memorial to the thoughtful soul. . . . For what our ancestors have left behind stirs in us the desire to follow in their footsteps, and to produce for our times what they produced for theirs; to strive to be useful even as they strove."[79] In other words, these monuments constitute a moral lesson for Egyptians in the present; they are important because they can inspire men to produce monuments for their own time. Nor does Mubarak advocate preserving all of these monuments materially. What is most important for him is that their true histories be known so that their moral lessons may be understood and may act as a catalyst for right action in the present and the future. Indeed, 'Ali Mubarak believed that a man's ties with his community were important above almost all else, and that men had a moral duty to work for the good of their communities.[80]

This view of the organic relationship of monuments to the present and future was a corollary to Mubarak's view of Islam, as well. Europeans, on and off the Comité, saw Islam as, at best, medieval, and as a medieval religion, it could be understood only in terms of the predominance of what they viewed as superstition and misguided belief. If one were to understand it at all, it had to be through recourse to Islam's classical texts. The European understanding of Islam is, if we decontextualize it, remarkably similar to the position of the followers of *taqlid* according to the reformers. Europeans saw immutability as an essential element of a true Islam, as did traditionalists. That Islam was authentic as a living faith, accessible and understandable through its vibrant and changeable ritual practices, never occurred to most Europeans who visited and studied the East. In a fashion similar to the British view of Hinduism and Islam in colonial India, religion was to be reconstructed through its classic texts and archaeological monuments, not through the practice of its living adherents. In India, John Marshall had suggested

> on discovering that after the handing over of the Bukbara Mosque at Bijapur to Muslims, it had been 'whitewashed, that prayer matting had been spread, lamps suspended, and prints pasted on the back wall' . . . that no mosques or other buildings, which have once been the property of the government should be handed back to Muslims and that they should only be allowed to pray subject to strict regulations . . . the spirit of such conservation was clearly positioned against the indigenous inhabitants [as] eviden[ced] in the Viceroy's comments regarding the same case (Indian Archaeology: 217): ' . . . having saved them from the destructive carelessness or the uncultured neglect of white men, we were not going to hand them back to the dirt and defilement of Asiatic religious practices'.[81]

The Comité, informed by these assumptions about religion, looked to restore monuments as representatives of the only Islam that they could recognize, an Islam that was, for them, continuously medieval. They could deem worthy of preservation only those monuments they could recognize in the historical and aesthetic framework they had constructed. It is not surprising that they restored many buildings that were irrelevant in the late nineteenth century to daily religious life, and did so in a way that guaranteed their continued irrelevance. Mubarak also seems to have assumed a large number of these mosques to be irrelevant, and so was willing to tear them down in order to build the wide and straight streets that are part of his urban legacy. The Comité fought demolitions and conserved buildings. Whether through dismantling or preservation, Mubarak and the Comité both rendered these structures into a continuing irrelevance to ongoing religious life in the city.

The Comité's view of the relationship of its own activities to religious life in the city is clear in one of its earliest decisions, namely, that its funds would not be spent on work to make mosques (even 'historic' mosques) functional for worship: ". . . il est confirmé que le Comité ne prendra à sa charge que ceux des travaux qui seront exécutés dans le but de la conservation des bâtiments qu'il classera dans la catégorie des monuments historiques, car tous les travaux qui sont nécessaires à l'exploitation d'un monument servant au culte ne rentrent pas dans l'espèce des travaux à payer sur le budget du Comité."[82] Europeans on and off the Comité could thus conclude that mosques should be preserved in their antique state because they were faithful to the picture of Islam as a 'medieval' or 'oriental' religion that they brought with them to Egypt. Mubarak could conclude that they might be demolished because he understood that Islam was a living tradition, and that daily religious life would be compromised little, if at all, by either the preservation or destruction of some of these mosques, which had already fallen out of the rhythms and patterns of religious life in the city of Cairo. Why bother to preserve materially a mosque that had little if anything to do with the religious life of the city's inhabitants? He was already undertaking the literary preservation of buildings in his *Khitat*, recording the circumstances of their foundation and how they changed over time, all as part of a large project in which the moral lessons of monuments remained accessible to Egyptians.

3

Cairo of the *Arabian Nights*

Lord Curzon's Lamp

In 1906, Lord Curzon, chief British colonial administrator of India, was engaged in an important project: the restoration of the Tàj Mahal. Not finding any mosque lamps that he thought suitable for his project, he wrote to his former protégé, Lord Cromer, Consul General of Egypt, and asked him to have a lamp designed on the model of those in Cairo's Mamluk mosques (Figure 9). When that plan fell through, Curzon tried (and failed) to obtain a copy of an illustrated *Arabian Nights* from his childhood, recalling an illustration of a mosque lamp that he thought suitable. Disappointed, he finally settled for a design based on some lamps he saw on a visit to Cairo.[1] But why did Curzon think that either a Mamluk mosque lamp or a design from his childhood *Arabian Nights* was a suitable model for the Taj Mahal in Agra, India? Although Curzon's quest took place in the first decade of the twentieth century, the story is embedded in the imperial cultures and politics of the nineteenth century. We can understand Curzon's search only by considering in a new way the two monuments to which he turned when he sought the model for his lamp: the *Arabian Nights* and Medieval Cairo.[2]

In the previous two chapters, I reframed the story of conservation in different ways—in imperial and local contexts, in the context of nineteenth-century religious life—to demonstrate how different economic, architectural, religious, and political policies and practices accumulated over time and how together they produced Medieval Cairo. My goal throughout has been to show the historical contingency of Medieval Cairo, to persuade readers that this version of a medieval city emerged from the convergence of a particular set of historical circumstances. But why does an argument that insists on the contingency of Medieval Cairo matter?

In this chapter, I try to answer that question by engaging in a different kind of historical contextualization, one that weaves together two stories that are ordinarily considered to be separate, that of Medieval Cairo and of the *Arabian Nights*. When told together as a *modern* story of 'Cairo of the Arabian Nights,' this account highlights the historical processes of which I have been speaking. Looking at two great monuments together—one literary, the other urban and architectural—sheds light on specific processes that produced these monuments and helps to explain why they could be regarded in different ways by multiple readers, viewers, and restorers.

Throughout this chapter, I argue for an understanding of the *Nights* and of Medieval Cairo as distinctly modern creations.[3] I also demonstrate something that I believe is very important in understanding how Medieval Cairo as well as the *Nights* came into being: they are constructed not only through the conservation of residual fabric (whether material or literary) or even of outright fabrications and additions, but also through a process of amalgamation that makes it difficult to distinguish old from new, and in which new (or newer) elements come to be redefined as old. I will show here how this process of amalgamation was at work in the creation both of Medieval Cairo and the *Nights*.[4] In so doing, I am trying to demonstrate not only the *processes* through which these material and literary works of the 'Orient' were constructed, but also some of the precise *mechanisms* through which orientalism's underlying conceptual framework found expression at identifiable historical moments. I am, therefore, trying to make an argument for the historical specificity of at least some of orientalism's particular effects and expressions. Finally, telling these two stories together draws attention to the connection between India and Egypt that is a theme of this book, and which is also a central concern of Chapter 4.

The *Nights* and Its Modern Contexts

The French and English Nights

The story of the *Arabian Nights* that I will tell here is primarily a tale of the eighteenth and nineteenth centuries. It begins with the introduction of the *Nights* to European literature, long before the first printed Arabic edition appeared, translated by Antoine Galland, and published between 1704–17. Galland's translation was a landmark event in the history of the *Nights*. Muhsin Mahdi, whose authority on the textual history of the *Nights* is unsurpassed, demonstrates that Galland's *Mille et Une Nuits* set the stage for the history of all versions of the *Nights* that we know in the modern world.[5]

Galland (1646–1715) was a Greek interpreter for the French ambassador to the Ottoman sultan. A genuine orientalist, he had spent five years in the Levant (1670–75) studying Turkish, modern Greek, Arabic, and Persian and two decades traveling in the eastern Mediterranean. He was interested primarily in the political maxims of orientals and the Church Fathers, which led him to other oriental texts. Galland's *Mille et Une Nuits* is based, serendipitously, on the oldest known manuscript of the *Nights*, and this manuscript accounts for the first 280 nights of Galland's translation. But his edition contains numerous other stories, including the stories of Aladdin as well as Ali Baba and the Forty Thieves. Galland's account is that he heard the Aladdin story from an Aleppan Christian storyteller.[6] It is possible that this man wrote the Aladdin story down later and gave it to Galland for his translation, but there is no direct evidence of that. The first time the story is known to have appeared in Arabic was in 1787, found in a manuscript by a Syrian priest living in Paris. This manuscript was purported to complete the missing portions of the fourteenth-century Syrian manuscript that Galland used for part of his translation. The story then also appeared in a very early nineteenth-century Arabic manuscript of a Syrian who claimed that he had copied it from an eighteenth-century Baghdad manuscript. These written versions, however, have both clearly been shown to be translations from Galland's French into Arabic. The Sindbad stories, which are part of Galland's translation, exist in Arabic originals that predate Galland's translation, but were not a part of the *Nights* tradition.[7]

Whatever the provenance of many of the stories of the Galland translation may be—and whatever its relationship to the printed Arabic editions that came out between 1814 and 1842—these are the versions of the *Nights* that were known in the European literary tradition and that helped shape the imagination of Europeans during the nineteenth century.[8] The French and later the British accepted these, the only versions of the *Nights* that they really knew, as authentic. Immediately after Galland published his *Nights*, other translations began, but they were translations of Galland's *Mille et Une Nuits*, not of any Arabic version of the *Nights*. Galland's French translation had been circulating for nearly a century when both the first Arabic printed editions and the first English translations were published.

Galland's translation also exemplified one of the clearest impulses in the eighteenth- and nineteenth-century history of the *Nights*: the impulse for completion. Whether in translations or the printed Arabic editions that followed, editors and compilers felt compelled to produce a work with all of the one thousand and one stories promised (in their view) by its title. The desire for completion was rooted partly in a profoundly philological impulse. Nineteenth-century literary reconstruction was part of the philological enterprise. Philology, which had begun as an effort to reconstruct the classical tradition, was by the mid-nineteenth century a specific methodology used in many different disciplines, including the orientalist sciences and, in particular, the literary study of the Hebrew Bible. By the later nineteenth century, various philological disciplines boasted chairs at Oxford and Cambridge. But the desire for completion was not only a literary impulse; it found its expression in architecture as well. The Frenchman Eugène-Emmanuel Viollet-le-Duc, arguably the nineteenth century's most famous architect, could just as easily have been talking about literary artifacts as architecture when he defined restoration as a process by which one re-established a building in a complete condition that may never have existed.

Concerns about the authenticity of Galland's *Nuits* emerged even among his eighteenth-century readers. James Beattie, in 1783, wondered "whether the tales be really Arabick, or invented by Mons. Galland, I have never been able to learn with certainty. If they be oriental, they are translated with unwarrantable latitude; for the whole tenor of the style is in the French mode: and the Caliph of Bagdat, and the Emperor of China, are addressed in the same terms of ceremony which are usual at the court of France."[9] Some of these concerns were specific to the *Nights*, while others grew directly out of debates about the enterprise of translation itself.[10] Among the debates then current were questions about the possibility of word-for-word translation and, particularly concerning Homer and the Bible, whether the translations were superior to the originals. By the early nineteenth century, new translations of the *Nights* were being proposed to address what were seen as the shortcomings of the earliest translations.

One of the first of these new translations was by Edward William Lane. Born in 1801, the son of a clergyman, Lane went to Egypt in 1825 on account of his poor health, intending to earn a living as a lithographer and looking for picturesque material to reproduce. He returned to England in 1828 and started work on his *Manners and Customs of the Modern Egyptians* (1836), then returned to Cairo in the late 1830s to work on his translation of the *Nights*, and finally, from 1842–49, he worked on his *Arabic-English Lexicon*. His sister, Sophia Lane-Poole, left her husband behind in England to live with Lane in Cairo, bringing with her two orphaned grandsons who grew up in Lane's house. The men these two boys grew up to be are well known to historians: Stanley Lane-Poole, who became an eminent orientalist, and his brother, Reginald Lane-Poole, one of the founders of the *English Historical Review* and an eminent medievalist.

The best known, at least popularly, of all English translations was that of Sir Richard Burton, who was already a famous adventurer and explorer when he published his own version in the late nineteenth century. He marketed his *Nights* through a subscription list in order to diminish the risk of being prosecuted for obscenity. He viewed his translation, which depends very heavily upon an earlier translation by John Payne, primarily as entertainment. Unlike Lane's, it had no formal footnotes, and he did not censor the text: all of the available stories in circulation, however vulgar, however bawdy, were included. In fact, the racier the better. Burton did, however, append several essays on various subjects, including a famous, highly imaginative one on the sexual habits of the Arabs and Africans. By the 1880s and 1890s, the *Nights* had been fully assimilated into European literature in the category of oriental tales. Numerous editions had been published and they were enormously popular, especially in Victorian England where there were dozens of nursery editions, and where it became a classic of Victorian reading for children.

The Arabic Nights *in Egypt and India*

Nights manuscript scholarship has concerned itself primarily with the problem of providing an authentic *Nights*. For eighteenth- and nineteenth-century editors and translators, authenticity was very often understood as completeness (that is, providing a version of the *Nights* that included all one thousand and one nights that were assumed to have been [or which they believed *should* have been] in the classical language). Thus they produced editions of the *Nights* with all one thousand and one nights, and in the case of the Arabic texts, corrected the language. It is now a well-established fact that the *Nights* was never a classical literary text, that is, it was not written in classical Arabic; rather, it was written in Middle Arabic. Eighteenth- and nineteenth-century European editors, however, considered these versions of the *Nights* to be corruptions of what they assumed was an original classical text. They therefore corrected the debased and ungrammatical language of the *Nights* to produce an authentic version that was both complete and linguistically sound (that is, classical).

The history of the printed Arabic editions of the *Nights* is inextricably bound up with British imperial practice in India.[11] Of the four major printed Arabic editions, two were produced in imperial India: First Calcutta (1814–18) and Second Calcutta (1839–42) were direct products of British imperialism, both of the British East India Company and the British colonial government.[12] The European editors of the printed Arabic *Nights* shared the idea of the classical literary tradition as authentic that also characterized the editors of another great nineteenth-century literary monument of European imperialism, the Literary Survey of India, companion to the great Archaeological Survey of India (see Chapter 1).[13] This classicizing impulse, which included a rejection of vernacular language as well as popular religious practice, was also a feature of the production of the *Nights*.

First Calcutta was intended as a textbook for the teaching of Arabic to British East India Company officers. Warren Hastings, Governor General of Fort William, began to appoint British revenue collectors and established a system of courts with British judges to administer local laws in the late eighteenth century. The use of British rather than Indian officers in the bureaucracy now meant that the Company (and later the British colonial government) needed orientalists in their employ who knew Indian languages, in this case, Persian and Arabic.[14]

The broader debates over the proper place of indigenous languages in education in India also framed the editing and publication of Second Calcutta. While this edition was in production, orientalists, Anglicists, and evangelicals were battling over the use of Indian as opposed to English vernaculars.[15] Among the orientalists there were additional debates between those who wanted to teach high culture through Arabic and Sanskrit and those who wanted to reach a larger audience by using vernacular languages. Muhsin Mahdi refers to these groups as "classical" and "vernacularist."[16] By the early 1830s, British policy and practice had shifted definitively toward the English language as the medium for moral education and modernization. Many British in India, however, continued to believe that India's classical languages (Arabic and Sanskrit) were fundamental to the project of modernizing India through the recovery of its classical past. Although it was widely believed (and is true) that at least some of the medieval *1001 Nights* stories were ultimately of Indian origin, no known manuscripts were of Indian provenance. The orientalist belief that part of India's cultural heritage was rooted in classical Arabic texts is echoed in the justifications for the study of Arab art proposed at the 1874 Congress of Orientalists: that India's architecture is really Arabic (see Chapter 1). Second Calcutta was not produced to serve any pedagogical purpose, but rather as part of the Asiatic Society of Bengal's broader project of cultural recovery through the publication of texts in classical languages. This edition was advertised as the most 'complete' (read: authentic) version of the *Nights*, printed from a manuscript (so the editors claimed), transcribed in Egypt, and brought to India.[17]

Whereas eighteenth- and nineteenth-century scholarship on the *Nights* sought authenticity in terms of completeness, twentieth-century scholarship sought authenticity in an original, or verifiably medieval, version(s) of the *Nights*. For this reason, a primary focus has been the Syrian tradition, with its small number of manuscripts all datable to the fourteenth century. The authoritative philological work of Muhsin Mahdi provides us now with the *stemma* and a critical edition of the medieval Middle Arabic text.[18] The new scholarship on the *Nights* and Hussain Haddawy's translation of Mahdi's critical edition focus on this quest for medieval origins. What follows is a brief account of the medieval history of the *Nights* that has been reconstructed in recent years by Muhsin Mahdi.

The earliest versions (no longer in existence) of the *Nights* were almost certainly fusions of Bedouin stories of the Arabian peninsula and Persian tales that had been Islamicized. The precise origins of the stories themselves are diverse and largely unknown, but the *Nights* was known as a collection of stories (again, of widely divergent contents) from as early as the tenth century.[19] One version was an Arabic work that had been translated from a Persian collection called *Hazar Afsana* ('A Thousand Legends'). This Persian work (which does not survive intact) provided both the title and the famous frame story to one of these collections of stories that came to be known as *The Thousand and One Nights*.[20]

The 'original' version, that is, a version with the form and some of the stories that we conventionally identify as the *Nights*, did not emerge until the thirteenth century in Mamluk Egypt or Syria. This version, like the *Hazar Afsana*, was lost, but not before a copy had been made that became the archetype for later copies and versions. The later archetypal version, too, was lost, and its existence is assumed from the striking similarities among early known copies. From the lost archetype, two branches emerged, one Syrian, the other Egyptian. Comprised of a much smaller number of known manuscripts, the Syrian tradition came to be regarded as the more reliable guide to the original archetype. The Egyptian branch, on the other hand, produced, in the words of Hussain Haddawy, "an abundance of poisonous fruits that proved almost fatal to the original."[21] Haddawy's judgment demonstrates the trajectory of modern scholarship on the *Nights*. He searches for authenticity in a 'pure' *stemma* that can be traced to an original version in the Middle Ages. He deems the later Egyptian versions as "a large, heterogeneous, indiscriminate collection of stories by different hands and from different sources, representing different layers of culture, literary conventions and styles tinged with the Ottoman cast of the time, a work very different from the fundamentally homogeneous original, which was the clear expression of the life, culture, and literary style of a single historical moment, namely the Mamluk period. This is the more significant because the Ottoman period is marked by a sharp decline in Arabic culture in general and literature in particular."[22]

Haddawy's critique of the Ottoman era *Nights* is typical in many respects of other modern assessments of Egypt's culture under the Ottomans that form part of the larger context in which Medieval Cairo was created. We find the stereotypical argument of decline. And where the multiethnic, multilingual, and multireligious nature of the classical Ottoman Empire is typically viewed by western historians as one of its positive characteristics (especially when viewed in the light of the status of minorities, a particularly western concern), for the literary critic, this heterogeneity presents a problem. Within a strictly textual context, which presumes a clear distinction between oral and written traditions and privileges a foundational over other versions of a text, the Egyptian branch might well be viewed with skepticism. If approached differently, however, we might come to a different judgment. We might ask whether the fruit of the Egyptian tree is really poisonous, after all.

The manuscripts that belong to the Egyptian branch are late. Almost all were copied between the second half of the eighteenth and first half of the nineteenth century, probably in order to satisfy the demand created by Europeans seeking the *Nights* exemplar; only one manuscript dates to the seventeenth century.[23] These Egyptian manuscripts substantially alter through deletion or emendation the Syrian manuscripts. This suggests that rather than seeking to trace the genealogy of the Egyptian *stemma* from the archetype, we should try to understand the *Nights* in the context of the eighteenth and nineteenth centuries.

Nelly Hanna's recent research shows that there was a lively trade in books in Cairo in the seventeenth and eighteenth centuries, and that the book trade did not depend upon printing. The manuscript arts were still widely practiced in the Islamic world, and while the introduction of the printing press into Egypt at the time of Napoleon's invasion played a major role in the development of journalism, such a development might not have occurred had not Cairo already enjoyed a thriving book culture.[24] As Hanna explains, the expansion of book culture in Cairo during the seventeenth and eighteenth centuries resulted from the same confluence of circumstances (available economic means to purchase books, literacy, a decrease in book prices) that account for the spread of book culture in Europe.

Throughout the two centuries prior to the introduction of the printing press in Egypt, large numbers of books were copied and numerous works passed from oral into written culture. Hanna's research into manuscript collections reveals what can only be described as an explosion of book production in the eighteenth century, when the majority of available manuscripts were copied irrespective of their date of composition, a situation that applies equally to Coptic and Muslim manuscript production.[25] One of the factors accounting for the proliferation of book production was the availability of cheap European paper, which in the seventeenth and eighteenth centuries was exported to Egypt.[26] Multiple sources and qualities of paper were readily available in Cairo by the beginning of the eighteenth century. The impact of the printing press on book production in Cairo, then, was indirect: printing spurred cheaper paper production in Europe, and these cheaper papers made their way to Egypt well before the printing press arrived. The spread of cheap papers meant that books now circulated to the middle classes, to artisans and tradesmen, whereas before they had been largely the privilege of the upper classes.[27]

The seventeenth and eighteenth centuries, as Hanna shows (what follows is a précis of her account), were characterized by a widespread book culture that made its way into the middle classes and that absorbed significant aspects of local oral culture, colloquial dialect, and entertainment values. Far from being something that was restricted to the learned classes and their patrons, the culture of book production and of reading became relatively commonplace among the middle classes. Religious scholars as well as learned men who were not members of the *ulama* responded to the demand for books accessible to a newly literate general reading public by writing religious and ritual manuals in simple language, or by providing copies of widely read Sufi manuals.

Other authors responded to the demand for written entertainment by committing to writing the amusing anecdotes that circulated widely, by issuing collections of proverbs or incorporating colloquial Egyptian into their writing.[28]

The expanded use of colloquial language in writing was new in the sixteenth century. As Hanna notes, appearances of colloquial language in Mamluk literature were rare, and were used to mark humor and irony.[29] In the early seventeenth century, however, colloquial writing "became a means of expression by those who were well trained in language skills and had a great familiarity with the language as it was taught in institutes of higher learning. Even more significant, colloquial writing became a subject of academic concern: observed, studied, and written about in a scholarly fashion."[30] The most interesting and unusual example of this new trend was the colloquial dictionary of Yusuf al-Maghribi.[31]

Whatever the reasons for their interest, educated "writers were listening to and recording in writing the language of subordinate groups . . . the language of the ordinary person was being scrutinized, listened to, interpreted, and recorded."[32] Hanna argues that tracking language usage at different levels of society was one expression of the development of interest in specifically local culture, an "emphasis on what was local rather than on the universal" that became increasingly common throughout the nineteenth century.[33] She also speculates that the availability of books in easily accessible language might have been a response to the increasing Arabization of some members of the Mamluk ruling class, namely those who had actually been born in Cairo and whose command of Arabic was relatively poor.

Even Muhsin Mahdi's masterful reconstruction, which situates the history of First and Second Calcutta within the context of British imperial policy, does not consider the *Nights* in its early modern Egyptian or Ottoman context. Mahdi's interest in this complicated story is to elucidate the relationship of the printed Arabic editions to Galland's manuscript, and, ultimately, its relationship to the medieval archetype. Mahdi defines his task as follows: "[T]o inquire into the complex literary history of the *Nights* as far as it can be traced in the surviving manuscripts, bring to fruition the search for what can be known about the archetype that constituted the core of the surviving redactions, and throw light on its origin, composition, and language, as well as on the growth of the different collection of stories appended to that original core."[34] The medievalist bent of *Nights* scholarship may also account for the fact that the *Nights* do not figure in Hanna's account of book production and book culture in seventeenth- and eighteenth-century Egypt, although the history of the *Nights* would fit comfortably within the scope of her project: it is a complex work that enjoyed a rich history of manuscript production before the introduction of the printing press; it draws on both oral and written traditions and demonstrates the fluid relationship between the two; the features of the Arabic and the thematic concerns of the stories are consistent with other literatures of the same period. And yet there is not a single mention of the *Nights* in her book, which calls into question nearly every bit of conventional wisdom in the field.

If we consider the *Nights* on its own terms as a cultural product of the eighteenth and nineteenth centuries, then the quest for an original version and its traces in later editions can be put aside in favor of different questions. In this new context, the features that troubled modern editors and redactors, and which they sought to correct or omit—its colloquial and Middle Arabic vocabulary, the often bawdy tone, the heterogeneous nature of its stories—become essential elements of its modern character and allow us to imagine a different kind of authentic *Nights*.[35]

We can now, for example, reconsider Lane's view of the *Nights*. Lane's translation was an extension of his earlier work aimed at depicting and explaining the manners and customs of the modern Egyptians, which Lane (like other Europeans) considered to be unchanged since the Middle Ages. He regarded the *Nights* as an ethnographic text.[36] Unlike both his predecessor, Galland, and his successor, Richard Burton, Lane intended his work not as an entertainment, but as an instructional work. He deleted stories that he regarded as excessively vulgar, and his sober, scholarly translation is filled with long footnotes.[37]

Lane's approach to the *Nights* was in most respects typically orientalist in his insistence that these stories, which he believed to be of genuinely medieval origins, shed light on nineteenth-century Arab society and culture, which he believed to be unchanged over many centuries. In one, respect, however, Lane's view of the *Nights* was different and moved ahead of his contemporaries of the late eighteenth and early nineteenth century: he insisted on a distinction between Egypt and the rest of the East. He believed the *Nights* to be a portrait not of 'the East' as a whole, but of Egypt itself. It is true that he continued to believe that the manners and customs portrayed in the *Nights* had much to tell his readers about *modern* Egypt. He was not the first to claim that the *Nights* was a portrait of a people, a claim commonly made, but he was the first to insist that it was a portrait of Egyptian customs. Russell's *Aleppo*, another travelogue widely read by the English, was in Lane's judgment a portrait of Turkish, not Arab peoples. So committed to this notion was Lane that he wrote in his Preface to *Manners and Customs*: "There is one work, however, which presents most admirable pictures of the manners and customs of the Arabs, and particularly those of the Egyptians; it is 'The Thousand and One Nights'; or 'Arabian Nights' Entertainments'. If the English reader had possessed a close translation of it with sufficient illustrative notes, I might almost have spared myself the labour of the present undertaking."[38]

Lane's view was correct in one regard, but not in another. The *Nights* does have much to tell us about nineteenth-century Egyptian culture, but not because Egyptian culture had remained unchanged since the Middle Ages. Like his contemporaries, Lane considered the proper milieu for understanding the *Nights* to be the medieval period. His extensive notes to his translation were later extracted, reorganized, and published separately by his great-nephew, Stanley Lane-Poole, as *Arabian Society in the Middle Ages: Studies from the Thousand and One Nights*.[39] Lane's translation of the *Nights* drew from numerous manuscripts and printed editions, many of them from the Egyptian *stemma*. Ironically, then, his claim that the *Nights* provided a portrait of contemporary Egyptian life might have some merit. If we consider the *Nights* as a piece of modern Arabic literature, produced in a specifically Egyptian context, it might well provide us with a source for understanding some elements of the culture, values, concerns, and interests of the eighteenth- and nineteenth-century Egyptians who read, wrote, rewrote, and circulated these texts. Were literary scholars to engage in careful studies of the Egyptian *stemma* in its early-modern context, we might learn a great deal about Egyptian culture and society of those eras. Viewed in this way, it is as a document of the Middle Ages, not of modern Egypt, that the Egyptian *Nights* might be considered anachronistic.

The Nights *and Medieval Cairo*

Lane's view of the *Nights* as an ethnographic text was shared by the many travelers who had begun to flood the East in the nineteenth century, their travel eased over the course of the century by Thomas Cook and the steamship. They were convinced that the *Nights* provided them with the raw material for understanding oriental societies, which they assumed all shared common features and had remained unchanged for centuries. The *Arabian Nights* was considered essential reading for travelers to Egypt in particular and to the East in general. For these travelers, the city was a site of entertainments as well as monuments. This imagined Orient, imagined Cairo, was far preferable in European minds to the modern, European-style architecture and street plans of the new district of Ismailiya, which Khedive Ismail had ordered his minister of public works to reproduce after returning from Baron Haussmann's Paris. Most European visitors found Ismail's 'Paris by the Nile' repugnant. The new districts lacked the charm and authenticity of the old Arab city, and were seen as pale imitations of 'real' European cities. Travelers preferred the Orient of the *Arabian Nights*, which they constantly sought (and found) on their forays into the so-called Arab city.

Some of these travelers had come originally to Egypt to explore its pharaonic antiquities and become intrigued by the Arab ruins that they saw.[40] Although these ruined buildings appealed to their romantic longing for a distant and exotic past, the most serious among these travelers—artists, draftsmen, engineers—began to lobby for the preservation of Egypt's (and especially Cairo's) Arab art. They noted that the rich architectural heritage of Cairo was in danger of being lost altogether, as the vast majority of its 'ancient' or 'medieval' or 'oriental,' or 'Arab' (they used all these terms) monuments were in a state of utter dilapidation. No doubt, some of their preservationist fervor was an extension of the rage for conservation then prevalent in Europe. But some of it was also the outcome of the Orient of their imagination, which they had brought with them to Cairo. And this is where our modern story of the *Nights* as an artifact of European culture begins to converge with another imagined Cairo, the one that was being materially reconstructed in the last decades of the nineteenth century by the Comité.

As we have seen earlier, the Comité was established in Cairo in 1881. Although there were a number of Egyptians on the Comité, the most influential members were British, French, German, and Hungarian. The Comité began to list all the monuments of Arab art that they considered worthy of preservation, and this meant that they listed approximately six hundred buildings mostly from the thirteenth, fourteenth, and fifteenth centuries. In the early decades of the Comité's work, the 'modern' buildings of the Ottomans were largely ignored as being inferior and of little artistic interest.

The buildings they chose to preserve and their plans for preservation were intended to make these monuments available not to the local population, but to the touring European public. British administrators were quite frank about who the intended audience for these buildings really was. Although they did considerable research and carried out their mission conscientiously, their preservation decisions were based on European ideas about what the city should look like and European assumptions about what constituted proper Arab art—an approach similar to that taken by the translators of the *Nights*. I might even risk a characterization of their activities as a sort of architectural philology: their impulse was to locate an original version of the building and to fix that version of the building, much as a philologist might seek to uncover and fix an authoritative version of a text.

The difficulty with these enterprises of recovery and restoration was that, just as with literary texts, no single authentic version of a building really existed. Many of these monumental structures had undergone continual repair, restoration, and alteration at the hands of successive rulers and dynasties over four or five centuries. The monuments themselves had suffered many vicissitudes, including numerous earthquakes, and most were in a dilapidated state. By the time of Napoleon's invasion, for example, none of the minarets (and there were and still are hundreds) standing in Cairo had any of their finials, and many were lacking large parts of their upper sections. This did not stop European artists from providing full sketches and even determining a rigid dynastic chronology to minaret types: Fatimid, Ayyubid, early Mamluk, Circassian, late Mamluk, and so on.[41]

Many of the fallen minarets had been replaced by Ottoman-style pencil point minarets. One of the most urgent tasks of the Comité was to identify and restore these dozens of monuments to proper dynastic style. In many cases, this meant dismantling later elements, especially Ottoman minarets, and replacing them with 'authentic' Mamluk elements. Thus, the members of the Comité repaired and replaced crenelations, wooden supports, locks, doors, windows, plaster windows, and accessories such as lamps. They needed replacement parts, many of which were manufactured in Cairo by craftsmen who were also prefabricating parts for the neo-Mamluk buildings being constructed in the new city of Heliopolis, whose developer had determined that the preferred architectural style would be Mamluk.[42] Other parts could not be as easily manufactured in Cairo, for example, mosque lamps. Members of the Comité took several examples of Mamluk glass lamps, sent them to Paris, and had copies made by craftsmen there.[43]

The work of preservation carried out by the Comité had made it increasingly difficult to distinguish between old and new elements of Cairo's Arab monuments, just as the history of translation, addition, and completion of the *Nights* had made it difficult for readers to differentiate between its many authors, layers, anachronisms, and provenances. With the conviction that they could (and should) fabricate authentic versions of Eastern monuments, be they literary or architectural, the Comité produced a Medieval Cairo that was and remains an amalgamation of old and new, a collage of often discrete elements that are an inextricable nineteenth-century expression of a colonial moment.

The *Nights* itself is also a complex amalgamation, merging diverse elements that quickly became indistinguishable from one another. The copyists of the Egyptian branch (like its earliest translators) added stories from different oral and written traditions (Indian, Persian, Turkish, Arabic), bringing the number of nights into line with the title of 'One Thousand and One'. Many of those stories have their roots in Egyptian or other Arab cultures. Even the stories that are now regarded as Galland's forgeries—Aladdin and Ali Baba—may well have an Arabic oral provenance, having entered the written tradition through the medium of Galland's *Nuits*.[44] This would be entirely consistent with Hanna's argument that the line between oral and written literary cultures in the seventeenth and eighteenth centuries was fluid and shifting. Versions of many works existed in both mediums, and it was not at all unusual for stories that had a primarily oral provenance to become incorporated into a written work. If Galland's claims about his source for the Aladdin and Ali Baba stories are true, they would be consistent with the general literary culture in Egypt at the time. But it is not possible for the ordinary reader or listener, once these different elements are assimilated and homogenized, to distinguish them from the older elements.

One of the most striking examples of this amalgamation in a literary context is not just the Aladdin and Ali Baba stories, but the self-conscious attempt on Richard Burton's part to provide an authentically 'oriental' version of a *Nights* tale for which he had no Arabic manuscript. In a letter published in *The Academy*, under the title, "The Orientalisation of Galland's 'Arabian Nights,'" Burton answered readers' objections to his plan to render Galland's text into English by first translating the French into Arabic, and then translating the Arabic into English. The subscribers to Burton's *Nights* wanted a direct translation from French into English. Burton announced that the problem had been solved, explaining that he had found three different translations of Galland into Hindustani, thereby accomplishing the "orientalisation" of the French *Nights* for him. He needed now only to "assimilate the style of the Indian version with the Arabic."[45] Unlike Lane, who saw in the *Nights* evidence for a specifically Egyptian Orient, Burton made no such distinction. His Orient was undifferentiated and his *Arabian Nights* could as easily be 'orientalised' by a Hindu version as by an Arabic one. Indeed, his conviction that a translation could be 'orientalised' and then reintroduced in yet another European language, that this process of translation and retranslation was all that was needed to produce not only a complete but also an authentic version, demonstrates just how pervasive the process of amalgamation could be.

Finally, we should consider a more concrete intersection of the literary and the architectural, the illustrated editions of the *Nights*. Travelers' images of the East had been shaped not only by the words on the page, but also by drawings in illustrated editions of the *Nights* that began to appear almost as soon as it was translated. These illustrated editions became common as part of a wider trend of illustrating books. Many of the figures involved in the publication of illustrated editions of the *Nights* were also central to the story of illustrated books in general: Owen Jones, the Dalziel brothers, and Charles Knight, to name just a few. Children's illustrated editions of the *Nights* followed, and we may assume that Lord Curzon had one of these editions in mind when he sought a design for his mosque lamp. But what sort of edition might he have seen?

Illustrated editions of the *Nights* came in many variations and were produced for different markets. Lane's illustrated edition occupies an important place not only in the history of *Nights* itself but in that of illustrated Victorian books as well.[46] His first illustrator, William Harvey (1796–1866), was the premier pupil of Thomas Bewick, who developed (perhaps even invented) the process of engraving on wood, which was "the most widely used medium during the first half of the century."[47] Bewick was the most influential craftsman of wood engraving, and the successive generations of pupils trained by him or in his school not only perpetuated the craft in England but also revived it in France.[48] There were competing aims and markets: people wanted to produce cheap volumes with large circulations, but they also wanted to produce nicer books at higher prices for the limited market that could afford to pay for them.[49] It would be from the middle and later part of the nineteenth century on, however, that the direct intersection between architectural Cairo and illustrations of the *Nights* would come: Richard Burton thanked Yacoub Artin Pasha, a member of the Comité, for designing the Arabic ornamentations used in his volumes.[50]

Amalgamations

Medieval Cairo and the *Arabian Nights* were amalgamations. In the rest of this chapter, I analyze a series of images that demonstrate amalgamations that came to be regarded as 'authentically' medieval. I have chosen them from a popular work that takes for granted the category 'Cairo of the Arabian Nights,' Douglas Sladen's *Oriental Cairo: The City of the "Arabian Nights,"* to demonstrate my argument about amalgamation. The book is one of a number of early twentieth-century travel entertainments written by Sladen, an intrepid traveler and travel writer who visited and wrote about a variety of exotic places: Japan, Australia, North Africa, British East Africa, and America. My intention here is not to disparage or even criticize those nineteenth and early twentieth-century writers and readers, but rather to show how 'Cairo of the Arabian Nights' was created.

Oriental Cairo's Wheels

The photograph facing the first chapter of Douglas Sladen's *Oriental Cairo: The City of the "Arabian Nights"*, also entitled "Oriental Cairo: The City of the 'Arabian Nights,'" shows a typical lorry bearing the caption "Native Bus of the more refined kind, drawn by two asses, in the Ataba-el-khadra" (Figure 10).[51] But we need to ask what is wrong with this picture, the first illustration his readers see of 'Cairo of the Arabian Nights.' Simply, it shows a wheeled vehicle, and one that looks archaic (albeit refined) at that. But wheeled vehicles were entirely absent from Cairo during the Middle Ages and the subsequent Ottoman period. Its streets were too narrow and too poor for wheeled vehicles to be a practical or efficient mode of transport. Cairenes in those days used beasts of burden, mostly donkeys and mules, to carry their goods. Wheeled vehicles were introduced to Cairo only in the nineteenth century, when the Ministry of Public Works widened and straightened many of Cairo's streets so that they could accommodate such vehicles. These wider streets, of course, often came at the expense of old buildings, and an intermittent turf battle between Public Works and the Comité (under the aegis of the Waqf Ministry) over this issue is evident in the Comité's published minutes.

The wheeled lorry that came to be typical and was thought of as archaic was, in fact, mostly modeled on the Napoleonic cart, with its oversized wheels (Figure 11). These carts were often the subject of photos, positioned in front of 'medieval' tombs, and were considered to be typically Egyptian. Carriages were also considered to be an oriental sight. An article, entitled "Modern Egypt and its People," published in the *Journal of the American Geographical Society of New York* in 1881, has this to say: "One of the most picturesque and Oriental sights of Cairo is often beheld on a bright moonlight night. A great handsome carriage, drawn by a pair of large English horses and full of lovely, half-veiled, fair Circassian and Georgian women."[52] In the middle of the nineteenth century, however, Murray's Guide noted with amusement the use of outdated European carriages by Cairo's elites, adding the wry comment that it appeared that European museums were selling off their duplicates to unwitting Egyptians.[53] These wheeled vehicles—whether lorry or carriage—that were anything *but* oriental demonstrate the extent of the amalgamation that made it impossible to distinguish new from old, or the extent to which some elements of the 'old' were new fabrications. And the widened streets that allowed for the introduction and use of the wheeled vehicles that became a marker of Cairo's quaint archaism were also responsible for the dismantling of some of its old architectural fabric.

Storytelling

Another image from Sladen's book carries the caption "A Story-teller Reciting from the Arabian Nights/ In the background are the ramparts of the Citadel" (Figure 12). The photo is taken at the foot of the lower retaining walls of the Citadel. Sladen, who spoke no more than a few words of Arabic, could not possibly have known what was actually taking place here. There are many reasons why it is highly unlikely that the storyteller was actually reciting from the *Nights*. Cairenes of the eighteenth and nineteenth centuries certainly listened to stories, and storytelling was a widespread, if somewhat debased, occupation. But the stories they listened to were of an entirely different sort: the "Sirat Bani Hilal" and the "Romance of al-Zahir Baybars," both dealing with the heroic deeds of important groups and figures in Islamic history.[54] Furthermore, the preferred site for *Nights* recitations, when they happened, was in coffeehouses, not in the open air.

This scene also emphasizes what Sladen and others considered to be the largely oral character of local Egyptian culture, at least among ordinary people. The image, then, is highly misleading on many counts. Wide exposure to the *Nights* came to Arabic readers in the nineteenth century, and was not limited to oral recitation. From the 1820s on in Egypt, Muhammad 'Ali ordered a register printed under the title *Jurnal al-Khidiw*. It was the first printed Arabic periodical. A bilingual Turkish–Arabic publication, the *Jurnal* was aimed primarily at reporting state affairs to officials. It started as a handwritten publication before being lithographed and eventually printed daily. As Ami Ayalon discusses, it included official notices, reports on developments in the capital and in the provinces, and, to alleviate the rigor of official business, stories from the *Thousand and One Nights*, a charming measure that would later become a feature of many Arabic papers.[55]

If the *Nights* were widely read or listened to in the nineteenth century by Egyptians, it was not the result of a continuous practice dating from the Middle Ages, but rather one aspect (and only one) of the larger development of book culture and the book trade in Cairo. The stories from the *Nights* that Europeans read—and which they imagined were being recited—were not a part of the culture of oral recitation of the *Nights*, which had a different corpus altogether. We should also recall that these developments were recent and depended upon new technologies and the adaptation of older techniques in new commercial settings. In other words, the spread of the *Nights* was, like the construction of Medieval Cairo, modern, and it was not a single text, in any case.

The Fountain of 'Abd al-Rahman Katkhuda

A more explicitly architectural example of amalgamation is the *sabil-kuttab* of 'Abd al-Rahman Katkhuda.[56] In Sladen's photograph in *Oriental Cairo* (Figure 13) the caption proclaims the view as "the most beautiful, romantic, and mediaeval street in Cairo, with the most exquisite street fountain in Cairo at its end."[57] The *sabil*, constructed in 1744, was an amalgamation of Ottoman and Mamluk styles, a fact acknowledged by Herz Bey in the survey of Arab architecture that appears in his catalogue of the Museum of Arab Art. Herz Bey's assessment of the aesthetic merits of the *sabil* as a mixture "where Arab and Turkish art combined to produce work having some claim to beauty" diverges from his generally negative judgment of the architecture of the Ottoman period, especially the decline of ornament.[58] Part of what appealed to Herz Bey was no doubt the building's decoration, something that had fallen by the wayside during the preceding Ottoman Egyptian centuries and which 'Abd al-Rahman Katkhuda reintroduced and elaborated.[59] But Herz Bey's clear recognition of the Ottoman elements of the structure was not remembered popularly. In Sladen's view, the *sabil* was a purely medieval building. This centerpiece of 'medieval' architecture, which enjoys a full-page photograph that makes no mention of its Ottoman origins, was reproduced as a representation of the medieval at the 1893 World's Columbian Exposition (where it was perhaps the most frequently used backdrop in photographs of the personnel in the street) (Figure 14) and again at the 1900 Exposition Universale in Paris. The *sabil*, thus established, in

Nicholas Warner's words, as "a favorite exemplar of Islamic architectural style," was also reproduced in Cairo itself. In the 1920s, the Comité added a copy of 'Abd al-Rahman Katkhuda's *sabil-kuttab* to the northern façade of the seventeenth-century mosque of Yusuf Agha al-Hin after it was restored.[60]

Minarets of Cairo

Numerous books and websites boast an image of these domes and minarets, often described in captions as 'Cairo of the Arabian Nights' or 'Medieval Cairo' (Figure 15). But this image is an illusion created by a carefully framed photograph to produce an architectural collage. What seems to be a medieval skyline is, in fact, a composite of the rooftops of two mosques, the fourteenth-century mosque of Sultan Hasan and the twentieth-century mosque of al-Rifa'i.

As discussed in Chapter 1, the mosque of al-Rifa'i is a thoroughly modern structure, reflecting a series of changes in Cairo's urban environment and its architectural traditions that are specific to the nineteenth century. The Rifa'i–Sultan Hasan photographic collage is the perfect visual metaphor for the *Nights*: it assimilates neo-Mamluk to Mamluk elements in a single, persuasive, deeply evocative image, an image that represents better than almost any other the power of visual as well as literary amalgamation.

There is another sense in which the Rifa'i Mosque is an amalgamation: the Ottoman imperial context as a possible frame of reference for its construction and reception has been erased from its history by modern scholarship. Mohammad al-Asad concludes that the monument combines "a Mamluk morphology with a nineteenth-century Beaux-Arts classical-revival syntax." But as Robert Ilbert and Mercedes Volait demonstrate, "neo-Arabic" architecture was not limited to religious structures, and "historicist" constructions were clearly influenced by the architectural revivals of the central Ottoman lands.[61] Ahmet Ersoy's study of the *Usul* establishes that the "rich architectural vocabulary of the Ottoman Renaissance on the street incorporates a highly eclectic blend of forms mostly appropriated from sources outside the Ottoman tradition—ranging from elements derived from the European Orientalist repertoire to details along the current neo-Gothic line."[62] We do not know how

Herz Bey understood the context for his design, but we can say that the use of both "neo-Arabic" and Gothic or other European architectural elements could easily have been read by at least some of its audiences as contemporary Ottoman practice. Such amalgamated structures were also a well-known feature of British imperial architecture in India.[63]

The erasure of a possible Ottoman context for interpreting the mosque here, just as its erasure in Sladen's presentation of the *sabil* of 'Abd al-Rahman Katkhuda, also represents amalgamation. This process of amalgamation, however, was not restricted to architecture or literature. We see it also in the treatment of religious practices as they were described and interpreted in nineteenth-century Cairo. Some of the features of nineteenth-century religious life that were most commonly associated with a seemingly unchanging Arab past had actually been introduced, reintroduced, or reconfigured during the Ottoman period. In Egypt, the Ottomans restored old shrines, created many new ones, and reassigned existing shrines. The cult of Sayyida Zaynab, for example, was introduced to Egypt by the Ottomans, who attributed to her a shrine that had previously been linked to a later descendant of the Prophet.[64] The Ottomans also reintroduced *mawlid*s that had been abandoned.

Some practices in Ottoman Egypt changed visibly from Mamluk times. The Ottomans segregated certain activities that had been fully integrated into mosque life under the Mamluks. Under the Mamluks religious institutions were largely multifunctional, meaning that within the same institution, prayer, jurisprudence, and sufi *dhikr* might take place; under the Ottomans, the broad assimilation of Sufi practices to the mosque disappeared. This was a reflection, also, of conventions within the Ottoman lands, where Sufism played a large and important role in the Ottoman state, but where Sufi practice and Sunni orthodox practice were generally segregated in distinct institutions.[65] Sufis, for example, were often appointed as Qur'an readers in Mamluk Egypt, but not in Ottoman Egypt.

Other practices changed more than once under the Ottomans: in early Ottoman times, the *mawlid* of the Prophet Muhammad had clearly been suppressed, but by the late nineteenth century, it was once again an official state occasion in Egypt.[66] The historian al-Jabarti (1753–1825) describes the retreat of the French after their three years of rule, and notes that "[f]or seven consecutive nights the minarets were lit up." He continues to describe the festivities for the *mawlid* of the Prophet, which began the next day. It was announced on both Tuesday and Wednesday that "the streets would be decorated . . . sweeping and sprinkling [of water, to keep the dust down] were ordered. People got busy, decorated their stores with pieces of silk, and Indian cloth . . . [t]oward evening lanterns and tapers were lit, also the minarets; and as usual al-Kulshani Takiya was crowded. People were milling about throughout the night. They sang and played music in the several places, and read the Koran. The children were noisy in the streets, and this spread through the city quarters of Cairo and Bulaq." Finally, al-Jabarti comments that in the past, "this was practiced" (meaning the festivities for the *mawlid*) only in Bulaq and in Azbakiya at the residence of Shaykh al-Bakri, who was in charge of the festivities of the Prophet's *mawlid*.[67] It is clear, then, that the celebration of the Prophet's *mawlid* was closely associated with particular neighborhoods under the French, and perhaps for an even longer period of time, and that its widespread celebration marked the end of French rule. All of these practices, however, were believed—assumed—to be centuries old, to be medieval.

Conclusion

Whether in the Streets of Cairo at World's Fairs and Exhibitions or in Cairo's own streets, these amalgamations become visible only when we look for them. New urban and architectural forms are present, even if they at times masquerade as Mamluk structures. What all these amalgamations have in common is that, while appearing to be 'oriental' or 'medieval' in the eyes of European observers, they are decidedly *modern*. Their presumptive interpretation as 'medieval' shows both how necessary and how successful the complex process of amalgamation was in the construction and canonization of Medieval Cairo and its life as Cairo of the *Arabian Nights*. An important part of the process of amalgamation involves assimilation and erasure, that is, the redefinition of new as old, and the assimilation of one style, category, or period so completely into another that its recent origins become completely invisible.

Just as the *Nights* is the product of a history that "combin[es] textual and oral processes over a long period of time," so, too, is Medieval Cairo the product of a history that combines different but overlapping processes over an equally long period of time. Both are, as Ibrahim Muhawi has stated in respect of the *Nights*, "heterogeneous."[68] But they are heterogeneous products that, in their canonized forms, have an antiquity and coherence that have been accorded to them through modern cultural and political processes of canonization and authority that assert a particular notion of authenticity. Those canons and notions of authenticity are not ageless. For both the *Nights* and Medieval Cairo, they are rooted in colonial practices that have themselves receded from our historical memory. In Chapter 4, I explore how the continuing process of amalgamation has led to the erasure of Medieval Cairo's colonial roots, and I discuss how recovering those forgotten colonial practices reveals a new way of understanding one of the most heated controversies over preservation in Medieval Cairo today.

4

Keeping Cairo Medieval

World Heritage and the Debate over Fatimid Monuments

Medieval Cairo, I have argued, was constructed in the late nineteenth century and became canonical soon thereafter. By the first decade of the twentieth century, Medieval Cairo, with its characteristically Mamluk appearance, was a given, regardless of the many names by which it was (or would later be) called: 'Cairo of the Arabian Nights,' 'Arab Cairo,' 'Medieval Cairo,' 'historic Cairo,' 'the historic center of Cairo,' 'Cairo's historic district,' and, sometimes, 'Fatimid Cairo,' in a nod to the dynasty that founded the palace city of Cairo in the tenth century. Throughout the twentieth century, Medieval Cairo continued to draw the attention of travelers, of local Egyptians, of the Comité in its various forms, and beginning in the 1960s, of the emerging World Heritage community and some Muslim communities with deep historical (though not recent) ties to the Fatimids and, thus, to Cairo itself.

In the 1970s, little attention was paid to the Islamic monuments of Cairo. In a manner somewhat reminiscent of the nineteenth century, American and European admirers and students of Medieval Cairo began to clamor actively for attention to the monuments. A grassroots organization, the Society for the Preservation of Arab Architecture in Egypt (SPARE) was formed. Its membership was almost entirely non-Egyptian. It published a periodic newsletter and actively lobbied for preservation. At roughly the same time, the World Heritage community began to take an interest in Medieval Cairo and, in 1979, an application was submitted to place 'historic Cairo' on the World Heritage list.

In these years, also, the Dawoodi (Daudi) Bohras, a sect of Ismaili Shi'ites from the Indian subcontinent, secured concessions to restore several Fatimid-era monuments in Cairo. Thus began a chapter in the history of conservation controversies that has continued for over a quarter of a century. These controversies over the Bohra restorations in 'Fatimid Cairo,' the response of the international conservation and World Heritage communities, and of local Egyptian officials and observers, however contemporary they may be, have deep roots in the nineteenth century. The controversies over the Bohra restorations in Cairo demonstrate clearly, in my view, what the stakes of a fully historicized Medieval Cairo are. The issues in Cairo are no longer over the relative merits of Ottoman versus Mamluk sites. That particularly nineteenth-century concern has receded, as other concerns (equally rooted in nineteenth-century contexts, and more importantly, unacknowledged assumptions) have emerged to inform the practice of and debates over preservation in Cairo.[1]

India in Egypt Redux

One of the liveliest debates in recent years has been over the relative merits or deficiences of the restorations carried out by the Dawoodi Bohras, a community of about one million Musta'lian Ismaili Shi'ites living mainly in India and Pakistan, with communities also in East Africa, Great Britain, Canada, and the United States. The Bohras trace their spiritual lineage to the earliest Hindu converts at the time of the Fatimid caliph al-Mustansir in the second half of the eleventh century. In the twelfth century, the Ismailis of the Yemen and India largely followed the mission *(da'wa)* of the Tayyibi schism, with the Dawoodis emerging as one of several Bohra communities, each recognizing a different line of missionaries (*da'is*).

The current Bohra *da'i* has considerable authority, including a claim to infallible judgment. He is addressed as *Mulla ji Sahib* or *Syedna* and carries the title 'His Holiness.' In the twentieth century, the Dawoodi Bohra religious hierarchy was headed by Tahir Sayf al-Din and his son, Muhammad Burhanuddin, who successively held the title *da'i mutlaq*. The community has also been rent in the last century by disputes over—among other things—the scope of the *da'i*'s authority and the finances of the community. This split resulted in the emergence of a reformist or progressive movement in the nineteenth century which has remained an active dissenting voice until the present day.

The restorations carried out by the Dawoodi Bohras have been roundly criticized by the Euro-American preservation community, and the debates they have generated over the proper appearance of restored monuments bring us back full circle to the colonially produced relationship between Egypt and India of the nineteenth century. The Bohras and the international heritage community represent viewpoints that have their roots in different colonial architectural traditions. One, the Indo-Saracenic form of architecture, is a product of the shared colonial experience in India; the other, canonical Mamluk Cairo, is the product of the shared quasi-colonial experience in Egypt. In the twentieth and twenty-first centuries, these canonical architectural traditions have been viewed as mutually exclusive, but they are both, in reality, indigenized colonial traditions. What we see in the debates over the fate of the Fatimid monuments is the collision of two indigenized colonial traditions—one Indian, one Egyptian—in Islamic Cairo. Both are the products of colonialism, but they emerge out of distinct colonial experiences with different histories and trajectories. Peter van der Veer has shown in his discussion of religion and empire that many issues "are rooted in the same history of empire but experienced on opposite sides of the colonizing process."[2] Following his analysis, we might say of the contenders in the debate over Fatimid monuments that they represent different long-term conclusions to histories that were experienced on the *same* side of the colonizing process, but in discrete colonial settings, each of which followed a different trajectory that, while colonial, is historically specific.

The Critique of Bohra Restoration

The terms of what is now a quarter-century battle over the aesthetic merits and authenticity of the Bohra restorations of Fatimid monuments in Cairo were framed not by preservation professionals, but by a grassroots advocacy organization devoted to the conservation of Egypt's Islamic antiquities. In its inaugural newsletter, published in November 1979, the newly formed Society for the Preservation of the Architectural Resources of Egypt (SPARE) noted with approval that medieval Cairo had been placed on UNESCO's World Heritage List. The same article, however, admonished readers that it would be "a mistake to imagine that any and all restorations are acceptable. Highly unsatisfactory work, for example, is in progress in the eleventh-century mosque of al-Hakim under the hands of a group of Indians belonging to the Bahariyya *[sic]* sect, for whom al-Hakim has a special religious significance. Though their method of financing the project is intriguing, their concrete arcades can only be deplored (Figure 16)."[3]

Although the Bohra restoration of the mosque, which included removal of a small Mamluk tomb, was clearly controversial, the assessments were not all negative. A year later, on the occasion of the official opening of the mosque, the Anglophone *The Egyptian Gazette* ran an appreciative article and editorial commending the transformation of "the saddest building" on the street, which had once been the major thoroughfare of Fatimid Cairo. They concluded, "No one who saw the mosque before the Bohara group began its task would deny the improvement." Not only had the mosque been dilapidated for several centuries, but the area in front of it had long been the site of a large onion and garlic market (Figure 17). Noting that "the Bohara sect did not go to Unesco for financial aid, or to their national government," they expressed the hope that the example of this "self-help" project would "not be lost on well-to-do Muslims closer to home." The paper recounted the controversy over the removal of the tomb ("born more from xenophobia than from concern for Egypt's cultural heritage") and cited a defense reported by *Al-Ahram*, the semi-official newspaper of the Egyptian government. There, the president of the Egyptian Antiquities Organization (EAO), Dr. Shehata Adam, defended the tomb's removal on the grounds that it was not contemporary with the Fatimid period.[4]

The debate did not end with the opening of the newly restored mosque. For more than two decades, the Bohras and the historic preservation community have pursued competing and mutually exclusive programs in 'historic' Cairo. The Bohra restorations have been criticized by professional architectural conservationists, old Cairo hands, as well as Islamic art and architectural historians.[5] The preservation community's condemnation of Bohra restoration efforts is founded upon the internationally accepted standards of preservation as articulated in the Venice Charter.[6] Those standards place the principle of reversibility—that is, that any intervention in a building or an object of art should be fully reversible—at the center of contemporary preservation practice. In addition to indicting the methods of restoration used by the Bohras, their critics also bemoan the resulting appearance of the monuments. The Bohra community has not, as far as I am able to determine, engaged in any criticism of the preservation community's practices.

The World Heritage List and 'Islamic Cairo'

The starting point for the contemporary conservationist program is the historical and cultural importance of 'Islamic' or 'historic' Cairo. The importance of the 'historic' city was articulated in Egypt's 1979 application to UNESCO nominating 'Islamic Cairo' for inclusion on the World Heritage List. That seminal document defines Islamic Cairo as "the historic centre of the City of Cairo (= al-Qahira), capital of Egypt." It uses the terms 'Islamic,' 'historic,' and 'medieval' interchangeably.[7] These terms are so conventional that they do not appear, at first glance, to need further investigation. But they and the ideas about the history of architecture that they stand for developed slowly and took different turns. As we saw in Chapters 1, 2, and 3, at the turn of the nineteenth century, 'medieval' Cairo did not exist. The city and its monuments were classified in the *Description de l'Egypte* as part of 'l'état moderne.' The medieval as a particular category in the periodization of human history had only recently fully emerged and had not yet been used in the periodization of the non-European past. 'Medieval Cairo' (and its corollaries, 'historic' and 'Islamic' Cairo) was the end product of a convergence and interaction of several different local and imperial contexts, cultural ideas and practices, and historical trajectories.

But none of this complex history is considered in the World Heritage List nomination.

The structure of the conservationists' narratives is bipartite: the history of the city is narrated separately from the history of preservation, as if the latter had no implications for the former. The World Heritage List nomination, following the conventional categories of the World Heritage application form, does not include information about the Comité's activities in its narrative history of the city; the Comité is mentioned, instead, in the section entitled "History of preservation/conservation." The summary history of Cairo briefly mentions the Fatimids as founders of the "nucleus of mediaeval Cairo," the connection of Fustat to Cairo forged by the Ayyubids, and the expansion and dramatically increased monumental density under the Mamluks. Unburdened by the anti-Ottomanism of either their early nationalist forebears or of the nineteenth-century European preservationists, the Egyptian authors of the World Heritage application also include in their narrative the Ottomans' faithful preservation of the original functions of medieval structures, particularly religious buildings. The historical narrative ends with the "construction of the modern Europeanized city to the west and to the north of the old city." The importance of this separate Europeanized city is emphasized in the final sentences of the history: "Thus the historic parts of mediaeval and Ottoman Cairo were left virtually untouched. Cairo was spared the irreversible and deplorable destruction that has been witnessed in most other cities of great historic past. And thus, till today the unequalled wealth of Cairo's historical monuments is an impressive testimony to the international rank of Cairo in the mediaeval period."

Medieval Cairo is thus presented to the reader as intact, a historic area that is available to the modern viewer in a basically unaltered state. The underlying assumptions are clear: the work of restoration has no implications for the *history* of the city. Conservation merely makes visible and available what is already there. Indeed, the "Diagnosis" subsection of the "State of preservation/conservation" section states baldly, "The historic fabric of Islamic Cairo has been preserved in some areas up to two fifths of the original. Such a state of preservation can be considered as exceptional." There is no calculation of the extent of the Comité's interventions or their role in the (re)configuration of these monuments.

The "Justification for Inclusion in the World Heritage List" drives the point home: "In an unbroken sequence, all periods of architectural development—from early Islamic times till the nineteenth century—are richly documentated *[sic]*. Most remarkable of all is the amount of constructions dating back to the Middle Ages, which accounts for nearly half of the surviving monuments. Thus Cairo is graced by the greatest density of mediaeval monuments to be found in any Islamic city, and is likewise an outstanding example of a mediaeval city anywhere in the world . . . the Islamic city of Cairo has retained much of its mediaeval character."[8]

Although the Comité's activities and conservation philosophy have been unusually well documented, until very recently, there had been almost no discussion in the heritage and preservation communities of the assumptions that underlie its works. Even recent publications on the architectural history of Cairo underplay the Comité's interventions.[9] For example, the introductory text *Islamic Architecture in Cairo* by Doris Behrens-Abouseif discusses over fifty Cairene monuments. In the narrative history of each monument, she provides a short discussion of restorations, but she generally discusses only restorations carried out in the Middle Ages. The Comité is mentioned occasionally in passing, with few details provided, although nearly all of the monuments she discusses were listed and restored by them, some to a very considerable extent. The first four editions of the *Practical Guide to Islamic Monuments in Cairo* make almost no mention of the Comité's restoration efforts; the fifth edition, significantly revised by Caroline Williams, provides considerable information on a monument-by-monument basis about the Comité activities. The most complete information about Comité activities is now to be found in Nicholas Warner's masterful *Monuments of Historic Cairo*.[10]

One important exception to Behrens-Abouseif's general disregard for the Comité's role in conservation is her discussion of the mosque of al-Salih Tala'i'. There she takes issue with the Comité's nearly complete reconstruction of the mosque. On the other hand, the latest restorations mentioned for the Sultan Hasan complex are those of 1671–77, although this monument received a considerable amount of attention from the nineteenth century onward. As is typical also in art and architectural history texts, the photographs that illustrate the text are undated; the monument is presented for scrutiny, usually in the form modern restoration has given it, without comment.[11] The same phenomenon may be observed in Arabic architectural histories, where the activities of the Comité are mentioned only occasionally and briefly.[12] Among twentieth-century historians of Islamic architecture, only K.A.C. Creswell (himself a member of the Comité), whose *Muslim Architecture of Egypt* remains the canonical text for architectural historians, provides significant details about Comité activities and references to its minutes and technical reports in the primary narrative about the history of the monuments.[13] The dominant bipartite structure of the World Heritage List nomination's historical narrative persists, even among works written by preservationists, including those published by the Supreme Council of Antiquities (formerly the Egyptian Antiquities Organization) itself.[14]

One of the primary justifications for including Cairo on the World Heritage List is the homogeneity of its architecture: "The homogenity *[sic]* of Islamic Cairo is further based upon a consistent architectural style of great artistic refinement . . . stylistic achievements of other regions were assimilated into the highly developed local architectural tradition . . . ." This architectural homogeneity may, however, be as much an artifact of the Comité's practices as it is a marker of dynastic style. Although nearly all of the minarets of Cairo fell in earthquakes during the Middle Ages (some were reconstructed by later Mamluk rulers, some by the Comité, and still others by contemporary preservationists), the extent of the Comité's role in shaping the fabric of Islamic Cairo has been largely written out of Islamic architectural history. As Irene Bierman has discussed, the Comité's decisions about restoration were often overdetermined by an insistence on pure dynastic typology.[15]

Nairy Hampikian has shown that the Comité routinely used replacement elements (wooden balconies for minarets, parapets, mashrabiyas, moldings) that were manufactured in the workshops of Cairo for the construction of the new, neo-Mamluk suburb of Heliopolis.[16] As reconstructed and canonized by the Comité, 'Medieval Cairo' was defined by dynastic typology and characterized by its Mamluk appearance. What have become unquestioned typologies are nowhere clearer than in the standard architectural history works and in the *Practical Guide to Islamic Monuments in Cairo*. Each successive version of this title, now in its fifth edition, provides readers with a denser monumental landscape, increasingly detailed descriptions of particular monuments, and increasingly rigid typologies of architectural style, but there is no discussion of the Comité. Although the authors of the first edition (1974) of *Islamic Monuments in Cairo* made no claim to professional expertise,[17] the volume, with its typologized descriptions of Islamic architecture in Cairo, its large map peppered with monuments, and its easy accessibility to the non-Arabist, was included as part of the supporting documentation of Islamic Cairo's nomination for inclusion on the World Heritage List.[18]

Contemporary debates over the Bohra restoration of the mosque of al-Hakim and the dismantling and relocation of the Mamluk tomb demonstrate how the preservation community's critique appeals to the authority of authenticity and well-established, albeit historically constructed, typologies. Nineteenth-century travelers, and even observers contemporary with the early Comité's activities, did not share the passion for classifying and typologizing that underlay so much of the Comité's work. Before its restoration by the Bohras, the mosque of al-Hakim did not differ so dramatically in appearance from the other structures on the street that it was held to represent any particular dynastic style. Nineteenth-century observers were most interested in the mosque's similarities to, not its differences from, monuments from other periods: it had Ibn Tulun-like arcades (Figures 18, 19), minarets resembling that of the complex of al-Salih Najm al-Din Ayyub (Figures 20, 21), and monumental Kufic inscriptions on its exterior. And, of course, it had a typically Cairene ruined interior (Figure 22).[19] The mosque hovered comfortably and ambiguously on the continuum of Arab (later 'Islamic') architecture.

The insistence in the contemporary debate on dynastic typology is organized largely around the visual impact of the Mamluk tomb. How did this undistinguished little tomb of a minor figure, a structure with neither a foundational inscription nor a date, become a *cause célèbre*, an emblem of an intrusion that makes the *qasaba* unreadable to those who now look at it, a site for polemic and debate in the twentieth and twenty-first centuries? It certainly had nothing to do with any recognized importance, either architectural or historical, for it appears that no one knew much of anything about its resident, one Qurqumas.[20] In 1847,

Sir Gardner Wilkinson commented on the danger to the mosque's doorway and its inscription, but neither he nor any other nineteenth-century travel writer mentions the small tomb.[21] Nineteenth- and early twentieth-century visitors seem to have edited the little structure out of the picture altogether. In 1893, Florence Groff's *Guide to Cairo and Environs, Catalogues to the Museums of Egyptian Antiquities at Gizeh and Arab Antiquities at the Mosque of El Hakim* briefly described the mosque and its courtyard, which housed the first Museum of Arab Antiquities. In three pages describing the layout of the Museum of Arab Antiquities and discussing the logistics of reaching the interior of the mosque, there is no mention of the small tomb abutting the entrance: "The entrance to the mosque is on the right-hand side of the street and is usualy *[sic]* occupied by market people seated on the ground, climbing over them one reaches the door."[22] It is possible that the number of "encroaching buildings" was so great that the tomb might not have been recognizable as a separate structure. When the Comité cleared the "mean" structures (the term is Creswell's) from the mosque's façade, the tomb was clearly visible, but it was initially thought to have belonged to the eleventh-century Fatimid general Badr al-Jamali.[23]

Creswell had little to say about the tomb in his meticulous account of the mosque in volume one of *Muslim Architecture of Egypt*. In 1974, Richard Parker and Robin Sabin wrote a blasé paragraph about the little tomb in the first edition of *Islamic Monuments in Cairo*: "On the north side of the entrance to the Mosque of Hakim stands the Tomb of Qurqumas, a typical late Mameluke (1511) tomb. It is simply a square chamber with a dome. The entrance is on the north, but it is now left high and dry by the removal of an accumulation of dirt and debris, the high-water mark of which can be seen in the line between the light and dark colored masonry on this tomb and on the outer wall of the Mosque of al-Hakim." As for the identity of the tomb's occupant, there was little to say: "Qurqumas (Neverfear) was a fairly common Turkish name. I have been unable to find out who this one was. There is no inscription and no date." By 1985, in the third edition, revised by Caroline Williams, a historian of Fatimid architecture, the tomb, now located in the Northern Cemetery, no longer merited even the most meager description. It was notable primarily because it had been moved from its original location: "This tomb originally stood beside the monumental entrance of the Mosque of al-Hakim on the Qasaba or main street of Fatimid Cairo. When that mosque was restored this tomb was moved to its present site."[24]

It was this dislocation that elicited the outcry reported by the Arabic newspaper *al-Ahram* and the Anglophone *The Egyptian Gazette*. As reported in *The Egyptian Gazette* of Tuesday, 25 November 1980, Dr. Shehata Adam, President of the Egyptian Antiquities Organization, defended the action by appealing directly to the authority of typology. He echoed the view of the illustrious Egyptian architect Hassan Fathy (a consultant to the Bohra restoration team), who declared the problem to be the original erection of the *qubba*, not its removal. Pushing aside the long tradition of additions, accretions, and adaptations that are a feature of building in Cairo, Fathy had gone so far as to characterize the building of the *qubba* nearly half a millennium ago as an act of "vandalism." The authorities argued that the dismantling of the tomb was necessary because it was not contemporary with the Fatimid period. The January 1981 issue of the SPARE newsletter reluctantly acknowledged that the dismantling of the *qubba* had restored "an architectural purity that had not been visible for 450 years." The head of the Egyptian Antiquities Organization went even further, noting that the carefully dismantled tomb would be reassembled in the "traditional Mameluke burial ground of the City of the Dead" (Figure 23).[25] And so typology won the day: the Fatimid mosque was restored to architectural purity, and the Mamluk tomb was removed to a more suitable place, a Mamluk cemetery.

The episode raises interesting questions about the circumstances under which restorations adhere to typologies and those in which they do not, in which a particular architectural feature is considered to be consistent with the established typology or disruptive. Earlier in the century, the Comité's removal of the Ottoman minaret at the Fatimid mosque of al-Salih Tala'i' had not evoked any similar indignation (Figure 24) The long half-century debate over the mosque among Comité members revolved around the question of a proper replacement for the minaret, not over dismantling it. And the destruction of the Ottoman minaret (Figure 25) did not produce so much as a faint echo in other narratives of the mosque's history. Even Creswell's ordinarily meticulous documentation of Comité activities failed in this regard: his account of the mosque of al-Salih Tala'i' in *Muslim Architecture of Egypt* makes no mention of the minaret or its removal, although it is clearly visible in several of the accompanying photographs.[26] Neither the Comité nor the Bohras ever suggested, in the name of typological purity, dismantling the fourteenth-century Mamluk finials on the mosque of al-Hakim's minarets (Figure 26) In the case of the Comité, they were most likely saved not only because they did not carry the onus of an Ottoman appearance, but also because they did not look out of place in what was understood as the conventional historic cityscape. In the case of the Bohras, it is perhaps testimony to the success of the Comité's program, which canonized the generally Mamluk appearance of 'Medieval Cairo' as authentic, that they saw no inconsistency in leaving the later minarets. Why, then, did one dismantling evoke an outcry and the other a deafening silence? The *Egyptian Gazette* article presumes to provide an explanation for the outrage, which it attributes to "xenophobia [rather than] concern for Egypt's cultural heritage." In any case, the dismantling of the tomb signaled that the familiar landscape of Medieval Cairo was being challenged, and that a very different context for the mosque of al-Hakim was being constructed.

Neo-Fatimid Architecture

The Bohra restoration of the mosque of al-Hakim produced a very different version of the mosque, one that stood out dramatically from the other monuments on the street. Like other Bohra restorations, this one is characterized by interior and structural elements faced with large quantities of Helwan marble. Interior inscriptions are ordinarily gilded. The Bohras borrow elements freely from one Fatimid structure for another. The restored buildings have become collages of Fatimid ornaments and motifs. It is common to find roundels and ornamental motifs from the al-Hakim and al-Aqmar mosques in other Fatimid structures. The intertwined Muhammad-'Ali roundel of al-Aqmar is repeated on numerous façades.[27] A marble-and-gilt rendering of the Fatimid mihrab of al-Azhar is installed in the qibla bay of the al-Hakim Mosque, replacing the mihrab that had deteriorated beyond recognition. The roundel in the dome, with intertwined writing in a circle, also is taken from al-Azhar.

The Lu'lu'a Mosque (Figure 27) is a collage not only decoratively, but also structurally: the original ruin has been completely rebuilt as a three-story structure resembling the Bab al-Nasr; two groupings of three arches and roundels from both al-Aqmar and al-Hakim decorate its façade. At Sayyida Ruqayya, Sayyida Nafisa, Sayyida Zaynab, and the Husayn Mosque (that is, on mausolea or mosques dedicated to *ahl al-bayt* [members of the Prophet's family], regardless of when they were built), the Bohras have installed silver-and-gold grillwork enclosures over the internal tombs themselves. The mausoleum of Sayyida Ruqayya boasts a silver-and-gold grillwork enclosure (Figure 28) with an exact replica, at each corner, of the bevel of al-Aqmar Mosque (Figures 29, 30). Furthermore, the Bohras consider arches of any kind, pointed or not, and often grouped in threes, as Fatimid. Silver and gold enclosures installed at Sayyida Zaynab and Imam Husayn are complete with so-called Fatimid arches. The Bohras have thus established a conventional typology, one that is no less contingent than that of the Comité and its successors, by reproducing Fatimid-era motifs and ornaments and by classifying generalized architectural features as Fatimid.

The use of this new Fatimid architectural style is not restricted to Cairo. The Bohras have also created an architecture that uses the typology and vocabulary established in Cairo to provide visual coherence among their new mosques in East Africa, Europe, North America, India, and Pakistan, as well as the restored tombs of *ahl al-bayt* and venerated Bohra *da'is*.[28] A recent Bohra publication devoted to the new mosque in Dubai not only designates the "Fatemi arches" as its defining "Fatimid" feature, but also appropriates the arch as the dominant graphic for the layout of the volume.[29] The new Masjid al-Mu'azzam in India boasts a replica of the bevel of al-Aqmar Mosque. The Maqama Ru'us al-Shuhada' at Damascus has a silver grill enclosure with keel arches and another architectural touch: its corners are surmounted by small stylized versions of the upper part of the minarets of the mosque of al-Hakim

The definition of the al-Hakim minaret as specifically Fatimid moves beyond the particularization of generalized features like arches or Kufic calligraphy to another phenomenon, namely, the outright reclassification of a specific architectural element from a later period as Fatimid. The original minarets fell in the 1303 earthquake that destroyed all but one of the minarets along the major axis of Cairo. The existing minarets were restored in 1304, so they cannot in any sense be understood as 'genuinely' Fatimid.[30] Thus, the replication of the minaret at once reclassifies the Mamluk restoration as Fatimid and incorporates it into the vocabulary of neo-Fatimid architecture. Similarly, Kufic calligraphy cannot properly be considered to be a specifically *Fatimid* calligraphic style. The monumental Kufic inscriptions on the exterior of al-Hakim were the first of their kind of Cairo, but later dynasties appropriated the form, which flourished under the Mamluks.[31]

All these elements (definition of generalized architectural features as Fatimid, reclassification as Fatimid, repetition of particular Fatimid elements) are evident in the Qubba Badriya in Saurashtra, India. The shrine's overall appearance does not seem to have, at first glance, any direct connection to the Fatimid monuments of Cairo, but it is a striking example of neo-Fatimid architecture. The intended connections with Cairene Fatimid monuments are clearly stated in a publication dedicated to the shrine: "The edifice, in brick, mortar and marble, in its features manifests a theme of piety and purity, incorporates the ancient and historic Fatimi art . . . . The dome and cornice are inspirations from Jame-Juyushi . . . . The four entrances to the mausoleum depict and match the entrance gates of al-Aqmar . . . . The entrances are adorned with four silver doors of Fatimid design and lead into the inner sanctuary of the mausoleum."[32]

The authority of this new Fatimid typology is invoked regularly in new Bohra structures that imitate and evoke the restored, rather than the 'historic,' versions of these monuments. Restored Fatimid architecture and decoration have become iconic for the Bohras and are now fully integrated into their repertoire of visual symbols. In Houston, Texas, the community's mosque (Figure 31) clearly evokes the restored al-Juyushi Mosque (Figures 32, 33) The celebration of Sultan Burhan al-Din's eightieth birthday at the West Indian Turf Club in Bombay, India, took place in front of a set that was a stylized version of the restored, symmetrical façade of al-Aqmar Mosque (Figures 34, 35, 36).

Neo-Fatimid architecture is not only the vocabulary of architectural and decorative elements used in restorations and new religious constructions. It is also constituted in the rhetoric of the Bohra hierarchy, which has created an interpretive framework that contextualizes the architecture. This framework and its relationship to the architecture it contextualizes is disseminated in the numerous pamphlets and books that record these restorations and new constructions, and that provide authoritative interpretations of their meaning for the community. The pamphlets are published in English and commemorate important community events and celebrations, Sultan Burhanuddin's visits to Ismaili sites, his contributions to restorations, and his new constructions. This new textual tradition accords equal importance to both word and image, and it is through the pamphlets that the majority of Bohras come to know both restored and new monuments, and their primary significance and meaning as articulated by the administrative arm of the head of the Bohra community, the Dawat-E-Hadiyah.

The visual material and authoritative interpretations are also presented on numerous Bohra websites, which with printed commemorative pamphlets and books, regularly publish photographs of these new and restored sites, helping to establish the authority of the restorations by connecting them directly to the sultan's position as custodian of the faith. The pamphlet *Edifice of Faith* contains numerous full-page color photographs of restored Fatimid-era monuments as well as new grillwork enclosures installed in tombs of the *ahl al-bayt*, and it frames the restoration project as a whole as a religious act, one which brings *baraka* to the community.[33] The final page in the pamphlet shows a photograph of Sultan Burhanuddin, framed by a pointed arch On the one hand, the framing 'Fatimid' arch visually expresses the notion of the sultan as inheritor of the Fatimid spiritual legacy and his position as custodian of Fatimid heritage; on the other hand, it invokes his position as custodian of Fatimid heritage to authorize the restorations themselves. The textual tradition has helped to establish a self-referential authority that is rooted not (as was the Comité's and its successors) in disciplinary knowledge and expertise, but rather in the spiritual authority of the *da'i* himself. This system of visual references, which is presented alongside authoritative explanatory texts in the pamphlets, is completely woven into the fabric of contemporary Bohra restorations and neo-Fatimid architecture.

A Different Frame: Indian and Anglo-Indian Roots of Neo-Fatimid Architecture

We have seen above how the transnational neo-Fatimid architecture of the Bohra community, which they understand in a specifically Fatimid context, is comprised of a series of amalgamations constituted by reusing decorative motifs from Fatimid monuments, particularizing generalized features of Islamic architecture in Cairo (for example, arches, Kufic calligraphy) and reclassifying architectural elements from the Mamluk period as Fatimid. The Bohra community uses all of these amalgamations in its architectural projects, especially in religious buildings. These architectural and decorative elements have been used consistently to create a contemporary architectural tradition that unifies the far-flung Bohra diaspora community. But do its architectural roots lie only in Egypt? In fact, they do not. Closer scrutiny of the history of the Bohra community's architecture points to a more complex origin and the possibility of understanding it in other contexts. As we have done elsewhere, let us ask what difference it might make to consider the story of Bohra neo-Fatimid architecture in a different frame, the frame of Indian and Anglo-Indian architecture.

Telling the story of Bohra neo-Fatimid architecture in an Indian or Anglo-Indian context directs our attention to non-religious as well as religious architecture. The Dawoodi Bohras have a history of a communal architectural style in India that dates back some seven centuries.[34] The traditional style of Sidhpur, Gujarat—one of the earliest Bohra settlements in India—using the Post and Lintel construction technique was based upon the ruins of the Rudr Mahaliya, a neighboring Hindu temple that had been destroyed before Sidhpur was settled permanently. Zoyab Kadi, an architect who documented Sidhpur's domestic architecture, focuses his discussion on construction techniques, interior spatial arrangements, the assimilation of multiple architectural features and styles into a harmonious traditional architecture, and changes in traditional architecture over time. What is remarkable, for an observer familiar with the community's discourse about Fatimid architecture, is the fact that the author, a trained architect and a Dawoodi Bohra (whose attachment to the Bohra hierarchy is sufficient for him to place his gratitude for Syedna's spiritual guidance at the head of his acknowledgments) makes no mention of Fatimid or Egyptian origins for any of the architectural or decorative elements of the traditional Hassanpura private houses And yet, even a cursory glance at a photographic array of traditional Hassanpura façades is striking for what could, elsewhere, be described as Fatimid architecture: the motif of repeated arches arrayed on a façade, or the triple-arch motif. This architecture is defined as Bohra, but its roots lie elsewhere, and nowhere in the architect's discussion of the houses, their style, or architectural changes over time is mention of Fatimid style ever made.[35] This, in spite of the fact that the author acknowledges the importance of religion to the long-term development of Sidhpur, whose "historicity is . . . rooted in its religiosity."[36] Although primarily Hindu, he clearly understands the deeply rooted religiosity to be an important aspect of the Bohra community's participation in the area's architectural traditions.

How, then, does Kadi understand the genealogy of Dawoodi Bohra domestic architecture? His genealogy includes the Vastushastra traditional Hindu astrological building technique, the local Hindu temple ruin, Rudr Mahaliya, and both "European and Oriental treatments" on the external façades of the houses.[37] A further development of the traditional style manifested itself in a spatial and architectural innovation called Harariya. In the late nineteenth century, a radical new housing pattern emerged on the outskirts of Sidhpur called Harariya. The new plan was distinguished by an entirely new system of access to the houses, one geared toward vehicular access. The new city plan, therefore, abandoned the older system of alleys for an open street system with two main, intersecting arteries. Kadi accounts for these changes, as he does for many others, by the affluence of the mercantile Bohra community and a sudden population influx.[38]

The influence of traditional Vastushastra building principles remains obvious to the architect Kadi, who does not argue for a deliberate adoption of the Vastu guidelines. Rather, he suggests that the Dawoodi Bohras had little specific knowledge of the principles, but continued to copy familiar models that had been built in accordance with Vastu Shastra. In fact, Kadi believes that Bohra homeowners contributed little to discussions about either internal organization of space or the structure and decoration of façades. Since building was a specialized trade, quite apart from the traditional commercial activities of the Bohra community, the Bohras generally followed the local building culture.[39] The point here is a simple but important one: the conventional external appearance of Bohrawads, with their triple-arch motifs, seems to have had no explicitly Bohra origin nor does it appear to be connected in any way to Fatimid motifs. To the extent that any ideology informed the structures that were being built a century ago, it was either Vastushastra as practiced by craftsmen in the building trades or a generalized local style which the Bohras, as well as other communities, had long considered to be appealing and appropriate.

Kadi reads the architectural record as evidence for "an unmistakable progression in the use of motifs from the local Hindu style to Oriental (Siamese?), to European."[40] Indeed, he maintains that "except for a few general arched windows here and there, and some Arabic inscriptions on the gable, the use of Islamic motifs on the main façade is very limited . . . ."[41] Discussing other Bohrawads of a century ago, boasting façades replete with arches, Kadi reads them as unequivocally European, even if he cannot determine a precise genealogy for all of their elements: "[T]hese Bohrawads of Sidhpur . . . invoke a powerful and unforgettable imagery quite unmatched in scale or vividness by any other group of privately owned row housing in India. In fact, the initial reaction is to suggest straight away that they look very 'Europeanish'—an observation that may not be much off the mark. But whether the style came from France, Italy, Britain or anywhere else is now a matter only of passing interest."[42] Kadi sees complex, syncretistic origins for Bohrawad architecture, and he explains the assimilation of these different elements by pointing, as he often does, to the community's commercial character, which exposed its merchants to multiple cultures. While continuing to insist on the ultimately colonial character of Sidhpur's domestic architecture, he recognizes also its complex origins and multiple roots: the principles of Vastu Shastra are quietly assimilated into the new architecture.[43]

Competing Contexts and Exclusive Pasts

Let us return, then, to Fatimid Cairo, as it has been recontextualized by the Bohra restorations. *The Egyptian Gazette*, in a 25 November 1980 article, described in hyperbolic language the dramatically different appearance of the mosque of al-Hakim: "The brilliant white marble courtyard, large as a football pitch, and the freshly plastered and painted arches are dazzling, and contrast sharply with the drab, dilapidated buildings all around." Two different judgments proceed from this observation, stipulated by all parties to the debate, that the restored mosque of al-Hakim stands out starkly from its Cairene surroundings. The first appeared in the January 1981 SPARE newsletter, and is typical of Euro-American assessments of the Bohra work: "Certainly, this gleaming white monument now seems closer in spirit to the Taj Mahal than to the muddy streets and rubbish-filled ruins that surround it. It is precisely this contrast, however, that disturbs experienced conservationists."[44]

The second judgment is from one of the dozens of Dawoodi Bohra websites easily accessible on the Internet, in a panegyric to the Dai al-Mutlaqs entitled "A celebration of piety," which marks the coincidence of the *mawlid*s of the Imam al-Tayyib and the Dai al-Mutlaq in the month of Rabi' al-Thani. The relevant section is subtitled "Awaking a Fatimi Masjid":

> The Dawoodi Bohras are fondly attached to the times of the Fatimi Imams, who . . . built the university-mosque of al-Azhar, which survived through changes in rule to retain its position as the foremost Islamic University in the Middle East. But many of the other architecturally unique places of worship and institutes of learning reached the twentieth century in a state of disrepair, victims of the vicissitudes of time. To renovate these relics and restore to them their original purpose and glory was a costly exercise, one that would exceed anything done by the community before. The visionary, Syedna Mohammed Burhanuddin decided to embark on the project nevertheless. Al-Jame al-Anwar, the huge masjid of the sixteenth imam, al-Hakim (SA) had been subject to utter neglect. It was impossible even to envisage its original eminence. In 1980,

> Syedna Mohammed Burhanuddin completed its restoration, converting a disused structure into a vibrant masjid, an oasis of heavenly peace in a desert of uncontrolled commotion, an island of radiant beauty in surrounding filth . . . . The sleeping soul of a magnificent Fatimi masjid was awoken to fulfil its real purpose and epitomised the revolution that the soul of each believer would experience in its wake . . . . That act of devotion was followed by many more and in the meantime, Dawoodi Bohra masjids spring up today in all corners of the world.[45]

What both these judgments confirm is that through their interventions, the Bohras are reclaiming Fatimid sites from the rest of canonical Medieval Cairo, which is heavily identified with Sunni Mamluk architecture, and they are recontextualizing them as Ismaili ritual sites with an explicitly sectarian meaning.[46] The Bohras are, ironically, engaged in the very version of restoration as defined in the nineteenth century by the grandfather of modern restoration himself, Eugène-Emmanuel Viollet-le-Duc. This version of restoration is as problematic for contemporary observers as Viollet-le-Duc's was for nineteenth-century non-interventionists. The Bohra restorations *undo* the century-long process by which Medieval Cairo was constructed and made legible to modern audiences.[47] When the Bohras intervened in the appearance of the mosque, they replaced a version fraught with comfortable ambiguities with one that was stark, imposing, and disturbing in its precision.[48] What is so jarring about the Bohra work on the mosque of al-Hakim (as on al-Aqmar, al-Juyushi, and Lu'lu'a) is perhaps not that it violates any carefully constructed typology of 'authentically' Fatimid architecture, but rather that it makes Fatimid monuments too easily identifiable as something different from their surroundings.

This new precision has also created a different context for the Fatimid monuments of Cairo, one that reclaims them locally from the familiar landscape of medieval Mamluk monumentality as it was reconstructed and canonized in the nineteenth century and integrates them into a transnational landscape of Bohra piety. This enterprise has disrupted the conventional landscape of Cairo medieval monumentality and resituated the mosques and shrines of Cairo into the larger ritual map of Bohra shrines and mosques, both old and new, in the Subcontinent, East Africa, Europe, and North America. This project is, of course, at odds with the conservationist project, which is grounded in a version of Medieval Cairo that has been conventional for more than a century.

The difference between the default interpretive contexts for the Bohras and the conservationist community is very clear, for example, in the uses (or proposed uses) for restored Fatimid sites. The Bohras restore Fatimid mosques and tombs for ritual purposes: they are sites for prayer, for the veneration of the *ahl al-bayt*, or to honor especially revered *da'is*. These sites are a part not only of a larger visual landscape, but also a larger ritual map of *ziyara*, visiting the tombs of holy men and women, which occupies a central role in the Bohras' contemporary formation and continuation of 'Fatimid tradition.' The ritual of visiting tombs of the *da'is* in the Subcontinent has been ongoing for centuries, but the practice of *ziyara*s (visits) to shrines in Egypt, Yemen, and Syria is more recent, and dates from the restoration of the sites in Cairo and elsewhere. Now, members of the Bohra community participate in organized tours to Cairene sites in addition to their traditional visits to sites in the subcontinent.

For the Bohra community, the integrity of the mosque lies in awaking its 'sleeping soul,' that is, in restoring it to its original use, as a site for Ismaili worship. There is no claim, implicit or otherwise, to neutrality here. The renovation of Fatimid mosques and shrines is an "act of devotion," one that has a direct effect on "the soul of each believer." It is, in fact, an act of faith, embedded in a system of belief that is, by definition, exclusionary. The conservationist project, on the other hand, privileges 'original' or 'authentic' material, but it does not similarly privilege original use. Rather, the conservationist project imagines the conserved and/or restored monument in the framework of 'adaptive reuse,' and considers it to be a proper restoration if it meets international standards of reversibility and the use of original materials. But original use does not figure in its considerations. Thus, the recommendations for additional planning and rehabilitation appended to the UNESCO Report, "Conservation of the Old City of Cairo," proposed that "[t]he enormous courtyard of the Hakim mosque itself should be used as a green public space (garden or park)."[49] There is no suggestion in any of the studies of possible reuse that the mosque should be returned to its original function as a site of worship, Ismaili or otherwise. While the fact that the mosque has been returned to its original purpose does not soften the conservationists' critiques of the restoration, its importance was recognized in the November 1980 *The Egyptian Gazette* article: "The mosque has been restored however not merely for decoration but as a place of worship. Whereas other monuments in Islamic Cairo have been converted into libraries and artist's colonies after their restoration Al Hakim's mosque, after a lapse of one thousand years, will once again be able to fulfill the function for which it was intended."[50]

The conservationist emphasis on original fabric (but not use) is one of the key elements for meeting the test of authenticity and one of the primary criteria for inclusion on the World Heritage List. The Third Session of the World Heritage Committee, held in October 1979, declared that "authenticity of a cultural property remains an essential criterion."[51] The problem of authenticity remains a crucial one for the World Heritage Committee. The current *Operational Guidelines for the Implementation of the World Heritage Convention* requires that a monument, group of buildings, or site meet one or more of six cultural criteria "*and* (italics in original) the test of authenticity," which is defined in terms of "design, material, workmanship or setting and in the case of cultural landscapes their distinctive character and components . . . ."[52]

The *Operational Guidelines* make it clear that the very concept of authenticity is unquestioned. They assume that it is possible to apply tests that will allow the determination, against a standard that is taken to be neutral, of "authenticity or integrity" which provides the authority for the judgment that a property is of "outstanding universal value."[53] There is no hint that the concept of 'authenticity' may itself be subject to the very kinds of 'particularisms' against which the Convention seeks to guard. The World Heritage Convention (WHC) Third Session (1979), in a section meant to elaborate the Convention, disallows "[n]ominations concerning, in particular, historical events or famous people [that] could be strongly influenced by nationalism or other particularisms in contradiction with the objectives of the World Heritage Convention."[54] Where historical events or famous people might be subject to the sway of ideologies, buildings, it seems, are not.

Thus the very notion that architecture may be assessed independently of ideologies is enshrined in the *Operational Guidelines* and in the Cultural Criteria. The importance of this dissociation is underscored by the change in the wording of the Cultural Criteria over a period of some twenty years. The original (1978) version of the *Operational Guidelines* articulates Cultural Criterion VI as follows: "Be most importantly associated with ideas or beliefs, with events or persons, of outstanding historical importance or significance." In the October 1980 version, however, Cultural Criterion VI no longer includes persons, and "historical significance" has been replaced with the supposedly neutral "outstanding universal significance." The 1980 text requires a work to "[b]e directly or tangibly associated with events or with ideas or beliefs of outstanding universal significance (the Committee considered that this criterion should justify inclusion in the list only in exceptional circumstances or in conjunction with other criteria)."[55] The *Operational Guidelines* themselves maintain the myth of neutrality in their general principles: "The criteria for the inclusion of properties in the World Heritage List have been elaborated to enable the Committee to act with full independence in evaluating the intrinsic merit of property, without regard to any other consideration (including the need for technical co-operation support)."[56]

Each of these positions requires a different historical narrative to support its claims, and each produces a sanitized history that configures and uses the past differently. In the case of the conservationist project, the principle of "outstanding universal value," and the political neutrality that it posits implicitly, are in fact embedded in a nationalist metaframework that understands states as the "wardens of civilisation" and endows them with the responsibility of preserving historic monuments.[57] The nomination process for inclusion on the World Heritage List is entirely in the hands of states, and not communities of faith or belief. While the sites on the World Heritage List are considered to be part of the cultural heritage of the world as a whole, their 'ownership' is in the hands of states, and this legal ownership also implies an ownership of meaning and the determination of value. In the case of Cairo, the World Heritage List nomination submitted by Egypt accepts as its starting point an Islamic Cairo whose stylistic unity is embedded in a notion of Islam that is unified and monolithic. While the history of Cairo provided in the nomination credits the Fatimids as founders of "the nucleus of mediaeval Cairo," it does so without mentioning their Ismaili Shi'ism. The nomination notes the Fatimid claim "to be the true caliphs" and their success in "establish[ing] themselves as the major power of the region, rivalling and eclipsing the importance of Baghdad, the seat of the 'Abbasid caliphs. The architectural splendour of this new foundation is still to be witnessed at such famous mosques as those of al-Azhar, al-Hakim, [and] al-Aqmar . . . ." This is a history cleansed of all sectarianism, a history that converges with orientalism in its assumption of a monolithic Islam that does not allow for the coexistence of more than one Islam or multiple Islamic meanings. But this history also is implicitly nationalist: reporting the Fatimid claim to be 'true caliphs' who eclipsed Abbasid power, is a tale of national, not sectarian, success, particularly when Ismaili Fatimid Cairo is subsumed under the larger categories of 'medieval' or 'Islamic' Cairo, represented by the canonical Medieval Cairo with its Mamluk appearance. Such a narrative might well have met with the approval of Max Herz Bey and Stanley Lane-Poole, both of whom considered Mamluk architecture to be the national art of Egypt. In the end, this exclusive identification of "Islamic Cairo" as medieval, and of the medieval as Mamluk, and of Mamluk with 'Egyptian' completes the syllogism that was initiated more than a century ago. The conservationist project is committed to and constructs through the Mamluk medieval a specifically Egyptian context for Islamic Cairo.[58]

For the Bohras, however, Fatimid history and architecture are not specifically Egyptian nor is their meaning constructed primarily as an episode in Egyptian history. Fatimid Cairo, for the Bohras, is neither Egyptian nor medieval, and its meaning as an Islamic site is not the generalized and monolithic Islam of the conservationists' 'Islamic Cairo.' It remains 'Fatimid Cairo,' a site that is not imagined as a contiguous area bounded by the eleventh-century Fatimid walls, but rather a series of symbolically dense religious sites, unified by Fatimid architecture (in its restored version) and by common ritual purpose; it is not an artifact of modern architects and historians seeking to make sense of a distant past, but rather an Ismaili site that finds its meaning in the present. Its proper context, then, is the living Fatimid tradition. Thus, where the conservationist history of Fatimid Cairo sanitizes the city of its Ismaili significance, the Bohra history of Fatimid Cairo sanitizes it of everything *but* Ismailism. It does this by constructing a narrative that views the history of the monuments beyond the Fatimid period as one of steady decline, awaiting their reawakening through the Bohra restorations, by removing in some instances the material remains of later dynasties, and by reclassifying both general and specific architectural elements as Fatimid. The Bohra restorations make sense only if we read the monuments in a radically new context, one in which they are legible not as monuments of the past, but rather as the sites where a dynamic relationship with Fatimid tradition is continually being enacted, and it is in this context that the Bohras stake their claim to authenticity.

The fundamental disharmony between the Bohra and the conservationist projects cannot be reconciled, not merely because of differences in basic conservation philosophies and techniques. The dilemma posed by conflicts over the restoration of a cultural property is addressed in a core World Heritage Convention text, "The Nara Document on Authenticity."[59] The Nara Document attempts to bring "greater respect for cultural and heritage diversity to conservation practice" by recognizing the fundamental role of authenticity in conservation practice. The document further calls for "acknowledgment of the legitimacy of the cultural values of all parties" where values are in conflict. It proposes that the solution to such conflict is to be found in the concept of authenticity, and it states that "the essential contribution made by the consideration of authenticity in conservation practice is to clarify and illuminate the collective memory of humanity." In other words, it directs competing claims toward convergence by insisting on the predominance of "collective memory," which it posits as an antidote to "aggressive nationalism and the suppression of the cultures of minorities." The problem is, of course, that no such "collective memory" exists, nor can a "collective memory of humanity," one that is free of the very particularisms that UNESCO aims to guard against, exist. The Nara Document struggles, however, to find a reliable way of determining what constitutes authenticity in its own terms, and it finds its solution in the authority of cultural context, declaring that "the respect due to all cultures requires that heritage properties must [be] considered and judged within the cultural contexts to which they belong." The document's proposal for the appropriate method of determining authenticity offers no remedy for the continuing controversies over restoration in Fatimid Cairo, where contexts are multiple and contested, and where exclusive pasts have been constructed to frame the monuments.

Conclusion: Colliding Colonialisms

Where do these competing contexts and exclusive pasts come from? In fact, both are part of the complex legacy of British colonialism in the East. We have seen earlier that the preservation of historic monuments in both India and Egypt was one part of a colonial project, one that, to use Thomas Metcalf's formulation, insisted on making the present appear to be the past.[60] Although the political circumstances are different, the World Heritage community insists, just like its nineteenth-century predecessors, on a medieval appearance and framework for the monuments of Cairo. If the World Heritage community continues the colonial tradition of making the present appear to be the past, then the Bohra restorations most assuredly make the past appear to be the present.

What the Bohras are doing with their architecture is, in fact, reminiscent of nineteenth-century British colonial architecture. By this, I do not mean to say that the Bohras are engaged in their architectural project because the British did it, nor that their neo-Fatimid architecture, with its different elements, is merely a re-named Indo-Saracenic architecture. I would insist, however, that it is no accident that the Bohras use a distinctive architectural style to create cohesion in their diaspora community—a community that, not coincidentally, has settled in many of the places that had a British colonial presence and a marked British colonial architecture—India and Pakistan, East Africa, South Africa, and elsewhere. While the Bohras do not make any claims to empire, they use architecture in a manner that evokes the British use of Indo-Saracenic architecture in the Subcontinent more than a century ago: as a marker of legitimacy.

Bohra neo-Fatimid architecture both constitutes and represents the legitimacy of the Bohra hierarchy. It makes the case, over and over, for the legitimacy of a religious (not political) authority that has been hotly contested in recent years, and it defines its symbolic vocabulary in terms of Fatimid legitimacy, even as it assimilates multiple architectural traditions.

The British in the nineteenth century made no pretensions to religious authority and indeed did not wish to do so. Theirs was a political, military, and cultural claim, articulated in both discourse and in architecture, and elaborated in a way that ultimately came to represent not just British authority and legitimacy, but legitimacy more abstractly. Once abstracted from the particularist British context, Indo-Saracenic architecture continued to be read as legitimating authority and, in particular, as marking modernity. This vocabulary was available to the communities (including the Bohras) who lived under British rule and after independence; it was available as a means of legitimating other authorities, even those with remarkably different (for example, spiritual) claims. Finally, it came to be read as 'modern' in ways that were and remain very important to the Bohras. It is no coincidence that the historic mosque in Sidhpur boasts a clock tower over its main entrance, just as it is no coincidence that the town of Sidhpur's most visible monument is the Muhammad 'Ali Clocktower, erected in the nineteenth century in a British colonial style. Indeed, this is precisely what the architect Zoyab Kadi has to say about it. And it is this British colonial clocktower, this marker of modernity and not any of the hundreds of private house façades that are the subject of his study, that graces the dust jacket of Kadi's book on domestic architecture. The Muhammad 'Ali Mosque in Cairo, an early nineteenth-century Ottoman construction, also boasts a clocktower, but like other Ottoman architecture that could not easily be read as 'medieval,' it did not become a favored architectural element in Cairo's landscape.[61]

Indo-Saracenic architecture is a colonial architecture that can be read as both traditional and modern at the same time. It is meant to be rooted in the past, but read as modern, and this is one reason why it lends itself easily to assimilation by the Bohras, a community intent on expressing its rootedness in both the past and the present. This is quite different from the tradition of Mamluk architecture in Cairo, which has been constructed for more than a century as an architecture that can be read in only one way: as medieval—possibly as neo-medieval—but emphatically *not* as modern.

As we have seen, the notion that Medieval Cairo was essentially a Mamluk city stood as a founding principle for many of the officials involved with the preservation of the city. Max Herz Bey, like many of his contemporaries in Egypt (including Lane-Poole) considered Mamluk architecture to be the national art of Egypt. His commitment to a generally Mamluk appearance was expressed not only in his decisions about preservation and restoration, but also in his devotion to Mamluk revival architecture. When Max Herz Bey redesigned the mosque of al-Rifa'i as a neo-Mamluk design, he rejected an explicitly modern, symmetrical design in favor of a Mamluk design that would be stylistically consistent with the mosque–madrasa of Sultan Hasan and that would 'read' as medieval, insisting implicitly that the present is most appropriately represented as the past.

A century later, the World Heritage community reads as 'authentic' the Mamluk style, while new versions of these Fatimid monuments, which they cannot read as 'medieval,' are fraudulent and disruptive. It does not read the erasures of the Comité's preservation and restoration processes as problematic, nor is it troubled by neo-Mamluk architecture, whether we find it in the so-called historic zone of Muhammad 'Ali Square or in the suburb of Heliopolis. Neither the Bohras nor their critics remember their common colonial roots, but each is now playing the role that a century of colonial and post-colonial experience has carved out for it. Having begun on the same side of the colonizing process, but in different colonial sites, the Bohra restorers and the World Heritage conservators now find themselves on opposites sides of a debate that has been constructed by more than a century's worth of forgotten meanings.

Conclusion

In the first half of this book, I reframed the story of conservation in imperial and local contexts and in the context of nineteenth-century religious life in order to demonstrate how different economic, architectural, religious, and political policies and practices accumulated over time and how together they produced Medieval Cairo. What have we gained by restoring both the larger narrative of Medieval Cairo's creation and more particular aspects of its history to the broader contexts from which they have conventionally been isolated? In Chapter 1, we saw that situating the story of Medieval Cairo in the context of British India suggests motivations for the preservation of Arab architecture in Cairo that we might otherwise not have imagined, namely, as part of the British imperial project in India. Taking Donald Reid's admonishment that it is preservation that needs explanation, we saw another *political* motivation for the study and preservation of so-called Arab art in situ that was not apparent before. We also saw, however, that the creation of a specifically Mamluk Medieval Cairo had many roots, not all of them the consequence either of European intervention or of incipient Egyptian nationalism and, consequently, that it also had meanings which were sometimes contradictory without being mutually exclusive.

In Chapter 2, we saw how the architectural preservation of Medieval Cairo worked to express an imperial view of Islam that was very much at odds with important modernizing currents of reformist thought. In this framework, an important Egyptian actor, 'Ali Mubarak, emerges in a new light—as an advocate of a vibrant, living Islamic tradition which his contemporaries practiced on a daily basis. 'Ali Mubarak's notion of why buildings were important had more to do with the moral lessons they might teach Egyptians in the present than in their monumentalization of the past. We can no longer view him simply as an urban modernizer who worked with little regard for the monuments of the past, but must also see him as a religious modernizer whose concerns were closer to those of Muhammad 'Abduh than the members of the Comité—both Egyptian and European—who worked from a different set of assumptions about the place of religion in a modern society.

Through these reframings, we learned that this version of a medieval city emerged from the convergence of a particular set of historical circumstances and that its varied meanings changed over time and in different circumstances. But we should still ask, in light of what we have learned, why this kind of recontextualization matters. Simply put, I think it matters because the process of creating a 'historic city' involves as much erasure as it does preservation; deletions as well as additions may no longer be visible to observers even shortly after the work is completed. This is especially the case when a 'historic city' becomes canonical and when the political circumstances of its creation (or even the notion that it is the product of a particular set of historical circumstances that are modern) become obscured, either deliberately or simply by the passage of time. It is easy under those circumstances to begin to take for granted that the 'historic city' of Cairo is, indeed, just that: a medieval city that has been preserved largely as it was in the Middle Ages. And this matters because such an assumption carries with it the implicit claim that it is this, rather than any other, version of Medieval Cairo that is authentic.

It is that claim of authenticity that I examined in the second half of this book. I want to be clear in stating that I do not consider canonical Medieval Cairo to be 'fake' or 'fraudulent' or even 'inauthentic.' Rather, I advocate a notion of authenticity that takes into consideration and allows for the historical contingency of Medieval Cairo. In other words,

I believe that this particular version of Medieval Cairo—the one that was produced in the late nineteenth and early twentieth centuries—has an authenticity that is equally rooted in its origins *and* in the specific historical circumstances from which it emerged in the nineteenth century. This is a form of authenticity in which I believe all 'historic' cities share.

The implications of this more nuanced notion of authenticity were examined in Chapters 3 and 4. In Chapter 3, we saw how weaving together two stories that are ordinarily considered to be separate, that of Medieval Cairo and of the *Arabian Nights*, could shed light on specific processes that produced these architectural and literary artifacts and help to explain why they could be regarded so differently by multiple readers, viewers, and restorers. There, I read a selection of visual images together with the texts that accompanied them to expose the amalgamations of old and new elements upon which our conceptions of Medieval Cairo and the *Arabian Nights* as exclusively medieval are founded and continue to depend. Looking explicitly for this kind of blending also fosters new understandings of other elements of Egyptian culture—particularly Islamic religious practice—that have conventionally been assumed to be medieval but which are also modern products of similar processes of amalgamation, as we also saw in Chapters 2 and 3.

Recognizing these amalgamations also raises important questions about the assumptions that inform our inquiries. Taken together, Chapter 2's discussions of religion and Chapter 3's argument about amalgamation raise questions even about our basic vocabulary. For example, what does it mean to describe the 'historic' part of Cairo as the 'Islamic' city? Why is it more 'Islamic' than any place else in Cairo, where millions of Muslims live, work, and—in varying degrees and ways—observe their faith? If any alley can be turned into a makeshift mosque on Friday at noon, if small mosques are tucked into the most unlikely corners on every block, then does the term 'Islamic' city reify a notion of a true Islam—or an acceptable Islam—as being mummified in the past? Incapable of becoming modern?

Looking for erasures as well as additions, for patterns in which old and new elements are blended, is an undertaking as productively applied to our own historiographies as it is to the activities of nineteenth-century preservationists and politicians. We should ask why the historiography and practice of preservation came to marginalize religion (that is, religion as a living tradition) as one of the ways to contextualize the story of conservation. The marginalization of living religious tradition (a term I prefer to the more vexed 'popular religion') in the concerns of preservation bears some similarity to the debates between linguists and philologists in the late nineteenth century over which version of a language should draw their attention—classical or vernacular—as it also does to the tensions between the proponents of vernacular education and education in 'classical' literary genres.

The implications of these canonized amalgamations and of the historiographies to which we have conventionally been committed are still played out in twentieth- and twenty-first-century debates about preservation in Cairo. It is only when we consider Egypt in its larger imperial contexts, a direction that general Egyptian historiography has taken recently and that suggests analyses that might undercut the nationalist historiographies to which people are deeply committed, that we can make historical sense of the passions that are so evident in the polemics over Bohra restorations of Fatimid monuments. The emergence of post-colonial nationalist historiographies, which generally carve out a unique historical experience for their audiences, do not fit as comfortably with the kinds of analysis that imperial studies might provide. As we saw in Chapter 4, nationalist historiographies shape preservationist rhetoric even in the ostensibly international setting of World Heritage. But when we situate the story of preservation within imperial historiographies, we can see how profoundly the recent imperial past shaped Medieval Cairo. Even more strikingly, we realize that the passions of the World Heritage community in advocating for the Mamluk medieval and the Bohras in restoring Ismaili ritual centers are, paradoxically, both legacies of a common colonial past.

Unlike the compilers, redactors, and translators of the *Arabian Nights*, I have not tried to tell multiple tales within a single frame. Instead, I have sought to tell a single story within multiple frames and to see how it changes in the process. In so doing, I have come to understand that we are all the inheritors of nineteenth-century ideas and practices that we have reconfigured, but which still share a number of common assumptions. I have tried in this book, to borrow Carl Schorske's evocative phrase, to *think with history* about conservation in Cairo: to emphasize the historical contingency of Medieval Cairo, to ask why this city was so readily and easily canonized, to wonder why this version of Medieval Cairo was and remains persuasive, and to question the assumptions about Medieval Cairo with which I originally came to the project but which did not—at least for me—hold up in the face of rigorous historical contextualization. These recontextualizations matter precisely because so much of the construction, canonization, and preservation of Medieval Cairo depended—and still depends—upon decontextualizations of many different kinds. The Medieval Cairo about which I have written, then, is not the 'historic' city—a landscape of monuments preserved and frozen for us in time, one in which so many rich pasts have been obscured—but the *historicized* city: dynamic, fluid, changeable, and changing. By historicizing Medieval Cairo within different and larger frameworks, we can see the assumptions and practices that left their impression directly and indirectly on the city, and that continue to shape our sense of Cairo, its heritage, and its historic value in the twenty-first century.

Epilogue

A visit to the Mamluk mosque of al-Zahir Baybars in 1996 revealed a surprising addition to the mosque, then being restored by an Egyptian team: it was being paved in white marble. When asked about the marble, the workers on the site commented that the architects supervising their work had seen the restored al-Hakim mosque and liked it, so they decided to incorporate the white marble into their restoration. Now, a decade later, several other Mamluk-era mosques also boast white marble in their interiors. The process of amalgamation and recontextualization continues, and along with it, the competition among multiple contexts for authenticity and authority. Much is in the process of being forgotten as new canons and new memories emerge in Medieval Cairo.

Notes

Notes to the Introduction

1 See Zeynep Çelik, *Displaying the Orient: The Architecture of Islam at Nineteenth-Century World's Fairs* (Berkeley and Los Angeles: University of California Press, 1992); Zeynep Çelik, *The Remaking of Istanbul: Portrait of an Ottoman City in the Nineteenth Century* (Seattle: University of Washington Press, 1986); Timothy Mitchell, *Colonising Egypt* (Cambridge: Cambridge University Press, 1988). I use the terms 'Arab art' and 'Arab architecture' throughout this book to refer to the art and monuments that are now commonly called 'Islamic art' and 'Islamic architecture.' I do so with no aim other than to stick as closely as possible to the language that was commonly used in the nineteenth century, particularly by the British, in discussing the Muslim architecture of both India and Egypt. As I discuss below, these terms were used interchangeably with several others terms, including 'Saracenic' and 'Mohammedan,' throughout the nineteenth century and into the early twentieth century.

2 Donald M. Reid, *Whose Pharaohs? Archaeology, Museums, and Egyptian National Identity from Napoleon to World War I* (Berkeley: University of California Press, 2002). This is a subject on which Reid has written widely; see especially his "Cultural Imperialism and Nationalism: The Struggle to Define and Control the Heritage of Arab Art in Egypt," *International Journal of Middle East Studies* 24 (1992): 57–76.

3 For a similar sentiment expressed by an architectural conservator, see Hossam M. Mahdy, "Attitudes towards Architectural Conservation: the Case of Cairo" (PhD diss., University of Glasgow, 1992).

4 Robert L. Tignor, "The 'Indianization' of the Egyptian administration under British Rule," *The American Historical Review* 68, no. 3 (1963): 636–61; Roger Owen, "The Influence of Lord Cromer's Indian Experience on British Policy in Egypt 1883–1907," *St. Antony's Papers* 17 (1965): 109–39; C.A. Bayly, "Representing Copts and Muhammadans: Empire, Nation, and Community in Egypt and India, 1880–1914," in Leila Fawaz, C.A. Bayly, and Robert Ilbert, eds., *Modernity and Culture: From the Mediterranean to the Indian Ocean* (New York: Columbia University Press, 2002), 158–203. Roger Owen, *Lord Cromer: Victorian Imperialist, Edwardian Proconsul* (Oxford: Oxford University Press, 2004).

5 Among those who study the seventeenth and eighteenth centuries on their own terms, see the work of Daniel Crecelius, Jane Hathaway, Michael Winter, Doris Behrens-Abouseif, and Nelly Hanna. A small number of historians, including Hathaway, do place Egypt in the broader Ottoman context. However, this is still a relatively new approach to the study of Ottoman Egypt, which continues to be excluded from the study of the broader Ottoman empire, even in the most recent historiography, e.g., Suraiya Faroqhi, *Approaching Ottoman History: An Introduction to the Sources* (Cambridge: Cambridge University Press, 1999). On the general neglect of Ottoman Egypt, see Ehud R. Toledano, "Forgetting Egypt's Ottoman Past," in Jayne L. Warner, ed., *Cultural Horizons: A Festschrift in Honor of Talat S. Halman*, vol. 1 (Syracuse: Syracuse University Press), 150–67.

6 Edward William Lane's *An Account of the Manners and Customs of the Modern Egyptians* (numerous editions), for example, is most often used as a source for either modern or medieval social and religious customs. It is only rarely, if ever, used as a source for the period in which it was written or the later nineteenth century, when it was widely reprinted and distributed. Lane himself believed that the customs he was describing did, in fact, date to the Middle Ages, although much of what he wrote can be shown to be rooted in Ottoman practice.

7 Similarly, the continuity of history writing throughout the Ottoman period has been denied. For example, the historian al-Jabarti is considered to be an enigmatic and final link to the tradition of classical Arabic historical writing that is presumed to have lain dormant for several centuries and then reemerged, without explanation, in the wake of the French invasion of Egypt. See on this Yoav Di-Capua, "The Thought and Practice of Modern Egyptian Historiography, 1890–1970" (PhD diss., Princeton University, 2004), 5ff.

8 Alaa El-Din Elwi El-Habashi, "*Athar* to Monuments: The Intervention of the *Comité de conservation des monuments de l'art arabe*" (PhD diss., University of Pennsylvania, 2001).

9 Thomas R. Metcalf, *Ideologies of the Raj*, The New Cambridge History of India, ed. Gordon Johnson (Cambridge: Cambridge University Press, 1995).

10 Peter van der Veer, *Imperial Encounters: Religion and Modernity in India and Britain* (Princeton: Princeton University Press, 2001).

11 See Thomas R. Metcalf, "Past and Present: Towards an Aesthetics of Colonialism," in G.H.R. Tillotson, ed., *Paradigms of Indian Architecture: Space and Time in Representation and Design* (Surrey: Curzon, 1998), 12–25.
12 Owen, *Lord Cromer*, 95ff.
13 For these issues, see Owen, *Lord Cromer*, 123ff. Afaf Lutfi Sayyid-Marsot's *Egypt and Cromer: A Study in Anglo-Indian Relations* (New York: Praeger, 1969 [1968]) remains the classic study of this period.
14 See Robert L. Tignor, *Modernization and British Colonial Rule in Egypt, 1882–1914* (Princeton: Princeton University Press, 1966), esp. 82–86.
15 Evelyn Baring, Earl of Cromer, *Modern Egypt*, 2 vols. (London: Macmillan, 1908), 290–91. The first British official from India was Sir Colin Scott-Moncrieff, who was appointed British Under-Secretary to the Department of Public Works along with a staff of officials from India.
16 Cromer himself acknowledged the impact of these Indian lessons when he wrote that he had "'laid in a stock of knowledge on a variety of subjects connected with civil administration' which proved of the utmost value in later life." This quotation is from Owen, *Lord Cromer*, 85 and 85n77, citing "Biographical Notes," 196–99.
17 Sir Alfred Lyall, author of *Asiatic Studies*, wrote to Lord Cromer in 1900 after seeing a draft of *Modern Egypt:* "What strikes me as a general observation is that the Oriental situation is very much the same everywhere—the same or similar problems present themselves; and especially the European protectorate over an Eastern state involves the same military and political difficulties everywhere," in Owen, "British Policy in Egypt," 110 (citing Lyall to Lord Cromer, July 1900, Cromer Correspondence, TNA FO 633/12).
18 Owen, "British Policy in Egypt," 110.
19 These ideas about the specificity of governing practices, institutions, and architecture to particular nations and climates were common in the nineteenth century and were echoed also in Ottoman theories about eastern architectural practice.
20 Owen, "British Policy in Egypt," 116.
21 Ussama Makdisi, "Mapping the Orient: Non-western Modernization, Imperialism, and the End of Romanticism," in Helena Michie and Ronald R. Thomas, eds., *Nineteenth Century Geographies: The Transformation of Space from the Victorian Age to the American Century* (New Brunswick, NJ: Rutgers University Press, 2003), 40–54.
22 These were the essential features of British plans in India and Burma; see Owen, "British Policy in Egypt," 116–17.
23 Ibid., 114 and 114n15, citing Cromer.
24 Ibid., 115.
25 This concern echoes Makdisi's argument in "Mapping the Orient" regarding the distinct romantic impulses of the nineteenth century: one a response to the losses occasioned by European modernization, the other a response to non-western modernization in the East itself.

26 For a detailed and nuanced discussion of these issues from the Enlightenment to the 1970s, see Françoise Choay, *The Invention of the Historic Monument*, Lauren M. O'Connell, trans. (Cambridge: Cambridge University Press, 2001).

27 "Restaurer un édifice ce n'est pas l'entretenir, le réparer ou le refaire, c'est le rétablir dans un état complet qui peut n'avoir jamais existé à un moment donné." Eugène-Emmanuel Viollet-le-Duc, *Dictionnaire raisonné de l'architecture française*, vol. 8 (Paris: A. Morel, 1875), 14. The entry in which this famous line appears, "Restauration," is translated in Eugène-Emmanuel Viollet-le-Duc and Charles Wethered, *On Restoration* (London: Sampson, Low, Marston, Low, and Searle, 1875), see esp. p. 9. For a brief and very useful account of preservationism in Europe, see Hans Huth, "The Evolution of Preservationism in Europe," in *Journal of the American Society of Architectural Historians* 1, nos. 3–4 (July/October 1941): 5–12.

28 *The Ecclesiologist* 1 (1842): 65–70, cited in "Architectural Conservation and Restoration," in Jane Turner, ed., *The Dictionary of Art*, vol. 2 (New York: Grove, 1996), 320, and Jukka Jokilehto, *A History of Architectural Conservation* (Oxford: Butterworth-Heinemann, 1999), 156–57.

29 See Morris's letter to *The Athenaeum*, 10 March 1877, advocating the formation of the SPAB; subsequent letter excoriating the restorers, dated 7 April 1877; and the "Manifesto of the Society for the Protection of Ancient Buildings on its foundation in 1877," all published in May Morris, ed., *William Morris: Artist, Writer, Socialist*, vol. 1 (Oxford: Basil Blackwell, 1936), 106–12.

30 A. Lane Fox, "Society for the Protection of Ancient Buildings," under the rubric "Anthropological Miscellanea," in *Journal of the Anthropological Institute of Great Britain and Ireland* 7 (1878): 186. John Ruskin's ideas were set forth in his *Seven Lamps of Architecture* (London: Smith, Elder, and Co., 1849 [numerous successive editions and reprints]).

31 See El-Habashi's narrative in "*Athar* to Monuments," 65–82, based on two articles in particular, by Frank Dillon and Edward T. Rogers, as well as the articles themselves: Frank Dillon, "The Arab Monuments of Egypt," *The Nineteenth Century* 10 (July–December 1881): 276–83; Edward T. Rogers, "The Mosques of Cairo," *Art Journal* 19 (1880): 7. See also the response of Arthur Rhoné (also discussed in detail by El-Habashi), "Coup d'oeil sur l'état présent du Caire ancien et moderne," *Gazette des beaux arts* 24 (1881): 420–32; 25 (1882): 55–67.

32 Frank Dillon, Letter to the editor, "Arab Monuments in Cairo," *The Times*, 26 May 1884, 4. Dillon also expressed the hope that the Egyptians "will learn to look with gratitude upon the protectors of their religious edifices."

33 This is based on El-Habashi's extensive discussion in "*Athar* to Monuments," 76–80, of Rhoné's critique. See also Roger Owen (cited also by El-Habashi), "The Cairo Building Industry and the Building Boom of 1897–1907," in *Colloque International sur l'histoire du Caire*,

25 mars–5 april 1969 (Cairo: General Egyptian Book Organization, 1969), 337–50. On the question of architecture and contemporary religious practice in the nineteenth century, see Chapter 2.

34 *The Times*, "The Preservation of Medieval Cairo," 29 February 1896.

35 István Ormos, "Preservation and Restoration: The Methods of Max Herz Pasha, Chief Architect of the Comité de Conservation des Monuments de l'Art Arabe, 1890–1914," in Jill Edwards, ed., *Historians in Cairo: Essays in Honor of George Scanlon* (Cairo: The American University in Cairo Press, 2002), 125.

36 Stanley Lane-Poole, *The Story of Cairo* (London: J.M. Dent and Co., 1902 [1906]), 309.

37 Comité de conservation des monuments de l'art arabe. *Exercise 1896: Procès-verbaux des séances—rapports de la deuxième commission* (Cairo: Imprimerie Nationale, 1897), 105–12; see also Chapter 1. French and English versions of Lane-Poole's report were provided to each member of the Comité.

38 Cited in Ormos, "Preservation and Restoration," 127.

39 Ormos, "Preservation and Restoration," 128–29, citing Achille Patricolo, *La conservation des monuments arabes en Égypte, I. Histoire du comité* (Cairo: n.p., 1914) and Philipp Speiser, *Die Geschichte der Erhaltung arabischer Baudenkmäler in Ägypten. Die Restaurierung der Madrasa Tatar al Higaziya und des Sabil Kuttab Abde ar-Rahman Kathuda im Rahmen des Darb-al-Qirmiz-Projektes in Kairo* (Abhandlungen des Deutschen Archäologischen Instituts Kairo, Islamische Reihe, 8) (Heidelberg: Heidelberger Orientverlag, 2001), 69. I have not been able to locate a copy of the Patricolo history, and therefore rely entirely on Ormos's account.

40 Ormos, "Preservation and Restoration," 30.

41 M. Edmond Pauty, "La défense de l'ancienne ville du Caire et de ses monuments: Urbanisme et archéologie," *Bulletin de l'Institut Français d'archéologie orientale du Caire* 31 (1931): 135–76.

42 While there has been considerable activity from the 1970s onward and a corresponding interest, especially since the 1992 earthquake, in the history of the Comité (particularly its earliest years), no one has yet written a history of Egyptian conservation focusing on the twentieth century. This summary, then, is necessarily brief and tentative.

43 For a summary, see Medhat al-Minabbawy, "Restoration Work in Cairo: Past, Present, and Future," in Jere L. Bacharach, ed., *The Restoration and Conservation of Islamic Monuments in Cairo* (Cairo: The American University in Cairo Press, 1995), 17–21.

44 See, for example, the chapters in Ahmet Evin, ed., *The Expanding Metropolis: Coping with the Urban Growth of Cairo* (Singapore: Concept Media and the Aga Khan Award for Architecture, 1985) and Stefano Bianca and Philip Jodidio, eds., *Cairo: Revitalising a Historic Metropolis* (Turin: Umberto Allemandi and Co. and the Aga Khan Trust for Culture, 2004).

Notes to Chapter 1

1 Minute by the Governor General of India dated 22 January 1862, published as Appendix I of Dilip K. Chakrabarti, *A History of Indian Archaeology from the Beginning to 1947* (New Delhi: Munshiram Manoharial Publishers, 1988), 219–26. These papers appear to have been previously published in *Journal of the Asiatic Society of Bengal* 31 (1862): 95–104.

2 On Curzon's view that conservation was a specifically British and not general European responsibility, see Nayanjot Lahiri, "Destruction or Conservation? Some Aspects of Monument Policy in British India (1899–1905)," in Robert Layton, Peter G. Stone, and Julian Thomas, eds., *Destruction and Conservation of Cultural Property* (London and New York: Routledge, 2001), 269.

3 Thomas R. Metcalf, *Ideologies of the Raj*, The New Cambridge History of India, ed. Gordon Johnson (Cambridge: Cambridge University Press, 1995), 150; Chakrabarti, *Indian Archaeology*, 48ff.

4 Metcalf, *Ideologies*, 148ff.

5 Act (X) of the Government of India, cited by M.C. Joshi and B.M. Pande in "The Archaeological Survey of India," in *Architecture + Design* 6, no. 1 (November–December 1989): 29–31, a succinct survey of the Archaeological Survey of India's history, regrettably without notes or bibliography.

6 Similar concerns were still being expressed by Lord Curzon in a speech delivered at a meeting of the Bengal Asiatic Society in February 1900. The entire speech is published in Chakrabarti, *Indian Archaeology*, Appendix II, 227–36. In the same speech, Curzon lays out the responsibilities of government for the conservation of ancient monuments.

7 Metcalf, *Ideologies*, 150–51.

8 Ibid., 151n34, quoting NAI Home Public, 28 May 1870, no. 88–89, and 18 February 1871, no. 28–29. I discuss this rhetoric in its twentieth and twenty-first-century incarnation in Chapter 4 with respect to UNESCO's World Heritage Convention.

9 Ibid., 151.

10 Ibid., *passim.*

11 Ibid., 152.

12 Ibid., 151.

13 The speech is reported in full in the *The Times* of London, 18 September 1874, 5a and following. *The Times* reported extensively on the sessions of the International Congress of Orientalists, often reproducing in full opening addresses and some papers. I discuss the implications of interweaving architectural and literary artifacts as constructed by Europeans in Chapter 3.

14 For further discussion of the implications of this view, see Chapter 4.

15 Metcalf, *Ideologies*, 153–54.

16 Ibid., 154–55.

17 Ussama Makdisi, "Mapping the Orient: Non-western Modernization, Imperialism, and the End of Romanticism," in Helena Michie and Ronald R. Thomas, eds., *Nineteenth Century Geographies: The Transformation of Space from the Victorian Age to the American Century* (New Brunswick, NJ: Rutgers University Press, 2003), 40–54.

18 Pascal Coste, *Architecture arabe ou monuments du Kaire mesurés et dessinés de 1818 à 1826* (Paris: Firmin-Didot, 1837); Jules Bourgoin, *Les arts arabes* (Paris: Vve. A. Morel, 1873); Prisse d'Avennes, *L'art arabe d'après les monuments du Kaire* (Paris: Vve. A. Morel, 1869–77); Owen Jones, *The Grammar of Ornament* (London: Day and Son, 1856). These and other major figures are discussed in "Figures de l'orientalisme en architecture," eds. Catherine Bruant, S. Leprun, and Mercedes Volait, special issue, *Revue du Monde Musulman et de la Méditerranée* 73–74 (1996).

19 A typical judgment of this sort is offered by N.C. Burt in *The Far East; or, Letters from Egypt, Palestine, and Other Lands of the Orient* (Cincinnati: R.W. Carroll and Company, 1868), 25.

20 Donald M. Reid, *Whose Pharaohs? Archaeology, Museums, and Egyptian National Identity from Napoleon to World War I* (Berkeley: University of California Press, 2002), 223n30.

21 This is the full extent of the information reported in *The Academy* 6 (26 September 1874): 354, part of the comprehensive account of the meeting of the International Congress of Orientalists provided by the same journal, 350–58. *The Times* of London also reported exhaustively on the proceedings of the Congress (all dates are 1874, and the page and column indicate the beginning of the articles, which often extend for several pages): 15 September, p. 9b; 16 September, p. 7d; 17 September, p. 5a; 18 September, p. 5a; 19 September, p. 10c; 20 September, p. 7a; 22 September, p. 3d; 23 September, p. 10f. As far as I can tell, the account in *The Academy* is the only one published that gives the full text of the motion. Stanley Lane-Poole discussed the motion and elaborated upon it in a column entitled "Arab Art Monuments" in the same issue of *The Academy* 6 (26 September 1874): 361. See also Reid, *Whose Pharaohs*, 223ff., and Alaa El-Din Elwi El-Habashi, "*Athar* to Monuments: the Intervention of the *Comité de conservation des monuments de l'art arabe*," (PhD diss., University of Pennsylvania, 2001), chapter 2.

22 Lane-Poole, "Arab Art Monuments," 361a–b. Cf. the unsigned article, "The Protection of the Monuments of Cairo," *The Times*, 30 July 1883, 4: "these thousand monuments represent what is vaguely called Arab art in its purest form, free alike from the excessive elaboration of Alhambra and from the grotesque forms and ornamentation of India . . . ." Both the wording and the intimate knowledge of the activities of the Comité suggest that the author may, in fact, have been Lane-Poole.

23 Lane-Poole, "Arab Art Monuments," 361b.

24 See Joshi and Pande, "Archaeological Survey of India" and Metcalf,

Ideologies, chapter 4 and esp. pp. 148–59. On European ordering of knowledge in nineteenth century Egypt, see Timothy Mitchell, *Colonising Egypt* (Cambridge: Cambridge University Press, 1988).

25 See Lahiri, "Destruction or Conservation?"

26 The Earl of Dufferin to Earl Granville, Egypt. No. 14 (1883) *in British Parliament, House of Commons, Further Correspondence Respecting the Reorganization of Egypt* [C.3696], Inclosure No. 17 (Cairo, 2 April 1883), p. 14. Dufferin was appointed Ambassador to Constantinople in 1881, then Special Commissioner to Egypt, 1882–83. He was the primary representative of the Gladstone government during the occupation of Egypt in 1882.

27 Egypt, No. 14 (1883) C.3696, *Further Correspondence Respecting the Reorganization of Egypt*, Inclosure No. 28 (Foreign Office, 19 April 1883). The destruction of antiquities as a result of increased tourism was a source of increasing concern. See, for example, a small item in the "Fine-Art Gossip" column of *The Athenaeum*, 25 February 1882, 258, citing an article in *The Builder*: "In the thirty years that Egypt has been thus visited more harm has been done to its old buildings than in the centuries of so much abused neglect which have passed over the country. The destruction caused by the tourists is really serious . . . ." Stanley Lane-Poole lamented, "It is vain to try to restore the lost fragments that travelled Goths have stolen from the mosques and houses of Cairo," in "The Preservation of the Monuments of Cairo," *The Athenaeum*, 17 March 1883, 350–51.

28 Unsigned article, "Protection of the Monuments of Cairo," 4.

29 *The Egyptian Gazette*, 27 January 1885, 2.

30 British Parliament, House of Commons, *Report on the Finances, Administration, and Condition of Egypt, and the Progress of Reforms* [Egypt. No. 1 (1896)], House of Commons Sessional Papers C7978, Vol. XCVII (1896). The first report in 1896 is particularly extensive, and includes a report by Stanley Lane-Poole prepared at the request of Lord Cromer; see Inclosure No. 5, "Report by Mr. Stanley Lane Poole on the Preservation of Arab Monuments," *Report on the Finances* [Egypt. No. 2 (1897)], C8332 [Chadwyck-Healey 103.927]; [Egypt. No. 1 (1898)] C8815; Egypt. No. 3 (1899) C9231; Egypt No. 1 (1900) Cd.95; Egypt No. 1 (1901) Cd.441.

31 *The Academy*, 26 September 1874, 354.

32 Charmes lamented: "For, alas! the Tombs of the Caliphs are disappearing, and if care be not taken, in a few years they will exist no longer. It is sufficient to cast the eyes over the plates of the fine work of the French Expedition to be convinced of the damage and irreparable losses sustained since that period. . . . the Turks are one of the races the least artistic that ever existed; they have suffered very many other treasures to be lost, almost as rare.", in Gabriel Charmes, *Five Months at Cairo and in Lower Egypt*, William Conn, trans. (London: Richard Bentley and Son, 1883), 107; original French edition, *Cinq mois au Caire et dans la Basse-Égypte* (Cairo: Jule Barbier, 1880), 111–12.

On the subject of the systematic exclusion of Egyptians from the study of their own heritage, see Donald M. Reid, "Indigenous Egyptology: The Decolonization of a Profession?" *Journal of the American Oriental Society* 105 (1985): 233–46 and Reid, *Whose Pharaohs*, esp. chapters 3, 5, and 6.

33 To establish a *waqf*, the owner of a piece of real property placed it in a perpetual trust, to be administered by a superintendent who was accountable to local religious judges for the honest administration of the trust in accordance with the conditions laid down by its founder. The trust specified the purposes to which the revenues that the property generated could be assigned. In early Islamic times, *waqf* revenues were ordinarily generated from commercial properties whose rents or profits were assigned to the endowment. By the eleventh and twelfth centuries, revenues from agricultural lands were also being placed into trust. Since large tracts of both urban and agricultural land provided the revenues from which these endowments were funded, *waqf* also created direct links between urban and rural. It is no exaggeration to say that *waqf* is probably the single most important economic and social institution for historians of Islamic urbanism, and *waqf* endowment deeds (Ar. *hujjat* [pl. *hujjaj*] *waqf*, or more simply, *waqfiya*) constitute a major source of information for art and architectural historians as well as specialists in many other disciplines. Ever aware of the possibilities for misuse, founders of *waqfs* typically wrote into their endowment instruments a requirement for the deed *(hujjat waqf)* itself to be taken out once a year and read publicly in the presence of a judge *(qadi)*. The deeds that have been preserved also provide accounts of court cases and the resolution of disputes, which were typically written in the margins or on the verso of the deed when there was occasion to seek a formal judgment about the disposition of revenues, personnel issues, or the exhaustion of the trust's resources. See Muhammad Muhammad Amin, *al-Awqaf wa-l-hay'at al-ijtima'iya fi-Misr, 648–923 A.H./1250–1517 A.D.* (Cairo: Dar al-Nahda al-'Arabiya, 1980), *passim*.

34 Irene A. Bierman, "Art and Architecture in the Medieval Period," in Carl F. Petry, ed., *Cambridge History of Egypt*, vol. 1, *Islamic Egypt, 640–1517* (Cambridge: Cambridge University Press, 1998), 360.

35 Amin, *al-Awqaf*, 98. El-Habashi, "*Athar* to Monuments," 27. See also Nelly Hanna, *Construction Work in Ottoman Cairo (1517–1798)* (Cairo: Institut Français d'Archéologie Orientale du Caire, 1984), esp. 1nn2–3, and 18–23.

36 Hanna, *Construction Work*, 5–6.

37 Unsigned article, "Protection of the Monuments of Cairo," 4.

38 Some Islamic schools of law permitted *istibdal* in the event that *waqf* property was no longer usable, but other schools prohibited the practice absolutely. On *istibdal*, see *The Encyclopaedia of Islam*, new edition, ed. H.A.R. Gibb et al., 12 vols (Leiden: E.J. Brill, 1960–2004), s.v. *wakf*; Leonor Fernandez, "Istibdal: the Game of Exchange and Its Impact on the Urbanization of Mamluk Cairo," in Doris Behrens-Abouseif, ed., *The*

Cairo Heritage: Essays in Honor of Laila Ali Ibrahim (Cairo: The American University in Cairo Press, 2000), 203–22.

39 Doris Behrens-Abouseif, *Egypt's Adjustment to Ottoman Rule: Institutions, Waqf and Architecture in Cairo, 16th and 17th centuries* (Leiden: E.J. Brill, 1994), 155.

40 Ibid., 156.

41 Ibid., 156–58.

42 Ibid., 146–47.

43 For these paragraphs, see Gabriel Baer, "Waqf Reform," in *Studies in the Social History of Modern Egypt* (Chicago and London: University of Chicago Press, 1969), 79–92.

44 Michael Winter, *Egyptian Society under Ottoman Rule, 1517–1798* (London and New York: Routledge, 1992), 57.

45 See Baer's discussion of modern *waqf* criticism in "Waqf Reform."

46 *The Times*, 29 February 1896.

47 See, for example, the anecdote in al-Muwaylihi's *Hadith ibn Hisham, aw fatra min al-zaman* (Cairo: al-Dar al-Qaymiya li-l-Tiba'a wa-l-Nashr, 1964), which relates a complicated story revolving around the search for an endowment deed in the *daftarkhane*. The story is referred to by Yoav Di-Capua, "The Thought and Practice of Modern Egyptian Historiography, 1890–1970" (PhD diss., Princeton University, 2004), 69–70, citing Roger Allen's translation, *A Period of Time* (Reading, UK: Ithaca Press, 1992). Di-Capua relates that the *daftarkhane* was founded in 1828 in order to gather documents to assist in the collection of revenues. There appears to have been a fire in 1820, prior to the establishment of the *daftarkhane*, in which many documents were believed to have been destroyed. The missing documents were discovered in the twentieth century, but it is uncertain whether they were known to government officials earlier.

48 On the history of the 'Abdin archive, see Di-Capua, "Thought and Practice," 67–92. For the history of *waqf*, the standard source is Amin, *al-Awqaf*. The *waqf* documents are housed today in two locations: the *daftarkhane* of the *Wizarat al-Awqaf* and the Egyptian National Archives *(Dar al-Watha'iq)*, previously located at the Citadel and now in the main Dar al-Kutub building on the Nile corniche. *Waqfiyat* have extensive marginalia, usually representing court decisions in the light of disputes or simply amendments to the *waqf*, new appointments, and a variety of other legal issues, all of which had to be recorded and verified by a judge. Thus, a systematic study of marginalia might reveal how extensively these documents were being consulted beyond the beginning of the nineteenth century. In the absence of such a study, it is not possible to say with certainty how well known the documents were to Egyptians. What can be said with confidence is that the Comité, itself a branch of the *awqaf* department, did not use the *waqf* documents in their study of the monuments.

49 Darrell Dykstra, "A Biographical Study in Egyptian Modernization: 'Ali Mubarak (1823/4–1893)," 2 vols. (PhD diss., University of Michigan, 1977), 167ff.

50 See Dykstra, "A Biographical Study," 168 and 168n1, citing Fu'ad Karam, *al-Nizarat wa-l-wizarat al-misriya* (Cairo: Matba'at Dar al-Kutub, 1969), still considered to be an authoritative work on the history of Egyptian ministries and cabinets. More recently, see Ahmad Muhammad 'Abd al-Khaliq and Yunan Labib Rizq, *Ri'asat Misr, nizam mutakamil li-tasnif wa-tarmiz al-ri'asat wa-l-wizarat* (Cairo: Mu'assasat Ruz al-Yusuf, 2004). For detailed discussion of Mubarak's education innovations and policies, and the Edict of 10 Rajab, see Dykstra, "A Biographical Study," 244ff.
51 Hanna, *Construction Work*, 17–18.
52 See Behrens-Abouseif, *Egypt's Adjustment*, 232–44.
53 Mohammad al-Asad, "The Mosque of Muhammad 'Ali in Cairo," *Muqarnas* 9 (1992): 39–55, here p. 43.
54 Behrens-Abouseif, *Egypt's Adjustment*, 164ff.
55 Ibid., 165–66.
56 On the household as the foundation of Ottoman society in Egypt, see Jane Hathaway, "Egypt in the Seventeenth Century," in M.W. Daly, ed., *Cambridge History of Egypt*, vol. 2, *Modern Egypt, from 1517 to the End of the Twentieth Century* (Cambridge: Cambridge University Press, 1998), 34–58; Jane Hathaway, *The Politics of Households in Ottoman Egypt: The Rise of the Qazdaglis* (Cambridge: Cambridge University Press, 1997).
57 Behrens-Abouseif, *Egypt's Adjustment*, 167.
58 Mitchell, *Colonising Egypt*, and Khaled Fahmy, "Modernizing Cairo: A Revisionist Narrative," in Nezar AlSayyad, Irene A. Bierman, and Nasser Rabbat, eds., *Making Cairo Medieval* (Lanham, MD: Lexington Books, 2005), 173–99.
59 André Raymond, *Cairo*, trans. Willard Wood (Cambridge, MA: Harvard University Press, 2000), 202 and 216ff.
60 See Behrens-Abouseif, *Egypt's Adjustment*, for a full discussion of Ottoman policy and practice in the sixteenth and seventeenth centuries. For the Comité's decisions, see their *Exercice. Procès-verbaux des séances—rapports de la deuxième commission* (Cairo: Imprimerie Nationale, 1892–1911 [1882–1910]), which provide the most important 'archive' of material for their philosophy, policies, and practice. These issues are also discussed at length in El-Habashi, "*Athar* to Monuments."
61 See Comité bulletins and Hanna, *Construction Work*, 1.
62 See Jack Crabbs, "Historiography and the Eighteenth-Century Milieu," in Daniel Crecelius, ed., *Eighteenth Century Egypt: The Arabic Manuscript Sources* (Claremont, CA: Regina Books, 1990), 9–24.
63 André Raymond, "La population du Caire et de l'Égypte à l'époque Ottomane et sous Muhammad 'Ali," in *Mémorial Ömer Lûtfi Barkan* (Paris: Librairie d'Amérique et d'Orient Adrien Maisonneuve, 1980), 170–73 and 175; and André Raymond, "Essai de géographie des quartiers de résidence aristocratique au Caire au XVIIIème siècle," in *Journal of the Economic and Social History of the Orient* 6 (1963): 70ff.; both cited by Crabbs, "Historiography," 10.

64 Crabbs, "Historiography," 10 and 10n4 (comment by Crecelius).

65 Ibid., 11 and 11n7, citing various works.

66 Crabbs, "Historiography," 13. Raymond, *Cairo*, 210–12, notes that the two largest communities of foreigners in eighteenth-century Cairo were Turks and Maghribis.

67 Raymond, *Cairo*, 218.

68 Reid, *Whose Pharaohs*, 215n4, translating and citing Rhoné, "Coup d'oeil sur l'état présent du Caire."

69 Amelia Edwards, "The Destruction of Cairo," *The Academy* 546 (21 October 1882): 301, cited also in Reid, *Whose Pharaohs*, 215–16.

70 Unsigned article, "Protection of the Monuments of Cairo," 4.

71 See on this Mine Ener, *Managing Egypt's Poor and the Politics of Benevolence* (Princeton: Princeton University Press, 2003).

72 Hanna, *Construction Work*, 17–18 and 33ff.

73 See S.D. Goitein, *A Mediterranean Society: The Jewish Communities of the Arab World as Portrayed in the Documents of the Cairo Geniza*, vol. 4, *Daily Life* (Berkeley and Los Angeles: University of California Press, 1983), 21–24; Moshe Gil, *Documents of the Jewish Pious Foundations from the Cairo Geniza* (Leiden: E.J. Brill, 1976), *passim*.

74 The continued presence of such dilapidation does not mean that Cairo's residents or rulers generally neglected her architecture. Legal responsibility for the upkeep of a *waqf* building rested with its supervisor *(nazir)*, but anyone could petition the court to ask for repairs. Residents of a quarter often initiated court proceedings when a *waqf* in their neighborhood was in disrepair (Hanna, *Construction Work*, 12–18). Hanna observes that the important role of the court (the Bab al-'Ali) in Cairo's architectural heritage through the maintenance of its monuments has yet to be explored fully (p. 27).

75 'Ali Mubarak, *al-Khitat al-tawfiqiya al-jadida li-Misr al-Qahira wa-muduniha wa-biladiha al-qadima wa-l-shahira* (Bulaq: al-Matba'a al-Kubra al-Amiriya, 1886–89); second edition printed by Dar al-Kutub, 1969. References here are to the reprint of the Dar al-Kutub edition.

76 See 'Ali Mubarak, *Khitat*, vol. 1, 77 and 80, also cited in Michael J. Reimer, "Contradiction and Consciousness in Ali Mubarak's Description of al-Azhar," *International Journal of Middle East Studies* 29 (1997): 55.

77 Reimer, "Ali Mubarak's Description of al-Azhar," 56, citing 'Ali Mubarak, *Khitat*, vol. 4, 12–24, on al-Azhar.

78 Nasser Rabbat, "The Formation of the Neo-Mamluk Style in Modern Egypt," in M. Pollak, ed., *The Education of the Architect: Historiography, Urbanism, and the Growth of Architectural Knowledge. Essays Presented to Stanford Anderson on his Sixty-second Birthday* (Cambridge, MA: MIT Press, 1997), 363–86.

79 It is a common misconception that the original plan of the mosque was designed by the European architect Pascal Coste in 1820, on a neo-Mamluk model. According to that narrative, after Coste left Egypt a new design,

modeled on the mosque of Sultan Ahmet I in Istanbul, was begun in 1833 and completed in 1857. Mohammad al-Asad demonstrates that this is false: see "Mosque of Muhammad 'Ali," esp. 41–42. See also Raymond, *Cairo*, 309.

80 Al-Asad, "Mosque of Muhammad 'Ali," 45–46.

81 Ibid., 51.

82 For the complete history of the mosque of al-Rifa'i, see Mohammad al-Asad, "The Mosque of al-Rifa'i in Cairo," *Muqarnas* 10 (1993): 108–24. Herz Bey himself wrote an account of the building of the mosque, *La mosquée el-Rifa'ï au Caire* (n.p., [1912]). 'Ali Mubarak provides a history of the mosque also in his *Khitat*, vol. 4, 114–19.

83 Max Herz Bey, *A Descriptive Catalogue of the Objects Exhibited in the National Museum of Arab Art, Preceded by a Historical Sketch of the Architecture and Industrial Arts of the Arabs in Egypt*, trans. G. Foster Smith (Cairo: National Printing Department, 1907), xliv–xlv.

84 Ulrich Haarmann, "Ideology and History, Identity and Alterity: The Arab Image of the Turk from the Abbasids to Modern Egypt," *International Journal of Middle East Studies* 20, no. 2 (1988): 175–96.

85 Ibid., 177.

86 Ibid., 183.

87 Thomas Philipp and Ulrich Haarmann, eds., preface to *The Mamluks in Egyptian Politics and Society* (Cambridge: Cambridge University Press, 1998), xi.

88 For important revisions to the history of the *awlad al-nas*, see Ulrich Haarmann, "The Sons of Mamluks as Fief-holders in Late Medieval Egypt," in Tarif Khalidi, ed., *Land Tenure and Social Transformation in the Middle East* (Beirut: American University of Beirut, 1984): 141–68; Donald S. Richards, "Mamluk Amirs and their Families and Households," in Philipp and Haarmann, *Mamluks in Egyptian Politics*, 32–54; Ulrich Haarmann, "Joseph's Law—the Careers and Activities of Mamluk Descendants before the Ottoman Conquest of Egypt," in Philipp and Haarmann, *Mamluks in Egyptian Politics*, 55–84. On questions of identification and language, see Ulrich Haarmann, "Arabic in Speech, Turkish in Lineage: Mamluks and their Sons in the Intellectual Life of Fourteenth-Century Egypt and Syria," *Journal of Semitic Studies* 33 (1988): 81–114.

89 On the rank-and-file Mamluks, see Amalia Levanoni, "Rank-and-file Mamluks versus Amirs: New Norms in the Mamluk Military Institution," in Philipp and Haarmann, *Mamluks in Egyptian Politics*, 17–31.

90 On this theme, see Ulrich Haarmann, "Rather the Injustice of the Turks than the Righteousness of the Arabs—Changing 'Ulama Attitudes towards Mamluk Rule in the Late Fifteenth Century," *Studia Islamica* 68 (1988): 61–77.

91 Haarmann, "Ideology and History," 184. This negative judgment persisted into the twentieth century.

92 Michael Winter, "The Re-emergence of the Mamluks following the Ottoman

Conquest of Egypt," in Philipp and Haarmann, *Mamluks in Egyptian Politics*, 98, and Michael Winter "Attitudes toward the Ottomans in Egyptian Historiography during Ottoman Rule," in Hugh Kennedy, ed., *The Historiography of Islamic Egypt (c. 950–1800)* (Leiden: E.J. Brill, 2001), 199.

93 For this, see Winter, *Egyptian Society under Ottoman Rule*, 31ff. and "Attitudes toward the Ottomans," 198–99.

94 Cited in Winter, "Re-emergence of the Mamluks," 94.

95 See Ibid., 94–95 and parts on Turkish suitability for military.

96 See, for example, Raymond, *Cairo*, 204n3.

97 Winter, "Attitudes toward the Ottomans," 195.

98 Winter, "Re-emergence of the Mamluks," 104–105

99 Ibid., 105.

100 See Gabriel Baer, "Egyptian Atittudes towards Turks and Ottomans in the 17th and 18th centuries," in *Prilozi za orijentalnu filologiju = Revue de philologie orientale* 30 (1980): 25–34.

101 See Winter, "Re-emergence of the Mamluks" and *Egyptian Society under Ottoman Rule*; see also Jane Hathaway, "'Mamluk Households' and 'Mamluk Factions' in Ottoman Egypt: A Reconsideration," in Philipp and Haarmann, *Mamluks in Egyptian Politics*, 107–17, and her *Politics of Households, passim.*

102 Winter, "Re-emergence of the Mamluks," 105.

103 Ibid.," 105–06.

104 Michael Winter, "Turks, Arabs, and Mamluks in the Army of Ottoman Egypt," *Wiener Zeitschrift für die Kunde des Morgenlandes* 72 (1980): 97–122.

105 *The Athenaeum*, 12 February 1881, 239.

106 Amelia Edwards, letter to *The Times*, 13 January 1883, 12/a; unsigned article, "The Protection of the Monuments of Cairo," *The Times*, 30 July 1883, 4/e–f.

107 Rev. F.A. Walker, *Nine Hundred Miles up the Nile* (London: West, Newman and Co., 1884), 75.

108 Stanley Lane-Poole, *The Art of the Saracens in Egypt*, 2 parts (published for the Committee of Council on Education by Chapman and Hall, Limited, 1886), Part I, v.

109 *The Egyptian Gazette*, 27 January 1885, 2.

110 *Further Correspondence Respecting the Reorganization of Egypt* [Egypt. No. 14 (1883)], C.-3696 [Chadwick-Healy 89.687], No. 17, "The Earl of Dufferin to Earl Granville," Cairo, 2 April 1883.

111 A.J. Butler, review of *The Art of the Saracens in Egypt*, in *The Academy* 739 (3 July 1886), 14–15.

112 See, for example, *The Times*, 6 March 1896, 3/f, a note on preservation of Cairo's "medieval monuments."

113 Edward William Lane, *Cairo Fifty Years Ago*, ed. Stanley Lane-Poole (London: John Murray, 1896), but based on portions of Lane's *Description of Egypt* written during his first visit to Egypt in 1825–28 [British Museum Add. 34080–88], revised around 1835, and copied by Reginald Stuart Poole (Lane's nephew and Stanley Lane-Poole's uncle) in 1847. See also Edward

William Lane, *An Account of the Manners and Customs of the Modern Egyptians* (numerous editions); Edward William Lane, *Description of Egypt*, ed., Jason Thompson (Cairo: The American University in Cairo Press, 2000).

114 *The Academy* 51 (23 January 1897): 99–100: "The book is prefaced by a map of mediaeval Cairo . . . ." However, 'medieval' does not displace other terms: the review of the same book in *The Times*, 5 December 1896, 10/b, refers to the "old Arab city."

115 *The Times*, 3 January 1882, reporting the decree that established the Comité de conservation des monuments de l'art arabe.

116 *The Builder* 43 (1882): 452ff.

117 *The Athenaeum*, 22 March 1884, 383–84, reporting and summarizing the publication of the first procès-verbaux of the Comité.

118 Stanley Lane-Poole, letter to *The Athenaeum*, 17 March 1883, 350.

119 Stanley Lane-Poole, preface to *Cairo: Sketches of its History, Monuments, and Social Life* (London: J.S. Virtue and Co., 1892). See also the review in *The Times*, 3 November 1892, 11/a quoting this passage.

120 *The Times*, 29 February 1896, 6/d-e. On the Comité, see Donald M. Reid, "Cultural Imperialism and Nationalism: The Struggle to Define and Control the Heritage of Arab Art in Egypt," *International Journal of Middle East Studies* 24 (1992): 57–76; Alaa El-Habashi and Nicholas Warner, "Recording the Monuments of Cairo: An Introduction and Overview," *Annales Islamologiques* 32 (1998): 81–99; Bierman, "Art and Architecture," 343–45.

121 "The Citadel of Cairo," *The Athenaeum*, 26 June 1897, 848.

122 *The Athenaeum*, 21 March 1896, 372.

123 *The Athenaeum*, 19 July 1890, 89/a-c.

124 Karl Baedeker, ed., *Egypt, Handbook for Travellers, Part I. Lower Egypt and the Peninsula of Sinai*, 3rd ed. (Leipsic: Karl Baedeker, 1895); Karl Baedeker, ed., *Egypt, Handbook for Travellers*, 4th ed. (Leipsic: Karl Baedeker, 1898). Baedeker first consolidated its two publications, *Lower Egypt* and *Upper Egypt*, into a single volume in the 4th edition.

125 Baedeker, *Egypt*, 3rd ed. (1895), "Outline of the History of Egypt," civ–cxxii; Baedeker, *Egypt*, 4th ed. (1898), "Outline of the History of Egypt," xcv–cxxi.

126 See the obituary published in *The English Historical Review* 217 (January 1940): 1–7. On the Lane-Poole brothers, see Simon Bailey, "Poole, Reginald Lane (1857–1939)," *Oxford Dictionary of National Biography* (Oxford: Oxford University Press, 2004) [http://www.oxforddnb.com/view/article/35568, accessed 23 July 2007] and R.S. Simpson, 'Poole, Stanley Edward Lane– (1854–1931)," *Oxford Dictionary of National Biography* (Oxford: Oxford University Press, 2004). [http://www.oxforddnb.com/view/article/35569, accessed 23 July 2007].

121 The first five volumes in the History of Egypt series dealt with the First to Thirtieth dynasties, the Ptolemies, and the Roman period. Stanley Lane-Poole, *The Story of Cairo* (London: J.M. Dent and Co., 1902 [1906]).

128 Lane-Poole, *Story of Cairo*, vii.
129 Stanley Lane-Poole, *The Story of the Nations: Mediaeval India under Mohammedan Rule, 1712–1764* (New York: G.P. Putnam's Sons, 1903), iii.
130 Lane-Poole, *Story of Cairo*, 5.
131 Mitchell, *Colonising Egypt*, 67ff.
132 See on this issue Fahmy, "Modernizing Cairo."
133 "Mehemet Ali and Ismail may be considered by the artist and antiquarian to have done their best to vulgarise, that is, Europeanise, the City of the Mamelukes." Eustace Reynolds-Ball, *City of the Caliphs: A Popular Study of Cairo and its Environs and the Nile and its Environs* (Boston: Estes and Lauriat, 1897), 2.
134 Reynolds-Ball, *City of the Caliphs*, 3.
135 Ahmet Ersoy, "On the Sources of the 'Ottoman Renaissance': Architectural Revival and its Discourse during the Abdulaziz Era (1861–1876)" (PhD diss., Harvard University, 2000). I am grateful to Shirine Hamadeh for bringing this pathbreaking work to my attention.
136 On this point, see Makdisi, "Mapping the Orient."
137 Stanley Lane-Poole, preface to Max Herz Bey, *Catalogue of the National Museum of Arab Art*, ed. Stanley Lane-Poole (London: B. Quaritch, 1896 [Original edition in French, 1895]), ix.
138 "The Proposed New Street at Cairo," *The Athenaeum*, 30 November 1889, 749. The Mamluk period as emblematic of the nation would not fare as well in the twentieth century, and particularly in the aftermath of the 1952 Revolution, when Gamal Abdel Nasser would characterize the Mamluk period as yet another era in which Egypt had been ruled by foreign oppressors.
139 Robert L. Tignor, *Modernization and British Colonial Rule in Egypt, 1882–1914* (Princeton: Princeton University Press, 1966), 82–83. On the shift from Constantinople to Cairo, see Ronald Robinson and John Gallagher, *Africa and the Victorians: The Climax of Imperialism in the Dark Continent* (New York: St. Martin's Press, 1961), 254–73.
140 Cited in Tignor, *Modernization*, 156n13, where the full reference is given: Baring to Salisbury, No. 174, 21 February 1892, Cromer Papers, TNA, FO 633/6.
141 *The Athenaeum*, 27 November 1886, 712–13.
142 Ersoy, "On the Sources of the 'Ottoman Renaissance,'" see esp. p. 203ff.
143 Ibid., 1. Ersoy's dissertation is a detailed study of the *Usul*, the circumstances of its production, and its meanings in the context of Tanzimat era politics and culture.
144 The authors customized the different language versions of the *Usul* in accordance with the cultural background and assumptions of their intended audiences; ibid., 226.
145 All quotations from ibid., 221–25.
146 It is interesting and important to note here, as Ersoy explains (ibid., 227), how the language versions may reveal the imperial assumptions of its authors. For example, in the French version the term 'turque' is used to

mean 'Ottoman,' following the convention of European languages. However, in the Turkish text, the authors consistently use the term 'Osmanli,' since 'Turkishness,' as an ethnic category, was not used among Ottomans as a marker of imperial identity. Furthermore, the Turkic Seljuk roots of Ottoman architecture, a theme that would become conventional in twentieth-century Turkish nationalism, are not discussed.

147 Ibid., 236–41.

148 Ersoy uses the term "medieval Romanticism," in "On the Sources of the 'Ottoman Renaissance,'" but I believe that the formulation 'Romantic medievalism' is the more appropriate expression of the ideas he explains, for the Ottoman practice was clearly imbued with many of the same features as the European medievalism of the Romantic period. See Ibid., 248ff.

149 Ibid., 203–304.

150 World's Fairs and universal expositions had been organized beginning in 1851, and typically included exhibits of eastern countries. The Ottoman Empire participated in these early expositions, but did not launch major exhibitions that included architectural reproductions until the 1860s. For the complete history and discussion of the representation of the Ottoman Empire in world's fairs, see Zeynep Çelik, *Displaying the Orient: The Architecture of Islam at Nineteenth-Century World's Fairs* (Berkeley and Los Angeles: University of California Press, 1992); Selim Deringil, *The Well-Protected Domains: Ideology and the Legitimation of Power in the Ottoman Empire, 1876–1909* (London: I.B. Tauris, 1999), 150–65; Ersoy, "On the Sources of the 'Ottoman Renaissance,'" 64ff.

151 Ersoy, "On the Sources of the 'Ottoman Renaissance,'" 66ff.

152 Ibid., 68.

153 Translated by Ersoy in ibid., 69. Ersoy cites the official report of the Ottoman exposition commission, 4 October 1866.

154 Charles Edmond, *L'Égypte à l'exposition universelle de 1867* (Paris: Dentu, 1867).

155 He cites the saying, "Dis-moi *où* tu hantes et je te dirai qui tu es," in ibid., 176.

156 Muhammad 'Arif, *al-Juz' al-rabi' min khulasat al-afkar fi fann al-mi'mar* (Bulaq: al-Matba'a al-Kubra al-Amiriya, 1902). As far as I can determine, the sole copy of this important work available in the United States or Western Europe is held by the University of Utah. This version is a reprint of one volume of the 1887 work. I am especially grateful to Betsy Dain of the National Humanities Center (NHC), for her extraordinary efforts in obtaining this book in 2003, when I was a fellow at the NHC. I am also grateful to Cathy Rockwell, Middle East Librarian at the University of Utah, for her decision to lend this rare and fragile volume.

157 Ibid., 91–100, see paras. 111–13.

158 Ibid., 101, para. 114.

159 Ibid., 102. 'Arif's volume is not illustrated, but he states that the reason was time and lack of funds. Generally, the lack of illustrations in Egyptian architectural and topographical works distinguished these publications

not only from European works, but also from later nineteenth century Ottoman treatises on architecture, where illustrations and other visual representations (for example, drawings) were commonplace, indeed, popular. See Ersoy, "On the Sources of the 'Ottoman Renaissance.'"

160 On craft guilds, see Pascale Ghazaleh, *Masters of the Trade: Crafts and Crafspeople in Cairo, 1750–1850* (Cairo: The American University in Cairo Press, 2000).

161 For a comprehensive discussion of neo-Mamluk and other turn-of-the-century Islamic architectures, see Tarek Mohamed Refaat Sakr, *Early Twentieth-Century Islamic Architecture in Cairo* (Cairo: The American University in Cairo Press, 1993) and Mohamed Scharabi, *Kairo: Stadt und Architektur im Zeiltalter des europäischen Kolonialismus* (Tübingen: E. Wasmuth Verlag, 1989).

162 For a comprehensive introduction to the varieties of Egyptian nationalism in the late nineteenth and early twentieth centuries, see Israel Gershoni and James P. Jankowski, *Egypt, Islam, and the Arabs: The Search for Egyptian Nationhood, 1900–1930* (New York: Oxford University Press, 1987).

163 On Ottoman programs of modernization, see Deringil, *Well-Protected Domains*; Makdisi, "Mapping the Orient."

Notes to Chapter 2

1 I speak here only of religious reform. The classic work on nineteenth-century reform more generally in the Middle East is Albert Hourani's unparalleled *Arabic Thought in the Liberal Age 1798–1939* (London and New York: Oxford University Press, 1962).

2 On this, see Selim Deringil, *The Well-Protected Domains: Ideology and the Legitimation of Power in the Ottoman Empire, 1876–1909* (London: I.B. Tauris, 1999).

3 Alaa El-Din Elwi El-Habashi's discussion of Muhammad 'Abduh's program in Appendix 4 of his dissertation, "*Athar* to Monuments: the Intervention of the *Comité de conservation des monuments de l'art arabe*" (PhD diss., University of Pennsylvania, 2001), is restricted to the issue of material repair and does not deal with his much broader intellectual and religious program of *islah*. For an introduction to 'Abduh's program of *islah*, see *The Encyclopaedia of Islam*, new edition, ed. H.A.R., Gibb et al., 12 vols. (Leiden: E.J. Brill, 1960–2004), s.v. *islah*; Charles C. Adams, *Islam and Modernism in Egypt: A Study of the Modern Reform Movement Inaugurated by Muhammad 'Abduh* (Oxford: Oxford University Press, 1933); Malcolm H. Kerr, *Islamic Reform: The Political and Legal Theories of Muhammad 'Abduh and Rashid Rida* (Berkeley: University of California Press, 1966); Elie Kedouri, *Afghani and 'Abduh: An Essay on Religious Unbelief and Political Activism in Modern Islam* (London: Cass, 1966); Jamal Mohammed Ahmed, *The Intellectual Origins of Egyptian Nationalism* (London: Oxford University Press, 1968); Hourani, *Arabic Thought in the Liberal Age*; Muhammad Rashid Rida, *Tarikh al-ustadh al-imam al-shaykh Muhammad 'Abduh* (Cairo: Dar al-Fadila, 2003), 3 vols.

in 4. Two collections on Islamic modernism provide translations of primary texts and clear introductions: see Charles Kurzman, ed., *Modernist Islam, 1840–1940: A Sourcebook* (Oxford and New York: Oxford University Press, 2002) and Mansoor Moaddel and Kamran Talattof, *Modernist and Fundamentalist Debates in Islam: A Reader* (New York: Palgrave, 2000).

4 *al-Manar*, 16 Rabi' al-Awwal, 1322/1 June 1904; in Rida, *Tarikh*, 1:633–35.

5 Rida, *Tarikh*, 1:633. Others besides 'Abduh lamented the state of the *ulama* and excoriated the narrowly educated among them. 'Abdulla Nadim, like other journalists, used his journal, *al-Tankit wa-l-tabkit*, as a vehicle for this critique, publishing stories about a presumably fictional Shaykh Zifti who considered universal education and all that went along with it as innovation *(bid'a)* and a prelude to Hell. For Nadim, Shaykh Zifti and his ilk were idiots *(ghabi)* and narcissists ("limited to self-love"). The journalistic community espoused a notion of progress that echoed the theory first introduced in the 1830s by Rifa'a al-Tahtawi in his account of his student days in Paris *(Takhlis al-ibriz fi talkhis al-bariz)*. Tahtawi accounted for the rapidity of European progress by the broad learning of its scholars, the introduction of universal education, and the subsequent development of electricity, trains, etc. Ideas of progress similar to Tahtawi's were found in many places across the Ottoman Empire in the 1870s and beyond. Although there were certainly members of the *ulama* who shared their values, journalists continued to consider the *ulama* as the chief obstacle to progress, particularly given their custodianship of education in Egypt. This paragraph is based on Indira Falk Gesink, "Beyond Modernisms: Opposition and Negotiation in the Azhar Reform Debate in Egypt, 1870–1911" (PhD diss., Washington University, 2000), 224–25.

6 For the history of educational institutions and pedagogy over the course of Islamic history, see *The Encyclopaedia of Islam*, New Edition, s.v. *madrasa*, sec. 6 (courses of instruction and personnel).

7 There was no instruction in the Arabic language itself, although in the late eighteenth century, the Ottoman sultan 'Abd al-Hamid I introduced Arabic language instruction into his schools. Literary Arabic was largely unknown in these mostly illiterate societies, and Qur'anic Arabic was even less known and understood. The teachers, called *fiqis* (a corruption of *faqih*), were not necessarily highly educated, and were sometimes illiterate. Their primary qualification seems to have been that they knew the Qur'an by heart.

8 Adams, *Islam and Modernism*, 22–23, citing and translating 'Abduh's autobiography in *al-Manar*, viii, 381.

9 Ibid., 22 citing *al-Manar*, viii, 381–82.

10 See Ibid., 28ff. and J. Heyworth-Dunne, *An Introduction to the History of Education in Modern Egypt* (London: Luzac and Co., 1939).

11 On the importance of Mubarak's work for the history of religious life in nineteenth-century Egypt, see Gabriel Baer, "'Ali Mubarak's Khitat as a Source for the History of Modern Egypt," in P.M. Holt, ed., *Political and Social Change in Modern Egypt* (New York: Oxford University Press, 1968),

13–27; Gilbert Delanoue, *Moralistes et politiques musulmans dans l'Égypte du XIXe siècle (1798–1882)* (Cairo: Institut Français d'Archéologie Orientale du Caire, 1982) 522–23.

12 Translated and cited by Michael J. Reimer in "Contradiction and Consciousness in Ali Mubarak's Description of al-Azhar," *International Journal of Middle East Studies* 29 (1997): 63 and 63n56.

13 Ibid., 63.

14 'Ali Mubarak, *al-Khitat al-tawfiqiya al-jadida li-Misr al-Qahira wa-muduniha wa-biladiha al-qadima wa-l-shahira* (Bulaq: al-Matba'a al-Kubra al-Amiriya, 1886–89); 2nd ed., Cairo: Dar al-Kutub, 1969, vol. 5, 304.

15 For a detailed discussion of practices at the tomb of Sayyida Zaynab based on ethnographic research, see Nadia Abu-Zahra, *The Pure and Powerful: Studies in Contemporary Muslim Society* (Reading, UK: Ithaca Press, 1997). Abu-Zahra, an anthropologist, is the only scholar to my knowledge who discusses 'Ali Mubarak's view of *mawlids*.

16 On *mawlids*, see J.W. McPherson, *The Moulids of Egypt (Egyptian Saints-Days)* (Cairo: Ptd. N.M. Press, 1941); *The Encyclopaedia of Islam*, s.v. *mawlid*; Nicolaas H. Biegman, *Egypt: Moulids, Saints, Sufis* (London: Kegan Paul International, 1990). Al-Jabarti reports on a Turkish preacher who preached mostly to a congregation of Turks at the mosque of al-Mu'ayyad against the cult of saints, and in particular against the notion that saints can perform miracles after their death. Two local shaykhs apparently issued a *fatwa* (juridical opinion) declaring that saints could indeed perform miracles after death: see Thomas Philipp and Moshe Perlmann, eds., *'Abd al-Rahman al-Jabarti's History of Egypt, 'aja'ib al-athar fi-l-tarajim wa-l-akhbar*, 4 vols. in 3 (Stuttgart: Franz Steiner Verlag, 1994) 1:79–82 [= Bulaq ed., vol. 1, 48–50]; also mentioned by Heyworth-Dunne, *Introduction to the History*, 12n1.

17 On intercession, see *The Encyclopaedia of Islam*, s.v. *shafa'a*. On the history of the Prophet Muhammad's *mawlid*, see N.J.G. Kaptein, *Muhammad's Birthday Festival: Early History in the Central Muslim Lands and Development in the Muslim West until the 10th/16th Century* (Leiden: E.J. Brill, 1993). Ibn Taymiya (d. 1328) is perhaps the most famous critic of practices associated with the cult of saints. On the cult of saints in the medieval Islamic world, there is a growing literature: Christopher Taylor, *In the Vicinity of the Righteous: Ziyara and the Veneration of Muslim Saints in Late Medieval Egypt* (Leiden: E.J. Brill, 1998); Josef Meri, *The Cult of Saints among Muslims and Jews in Medieval Syria* (Oxford and New York: Oxford University Press, 2002); S.D. Goitein, *A Mediterranean Society: The Jewish Communities of the Arab World as Portrayed in the Documents of the Cairo Geniza*, vol. 5, *The Individual* (Berkeley: University of California Press, 1988), 18–25. The most famous of the guidebooks for pilgrims is al-Harawi's *Kitab al-isharat ila ma'rifat al-ziyarat*. This guidebook told pilgrims the location of tombs, what the resident of the tomb was known for (i.e., what kind of problem the saint's intercession might be good for), what

particular prayers or other offerings were appropriate, and, generally, the appropriate etiquette and decorum. See the recent translation into English by Josef Meri, *A Lonely Wayfarer's Guide to Pilgrimage: 'Ali ibn Abi Bakr al-Harawi's Kitab al-isharat ila ma'rifat al-ziyarat* (Princeton: Darwin Press, 2004). On al-Harawi himself, see *The Encyclopaedia of Islam*, s.v. *al-Harawi al-Mawsili*.

18 Michael Winter, *Egyptian Society under Ottoman Rule, 1517–1798* (London and New York: Routledge, 1992), 116n42.

19 Imam al-Shafi'i (d. 820), the architect of Muslim jurisprudence and founder of the Shafi'i school of Islamic law, is the only founder of a legal school who is buried in Egypt. His tomb is a site of immense popularity and importance, a major location for popular religious activities, but also an important legitimizing site for Sunni Islam. Many *ulama* were buried in the vicinity of al-Shafi'i's tomb, and so the whole neighborhood (which is, it should be remembered, a cemetery) acquired a *gravitas* that was recognized both popularly and by the religious and political establishments. New governors during the Ottoman period generally visited al-Shafi'i's tomb when they assumed their duties in Cairo. These sites were (and today still are) firmly within the mainstream of Egyptian religious life. Devotees of Imam al-Shafi'i still visit his tomb to ask for intercession on legal matters. After circumambulating the sepulcher inside the tomb, they throw chits on which they write their legal problem into its interior. James Rosberg, personal communication to author, Cairo, 1996.

20 Wilfrid Scawen Blunt stands in stark contrast to Cromer's view and that of most of his fellow British. He believed profoundly in Islamic reform and developed a close association with Muhammad 'Abduh. See his *Future of Islam* (London: Kegan Paul, Trench and Co., 1882). For a broader discussion of anti-imperialist British figures with a sympathetic view of Islam, see Geoffrey Nash, *From Empire to Orient: Travellers to the Middle East, 1830–1926* (London: I.B. Tauris, 2005).

21 This is echoed in a different context in Macaulay's "Minute on Indian Education" (1835) (Lord Thomas Babington Macaulay, "Minute on Indian Education," in Barbara Harlow and Mia Carter, eds., *Archives of Empire*, vol. 1, *From the East India Company to the Suez Canal* [Durham, North Carolina: Duke University Press, 2003], 227–38) in which he argues against the justification for teaching Sanskrit and Arabic on the grounds that "they are the languages in which the sacred books of a hundred millions of people are written." He retorts that, while the British must be neutral on religious issues, it is unjustifiable to study a "literature [that] inculcates the most serious errors on the most important subjects . . . ," that is filled with "monstrous superstitions" and "false history, false astronomy, false medicine . . . in company with a false religion."

22 Gregory Starrett, *Putting Islam to Work: Education, Politics, and Religious Transformation in Egypt* (Berkeley: University of California Press, 1998), 38ff.

23 On the discourses of stagnation in Egyptian historiography, see Gabriel Piterberg, "The Tropes of Stagnation and Awakening in Nationalist Historical Consciousness: The Egyptian Case," in James Jankowski and Israel Gershoni, eds., *Rethinking Nationalism in the Arab Middle East* (New York: Columbia University Press, 1997), 42–61.

24 Translated and cited in *The Encyclopaedia of Islam*, s.v. *islah*, section 3e, citing *al-Manar* 3 (1900): 244.

25 Evelyn Baring, Earl of Cromer, *Modern Egypt*, 2 vols. (London: Macmillan, 1908), vol. 2, 227.

26 Ibid., 201–202. On the relationship between theories of race and religion, see Susan Bayly, "Race in Britain and India," in Peter van der Veer and Hartmut Lehmann, eds., *Nation and Religion: Perspectives on Europe and Asia* (Princeton: Princeton University Press, 1999), 71–95.

27 Cromer, *Modern Egypt*, vol. 2, 203.

28 Ibid., 217.

29 Ibid., 231n1. Similar ideas about Europeanization are expressed often by Sir Richard Francis Burton, who was a central figure in the dissemination of orientalism. Burton, who had already grown weary of "civilization" when he undertook his famous pilgrimage, was convinced, in Ussama Makdisi's words, of "the crucial role [the Orient] could play alongside the science and civilization of the West." He therefore adamantly opposed non-western modernization. See on this Ussama Makdisi, "Mapping the Orient: Non-western Modernization, Imperialism, and the End of Romanticism," in Helena Michie and Ronald R. Thomas, eds., *Nineteenth Century Geographies: The Transformation of Space from the Victorian Age to the American Century* (New Brunswick, NJ: Rutgers University Press, 2003), esp. pp. 47–50.

30 For a general discussion of Cromer's views of Islam, see Robert L. Tignor, "Lord Cromer on Islam," in *The Muslim World* 52 (1962): 223–33; Nash, *From Empire to Orient*, 78–79.

31 Starrett, *Putting Islam to Work*, 38–40.

32 On the introduction of the Lancaster method into Egypt, see Timothy Mitchell, *Colonising Egypt* (Cambridge: Cambridge University Press, 1988), 69–71.

33 Peter van der Veer, *Imperial Encounters: Religion and Modernity in India and Britain* (Princeton: Princeton University Press, 2001), esp. chapter 5, "Monumental Texts: Orientalism and the Critical Edition of India's National Heritage."

34 See Thomas R. Metcalf, *Ideologies of the Raj*, The New Cambridge History of India, ed. Gordon Johnson (Cambridge: Cambridge University Press, 1995), 40–41.

35 This paragraph is based largely on Adams, *Islam and Modernism*, esp. pp. 109ff.

36 Ibid., 110, translating *Tarikh*, ii, 477.

37 For this, see *The Encyclopaedia of Islam*, s.v. *islah*, IV 151a.

38 *The Encyclopaedia of Islam*, s.v. *islah*, IV 151a. For a broad treatment of the question of modernity in a Syrian context, see Keith Watenpaugh, *Being*

Modern in the Middle East: Nationalism, Colonialism, and the Arab Middle Class (Princeton: Princeton University Press, 2006).

39 *The Encyclopaedia of Islam*, New Edition, s.v. *islah*, IV 152a.

40 Ibid., 152b.

41 See Muhammad 'Abduh, *The Theology of Unity*, trans. Ishaq Musa'ad and Kenneth Cragg (London: George Allen Unwin, 1966), 158.

42 Darrell Dykstra, "A Biographical Study in Egyptian Modernization: 'Ali Mubarak (1823/4–1893)," 2 vols. (PhD diss., University of Michigan, 1977), 359, citing Ahmad Amin, *Zu'ama' al-islah fi-l-'asr al-hadith* (Cairo: Maktabat al-Nahda al-'Asriya, 1949), 198–99.

43 See Dykstra, "A Biographical Study," 565ff.

44 Cited in ibid., 564n1.

45 Ibid., 567, citing Mubarak, 312–14.

46 Ibid., 574ff.

47 Ibid., 576ff.

48 Ibid., trans. 579n1, citing and translating *'Alam al-din*, 1:356–58.

49 Dykstra's discussion in ibid., 582

50 Ibid., 584–85.

51 On the question of interactions between Arab intellectuals and European orientalists in the nineteenth and twentieth centuries, see Ronen Raz, "The Transparent Mirror: Arab Intellectuals and Orientalism, 1798–1950," (PhD diss., Princeton University, 1997), who presents a different picture from that drawn in Edward Said, *Orientalism* (New York: Panthean Books, 1978).

52 Cromer, *Modern Egypt*, vol. 2, 180.

53 Ibid., 235–37.

54 Ibid., 236.

55 For a good summary, see Hugh McLeod, "Protestantism and British National Identity, 1815–1945," in Peter van der Veer and Hartmut Lehmann, eds., *Nation and Religion: Perspectives on Europe and Asia* (Princeton: Princeton University Press, 1999), 44–70.

56 Ibid., 51 and see note.

57 Ibid.," 56–57.

58 See van der Veer, *Imperial Encounters*, chapter 1, esp. pp. 22ff.

59 Cromer, *Modern Egypt*, vol. 2, 224.

60 Cited in Metcalf, *Ideologies*, 142.

61 Metcalf, *Ideologies*, 142ff. For a full account of Victorian attitudes toward religion, see Bernard M.G. Reardon, *Religious Thought in the Victorian Age: A Survey from Coleridge to Gore* (London: Longman, 1995 [2nd ed.]). See also Bayly's discussion in "Race in Britain and India."

62 Cromer, *Modern Egypt*, vol. 2, 145n1, citing Dean Stanley's *Lectures on the Eastern Church*, 334. Cf. also Sladen's comment in *Oriental Cairo: The City of the "Arabian Nights"* (London: Hurst and Blackett, 1911) about mosques, 324.

63 Cromer, *Modern Egypt*, vol. 2, 228.

64 Ibid., 228–29.

65 Metcalf, *Ideologies*, 142, citing W.W. Hunter.

66 As Thomas Metcalf has put it, Islamic reform "represented an ideal both of faith and of practice toward which, even as they denounced it, the British found themselves drawn. In part this attraction involved a romantic yearning for a simpler life of the sort they imagined to have existed in the 'merry England' of old, and which they sought now, as we shall see presently, to reconstruct on the Frontier. But Islam exerted an appeal of its own. The spread of Western education would, to be sure, help make Muslims 'less fanatical', and so propel them away from a 'mistaken' religion to a 'higher level of belief' in Christianity. Yet it also would mean, as Hunter saw it, that the Islamic faith, like that of his own Christian contemporaries, would become 'less sincere', with the educated sons 'less earnest' in their belief than their untutored fathers. Such a transformation was an occasion not only for rejoicing but for regret; for among late-Victorian Englishmen, who doubted their faith but still wished to believe, the rigorous monotheism of the Waḥabi preacher offered a reassurance they could no longer find in themselves." Metcalf, *Ideologies*, 142–43.

67 See Evelyn Baring, Earl of Cromer, *Abbas II* (London: Macmillan and Co., 1915) 32–33. See also Cromer's discussion of Gallicized Egyptians in *Modern Egypt*. For a succinct account of Cromer's attitudes toward Islam, see Tignor, "Lord Cromer on Islam."

68 Cromer, *Abbas II*, 37–38.

69 Ibid., 11.

70 Ibid., 14.

71 Cromer, *Modern Egypt*, vol. 2, 146ff.

72 Ibid., 146.

73 Ibid., 161.

74 Donald M. Reid, *Whose Pharaohs? Archaeology, Museums, and Egyptian National Identity from Napoleon to World War I* (Berkeley: University of California Press, 2002), where he states that for the historian, it is conservation and not its absence that needs to be explained.

75 Translated and cited by Reimer in "Ali Mubarak's Description of al-Azhar," 61, quoting from the Introduction to *Khitat*.

76 Reimer, "Ali Mubarak's Description of al-Azhar," 61.

77 On al-Maqrizi's *Khitat* as a "site of memory," see Nasser Rabbat, "Al-Maqrizi's *Khitat*, an Egyptian *lieu de mémoire*," in Doris Behrens-Abouseif, ed., *The Cairo Heritage: Essays in Honor of Laila Ali Ibrahim* (Cairo: The American University in Cairo Press, 2000), 17–30. I come to a different conclusion from Rabbat about Mubarak's *Khitat* as a "site of memory."

78 For a clear summary of theories and historiographies of memory among historians, see Daniel J. Sherman, *The Construction of Memory in Interwar France* (Chicago: University of Chicago Press, 1999), esp. 1–12.

79 Translated by Reimer in "Ali Mubarak's Description of al-Azhar," 61.
80 See Dykstra, "A Biographical Study," chapter 7, 550ff., citing Mubarak's article, "Sharh al-hadith al-nabawi: ihrith li-dunyaka ka'annaka ta'ish abadan wa i'mal li-akhiratika ka'annaka tamut ghaddan," in *al-Azhar* 4, no. 10 (May 1891): 309–15. Dykstra discusses this article of Mubarak's at some length in his chapter.
81 Nayanjot Lahiri, "Destruction or Conservation? Some Aspects of Monument Policy in British India (1899–1905)," in Robert Layton, Peter G. Stone, and Julian Thomas, eds., *Destruction and Conservation of Cultural Property* (London and New York: Routledge, 2001), 8, citing Curzon.
82 Comité de conservation des monuments de l'art arabe, *Procès-verbaux des séances* 1885 (French), p. xv; Arabic, pp. 15–16 ("al-A'mal al-daruriya li-taslih masjid yusalli fihi").

Notes to Chapter 3

1 The story is reported in two places by Thomas Metcalf: in his *Ideologies of the Raj*, The New Cambridge History of India, ed. Gordon Johnson (Cambridge: Cambridge University Press, 1995), 153–54; and his "Past and Present: Towards an Aesthetics of Colonialism," in G.H.R. Tillotson, ed., *Paradigms of Indian Architecture: Space and Time in Representation and Design* (Surrey: Curzon Press, 1998), esp. p. 24, where Metcalf cites (n. 18) "Curzon to Imperial Library, 4 and 14 April 1905, to British Agency in Cairo, 27 July 1905, to Louis Dan, 24 June 1906, and to J.P. Hewett, 24 November 1908, in Curzon Papers F111/621." I have not seen these documents myself.
2 I follow here Hasan El-Shamy's usage, in which he distinguishes between the narrative cycles that were part of 'native' editions and those part of European editions: "It would be useful to differentiate between two categories of this anthology: native, typically referred to as *Alf laylah wa laylah (Thousand Nights and a Night)*, and European, often labelled '*The Arabian* Nights.' The European being a composite of a number of native editions and other narratives not found in the native ones, thus, being more inclusive but less representative of the actual edition(s) circulating in one country (or area of domain)." See his "Oral Traditional Tales and the *Thousand Nights and a Night*: The Demographic Factor," in Morton Nøjgaard et al., eds., *The Telling of Stories: Approaches to a Traditional Craft* (Odense, Denmark: Odense University Press, 1990), 84. El-Shamy also discusses the implications of the title in the introduction to his *A Motif Index of The Thousand and One Nights* (Bloomington, IN: Indiana University Press, 2006). A brief statement with a different focus on the significance of the titles used for the European editions of the *Nights* appears in Eva Sallis, *Sheherezade through the Looking Glass: The Metamorphosis of the "Thousand and One Nights"* (Surrey: Curzon Press, 1999), 7–8. Numerous subjects on the history of the oral and written texts, as well

as a comprehensive account of all aspects of the *Nights*, are to be found in Ulrich Marzolph and Richard van Leeuwen, *The Arabian Nights Encyclopedia*, 2 vols. (Santa Barbara, CA: ABC-CLIO, 2004). A detailed discussion of the implications of folklore methodologies for the study of the *Nights* as a whole is in Hasan El-Shamy, "A Motif Index of *Alf Laylah wa Laylah*: its Relevance to the Study of Culture, Society, the Individual, and Character Transmutation," in *Journal of Arabic Literature* 36 (2005): 235–68.

3 For a different approach, see Derek Gregory, "Performing Cairo: Orientalism and the City of the Arabian Nights," in Nezar AlSayyad, Irene A. Bierman, and Nasser Rabbat, eds., *Making Cairo Medieval* (Lanham, MD: Lexington Books, 2005), 69–93.

4 Irene A. Bierman, "Urban Memory and the Preservation of Monuments," in Jere L. Bacharach, ed., *The Restoration and Conservation of Islamic Monuments in Cairo* (Cairo: The American University in Cairo Press, 1995), discusses the use of old forms (for example, the use of the façade of al-Aqmar on the Coptic Museum) "to fabricate a Cairene past and make linkages to it," p. 8.

5 Muhsin Mahdi, *Kitab alf layla wa-layla min usuliha al-'arabiya al-ula*, 3 vols. (Leiden: E.J. Brill, 1995). The three-volume set includes his critical edition of the Middle Arabic text, accompanied by an introduction and a volume of critical apparatus that reconstructs the complete *stemma* (all in Arabic). Mahdi also published a one-volume English version of his critical introduction and apparatus under the title, *The Thousand and One Nights* (Leiden: E.J. Brill, 1995). This approach has been described as "critical philology" by Kamran Rastegar in "The Changing Value of *Alf Laylah wa Laylah* for Nineteenth-Century Arabic, Persian, and English readerships," *Journal of Arabic Literature* 36 (2005): 285ff.

6 For a full discussion, see Aboubakr Chraïbi, "Galland's 'Ali Baba' and Other Arabic Versions" and, particularly, Sylvette Larzul, "Further Considerations on Galland's *Mille et une Nuits*: A Study of the Tales Told by Hanna," both in *Marvels & Tales: Journal of Fairy-Tale Studies* 18, no. 2 (2004): 159–69 and 257–71, respectively.

7 On the nineteenth-century editions and critical scrutiny of them, see Mahdi, *Thousand and One Nights*, 87–126.

8 Larzul notes the employment of terms from seventeenth-century decorative arts and the descriptions of processions in the Aladdin stories that are reminiscent of the Ottoman sultan's processions, 266. She also notes conventions of description that do not correspond to Arabic canons, especially the use of abstract expressions rather than detailed descriptions.

9 Cited in Robert Irwin, *The Arabian Nights: A Companion* (London: Allen Lane, 1994), 17.

10 Ibid., 18.

11 See Rastegar, "Changing Value" and Mahdi, *Thousand and One Nights*.

12 Mahdi, *Thousand and One Nights*, lays this out fully, 89ff.

13 See Metcalf, *Ideologies* and Peter van der Veer, *Imperial Encounters: Religion and Modernity in India and Britain* (Princeton: Princeton University Press, 2001).
14 For the complex history of these editions and their particular linguistic characteristics, see Mahdi's meticulous and comprehensive account in *Thousand and One Nights*, chapter 3.
15 See Mahdi, *Thousand and One Nights* and van der Veer, *Imperial Encounters.*
16 Mahdi, *Thousand and One Nights*, 109.
17 No manuscript has ever, in fact, been identified. Mahdi, *Thousand and One Nights*, 103.
18 This is volume one of Mahdi's *Kitab alf layla wa layla.*
19 S.D. Goitein, "The Oldest Documentary Evidence for the Title *Alf laila wa-laila*," in *Journal of the American Oriental Society* 78 (1958): 301–302. Many stories that were popular in the Abbasid period were set at the court of Harun al-Rashid, and many of the popular stories of that era dealt with the amatory themes typical also of the *Nights.*
20 Husain Haddawy, trans., introduction to *The Arabian Nights = Alf laylah wa-laylah* (New York: Norton, 1990).
21 Ibid., xii.
22 Ibid., xiii.
23 Rastegar, "Changing Value," 273 and 282ff.; Mahdi, *Thousand and One Nights.*
24 This very important issue of dissociating the spread of book culture from the introduction of printing has been discussed fully by Nelly Hanna, *In Praise of Books: A Cultural History of Cairo's Middle Class, Sixteenth to the Eighteenth Century* (Syracuse: Syracuse University Press, 2003), chapter. 4.
25 Ibid., 83.
26 Ibid., 86–87.
27 Ibid., 89. For the pre-modern history of paper in the lands of Islam, see Jonathan Bloom, *Paper before Print: The History and Impact of Paper in the Islamic World* (New Haven: Yale University Press, 2001).
28 John Lewis Burckhardt's *Arabic Proverbs, or, The Manners and Customs of the Modern Egyptians: Illustrated from their Proverbial Sayings Current at Cairo* (London: John Murray, 1830), therefore, merits more serious consideration by scholars of the nineteenth century, whose focus on Lane's *Modern Egyptians* has turned their attention away from equally profitable and important sources for our knowledge of early nineteenth-century Egyptian culture. Burckhardt's translation may reflect both a European's sense of what was important and the widespread availability of proverb collections in Arabic at the time.
29 Hanna, *In Praise of Books*, 133.
30 Ibid., 133.
31 Ibid., 133ff. For a discussion of the manuscript, its author, and contents, see Elisabeth Zack, "Yusuf al-Maghribi's Egyptian-Arabic Word List. A Unique Manuscript in the St. Petersburg State University Library," *Manuscripta Orientalia: International Journal for Oriental Manuscript Research* 7, no. 3 (2001): 46–49. See also Ibn Abi al-Surur (d. 1676–77), *al-Muqtadab fi-ma wafaqa lughat*

ahl Misr min lughat al-'Arab, ed. Hisham 'Abd al-'Aziz et al. (Cairo: Akadimiyat al-Funun, 2006). Ibn Abi al-Surur's work is based on Yusuf al-Maghribi's word list.

32 Hanna, *In Praise of Books*, 134–35.

33 Ibid., 135.

34 Mahdi, *Thousand and One Nights*, 1.

35 The work of folklorists and scholars engaged in "critical philology" is central to a more complex understanding of the question of "authenticity" with respect to the *Nights*. See Rastegar, "Changing Value," and El-Shamy, "Oral Traditional Tales."

36 Sallis, *Sheherazade*, 73.

37 Lane was not the first to consider the *Nights* as an ethnographic text. Henry Weber was an early exponent of the idea of the *Nights* as "conveying in general a true and striking picture of the manners and customs prevalent amongst . . . the orientals (Henry Weber and François Pétis de La Croix, *Tales of the East, Comprising the Most Popular Romances of Oriental Origin: And the Best Imitations by European Authors* [Edinburgh: J. Ballantyne and Co., 1812]), cited in Rastegar, "Changing Value," 274.

38 Edward William Lane, in his preface to the first edition of his *An Account of the Manners and Customs of the Modern Egyptians*, which appears also in the standard fifth edition, xiv, n. 2.

39 Edward William Lane and Stanley Lane-Poole, *Arabian Society in the Middle Ages; Studies from the Thousand and One Nights* (London: Chatto and Windus, 1883).

40 There is a vast literature on travel and travelers to Egypt. Two particularly rewarding discussions are in Donald M. Reid, *Whose Pharaohs? Archaeology, Museums, and Egyptian National Identity from Napoleon to World War I* (Berkeley: University of California Press, 2002) (for discussions of Egyptomania and Egyptology) and Paul Starkey and Janet Starkey, eds., *Travellers in Egypt* (London and New York: I.B. Tauris, 1998).

41 On the use of dynastic labeling, rather than other systems of classification, in Islamic architecture, see Doris Behrens-Abouseif, "The 'Abd al-Rahman Katkhuda Style in 18th Century Cairo," *Annales Islamologiques* 26 (1992): 118–19.

42 Robert Ilbert, *Héliopolis: le Caire, 1905–1922: genèse d'une ville* (Paris: Éditions du Centre National de la Recherche Scientifique, 1981).

43 Is this perhaps one of the mosque lamps that Curzon saw on his trip to Cairo?

44 See Chraïbi, "Galland's 'Ali Baba'" and Larzul, "Further Considerations." The possible folklore origins of some of Galland's material was already raised in the nineteenth century, see Henry Charles Coote, "Folk-Lore the Source of Some of M. Galland's Tales," *The Folk-Lore Record* 3, no. 2 (1880): 178–91. On this issue in general, see El-Shamy, "Oral Traditional Tales," 63–117; Hasan El-Shamy, "The Oral Connections of the *Arabian Nights*," in Marzolph and van Leeuwen, *Arabian Nights Encyclopedia*, 1:9–12.

45 "The Orientalisation of Galland's Arabian Nights," *The Academy* 30 (1886): 277.

46 On illustrated editions of the *Nights*, see Terry Reece Hackford, "Fantastic Visions: Illustration of the *Arabian Nights*," in *The Aesthetics of Fantasy Literature and Art*, ed. Roger C. Schlobin (Notre Dame, IN: University of Notre Dame Press, 1982), 143–75; Percy Muir, *Victorian Illustrated Books* (New York: Praeger Publishers, 1971), 1–3.

47 Muir, *Victorian Illustrated Books*, 5–6.

48 Ibid., 6.

49 Ibid., 4. Recent studies on the illustrated editions of the *Nights* include Kazue Kobayashi, "The Evolution of the *Arabian Nights* Illustrations: An Art Historical Review" and Akiko Motoyoshi Sumi and Claus Clüver, "Body, Voice and Gaze: Text and Illustration in the Frame Story of the *Thousand and One Nights*," both in Yuriko Yamanaka and Tetsuo Nishio, eds., *The Arabian Nights and Orientalism: Perspectives from East and West* (London: I.B. Tauris, 2006), 171–93 and 194–218, respectively.

50 See Richard Francis Burton, *The Book of the Thousand Nights and a Night*, Illustrated Library Edition, 1 (London: H.S. Nichols, 1897), xxxii.

51 Douglas Sladen, *Oriental Cairo: The City of the "Arabian Nights"* (London: Hurst and Blackett, 1911), facing p. 1.

52 R.E. Colston, "Modern Egypt and Its People," *Journal of the American Geographical Society of New York* 13 (1881): 133–64.

53 John Gardner Wilkinson, *A Handbook for Travellers in Egypt* (London: John Murray, 1867), 112–13, "Many of the private carriages are curiosities. They might have come from some European museum, which had preserved them unchanged for a century or two, and had taken advantage of the new want in Cairo, and of the inexperience of the purchasers, to sell off all the duplicates that could be spared." This observation is absent from the 1847 edition, indicating the rapid introduction of large numbers of carriages in the intervening twenty years. By 1888, carriages had clearly become commonplace, and Murray's seventh edition (p. 157) said merely, "Carriages now abound in Cairo . . . ."

54 The special position of the Sira of the Banu Hilal within Egyptian culture was recognized recently by its inclusion on UNESCO's Masterpieces of Intangible Cultural Heritage proclamation for the year 2003. For an explanation of the Intangible Cultural Heritage program, see http://portal.unesco.org/culture/en/ev.php-URL_ID=2225&URL_DO=DO_TOPIC&URL_SECTION=201.html (accessed 14 March 2007). "The Al-Sirah al-Hilaliyyah Epic" is described at http://www.unesco.org/culture/ich/index.php?cp=EG (accessed 14 March 2007). The Egyptian folklorist Ahmed Morsi, the primary author of the nomination, noted in an article in *Al-Ahram Weekly* (9–15 September 2004), that "*The One Thousand Nights and a Night*, better known as *The Arabian Nights*, only became widely known after it was translated into French and English . . . . This is the first time that we, as Arabs, have taken the initiative in proposing an example of

our own folk culture for appraisal by an international organisation." http://weekly.ahram.org.eg/2004/707/he1.htm (accessed 14 March 2007).

55 Ami Ayalon, *The Press in the Arab Middle East: A History* (New York: Oxford University Press, 1995), 14–15. Rastegar, "Changing Value," discusses a series of debates in the Egyptian periodical *al-Hilal* appearing between 1894–1901 on the question of the origins of the *Nights* and the proper way to classify its tales, 280–81.

56 'Abd al-Rahman Katkhuda was a prolific builder. His constructions are well documented: Philipp Speiser, "Das Brunnenhaus des 'Abd-ar-Rahman Kathuda," in Philipp Speiser, *Die Geschichte der Erhaltung arabischer Baudenkmäler in Ägypten*, 112–38 (Heidelberg: Heidelberger Orientverlag, 2001); André Raymond, "Les constructions de l'émir 'Abd al-Rahman Katkhuda au Caire," *Annales Islamologiques* 11 (1972): 235–51; Doris Behrens-Abouseif, "The 'Abd al-Rahman Katkhuda style," 117–26; Muhammad Afifi and André Raymond, "La fontaine de 'Abd al-Rahman Katkhuda, à Bayn al-Qasrayn, dans la waqfiyya 941 du ministère des waqfs au Caire," in Speiser, *Die Geschichte*, 205–12; Muhammad Abu al-'Amayim, *Athar al-Qahira al-islamiya fi-l-'asr al-'uthmani*, vol. 1 (Istanbul: Markaz al-Abhath li-l Tarikh wa-l-Funun wa-l-Thaqafa al-Islamiya bi-Istanbul, 2003), 157–60 (with photographs, elevations, and plans before and after restoration).

57 Sladen, *Oriental Cairo*, facing p. 4.

58 Max Herz Bey, *A Descriptive Catalogue of the Objects Exhibited in the National Museum of Arab Art, Preceded by a Historical Sketch of the Architecture and Industrial Arts of the Arabs in Egypt*, trans. G. Foster Smith (Cairo: National Printing Department, 1907), liv–lv.

59 Doris Behrens-Abouseif, *Egypt's Adjustment to Ottoman Rule: Institutions, Waqf and Architecture in Cairo, 16th and 17th centuries* (Leiden: E.J. Brill, 1994), 119.

60 Nicholas Warner, *The Monuments of Historic Cairo: A Map and Descriptive Catalogue* (Cairo: The American University in Cairo Press, 2005), 43–44 (see esp. fig. 33 for before-and-after photographs of the mosque of Yusuf Agha al-Hin); for the 1900 Paris Exposition Universelle reproduction of the *sabil-kuttab*, see Zeynep Çelik, *Displaying the Orient: The Architecture of Islam at Nineteenth-Century World's Fairs* (Berkeley and Los Angeles: University of California Press, 1992), 118 (fig. 77).

61 Robert Ilbert and Mercedes Volait, "Neo-Arabic Renaissance in Egypt, 1870–1930," in *Mimar* 13 (1984): 26–34.

62 Ahmet Ersoy, "On the Sources of the 'Ottoman Renaissance': Architectural Revival and its Discourse during the Abdulaziz Era (1861–1876)" (PhD diss., Harvard University, 2000), 308ff.

63 Thomas R. Metcalf, *An Imperial Vision: Indian Architecture and Britain's Raj* (Berkeley and Los Angeles: University of California Press, 1989), esp. ch. 3.

64 Behrens-Abouseif, *Egypt's Adjustment*, 161ff.

65 Ibid., 161–63.
66 See Michael Winter, *Society and Religion in Early Ottoman Egypt: Studies in the Writings of 'Abd al-Wahhab al-Sharani* (New Brunswick, NJ: Transaction Books, 1982), 176–79, citing Ibn Iyas.
67 Thomas Philipp and Moshe Perlmann, eds., *Abd al-Rahman al-Jabarti's History of Egypt, 'Aja'ib al-athar fi'l-tarajim wa'l-akhbar* (Stuttgart: Franz Steiner Verlag, 1994), 3:291–93 [=Bulaq edition, 3:190–91].
68 Ibrahim Muhawi, "Arabian Nights and Questions of Authorship," *Journal of Arabic Literature* 36 (2005): 323.

Notes to Chapter 4

1 It has continued, albeit in a somewhat informal fashion, for more than two decades, and it has become increasingly vitriolic as the international conservation community, with the authority of the World Heritage List behind it, has undertaken other projects. There has been no formal, sustained, and detailed critique of the Bohra project in writing. But criticism of Bohra restoration methods and results has become a part of the culture of conservation conversation in Cairo.
2 Peter van der Veer, *Imperial Encounters: Religion and Modernity in India and Britain* (Princeton: Princeton University Press, 2001), 30.
3 The Society for the Preservation of the Architectural Resources of Egypt (SPARE), Newsletter, no. 1 (November 1979): 1 (consulted at the library of the American Research Center in Egypt).
4 "Qubbat qurqumas lam tuhdam wa-innama nuqilat bi-kamiliha ila jabbanat-il-mamalik," *al-Ahram*, 10 November 1980, 6.
5 See, for example, Nasser Rabbat, "Restoration Projects in Islamic Cairo Critiqued," *Medina* 13 (2000): 48–51. The article has an English and an Arabic section. The English critique states, "The worst examples are the complete restorations, executed without any research or documentation, of four of the most important Fatimid monuments of Cairo. . . . These historically unfounded restorations were sponsored and carried out by members of the Buhara Isma'ili sect, with the apparent approval of the Egyptian authorities." The Arabic version, which is more elaborate in all respects, omits the statement about the Egyptian authorities, but notes disapprovingly that the Bohras have restored the monuments as religious centers commemorating an imaginary golden age.
6 For a history of conservation philosophy and practice, see Jukka Jokilehto, *A History of Architectural Conservation* (Oxford: Butterworth-Heinemann, 1999). The text of the Venice charter is available at http://www.international.icomos.org/charters/venice_e.pdf (accessed 14 March 2007). For a full discussion of the Venice Charter, its history, and its relationship to conservation ideology and practice, see the Proceedings of the Fortieth Anniversary Conference at http://www.international.icomos.org/venicecharter2004/index.html (accessed 14 March 2007).

7 Jim Antoniou, *The Conservation of the Old City of Cairo* (London: UNESCO, 1979–80), Appendix A, "Nomination Submitted for Inscription of Islamic Cairo on World Heritage List," Ref. No. RP/PP/1979–1980/47.6/05 (consulted at the ICCROM library in Rome, shelf no. Viii e 737/1–2).

8 Ibid., Appendix A, "Nomination."

9 There are now emerging some serious discussions and critiques of the Comité's practices and core assumptions. See Alaa El-Din Elwi El-Habashi and Nicholas Warner, "Recording the Monuments of Cairo: An Introduction and Overview," *Annales Islamologiques* 32 (1998): 81–99; Alaa El-Din Elwi El-Habashi, "*Athar* to Monuments: The Intervention of the *Comité de conservation des monuments de l'art arabe*" (PhD diss., University of Pennsylvania, 2001); Nairy Heraz Karkour Hampikian, "Complex of al-Salihiyya: Transformations through Time and a Proposal for the Future" (PhD diss., University of California, Los Angeles, 1997).

10 Nicholas Warner, *Monuments of Historic Cairo: A Map and Descriptive Catalogue* (Cairo: The American University in Cairo Press, 2005).

11 Doris Behrens-Abouseif, *Islamic Architecture in Cairo: An Introduction* (Leiden: E.J. Brill, 1989).

12 See, for example, Mustafa 'Abd Allah Shaykhuh, *al-Athar al-islamiya fi Misr min al-fath al-'arabi hatta nihayat al-'asr al-ayyubi* (Cairo: Maktabat al-Nahda al-Misriya, 1992); Dr. 'Abd al-Rahman Zaki, *al-Qahira: tarikhuha wa-atharuha* (Cairo: al-Dar al-Misriya li-l-Ta'lif wa-l-Tarjama, 1966); Dr. Abu'l-Hamd Mahmud Farghali, *al-Dalil al-mujiz li-ahamm al-athar al-islamiya wa-l-qibtiya* (Cairo: al-Dar al-Misriya al-Lubnaniya, 1996).

13 K.A.C. Creswell, *The Muslim Architecture of Egypt*, 2 vols. (Oxford: Clarendon Press, 1952–59).

14 See, for example, the EAO's series *al-Qahira al-islamiya* (*Islamic Cairo*), in Arabic and English, which documents contemporary Egyptian restorations: *al-Mashhad al-husayni* (1985); *Masajid maydan Salah al-Din* (1986); *Qasr al-amir bashtak, sabil wa-kuttab 'Abd al-Rahman Katkhuda* (n.d.); *Jami' 'Amr ibn al-'As* (1986). One notable exception is an article by Mohamed Abd el-Hady, "Re-restoration of the Ancient Restorations to Historical Buildings in Cairo," in *Restauration, dé-restauration, re-restauration . . . Paris, 5, 6 et 7 octobre 1995* (Paris: Association des restaurateurs d'art et d'archéologie de formation universitaire, 1995), 55–60 and esp. p. 56, who cautions: "Renovations of historical buildings in Cairo which date back to the nineteenth century were carried out using quite different techniques [from those of contemporary restorations] . . . [i]n fact, the personality of the restorer or architect was impressed upon the monuments, and for this reason some of the worst architectural damage to historical buildings was caused by the Faculty of Restoration Works during this period." The historiography is changing, however, as evident in El-Habashi, "*Athar* to Monuments."

15 Irene A. Bierman, "Envisioning the 'Walled' City of Cairo," unpublished paper (November 1997); Bierman, "Urban Memory and the Preservation of Monuments," in Jere L. Bacharach, ed., *The Restoration and Conservation of Islamic Monuments in Cairo* (Cairo: The American University in Cairo Press, 1995), 1–12; Hossam M. Mahdy, "Travellers, Colonisers and Conservatoinists," in Paul Starkey and Janet Starkey, eds., *Travellers in Egypt* (London and New York: I.B. Tauris, 1998), 157–67.

16 Nairy Heraz Karkour Hampikian, "Re-birth of 'Historical Cairo' and Birth of Heliopolis" (paper delivered at the symposium "An 'Authentic' City for a Modern World: Cairo in the Nineteenth Century," Berkeley, California, 29 October 1999).

17 The notes on the authors describe Parker as a career Foreign Service Office who was Political Counselor at the American Embassy in Cairo from 1965–67 and Sabin as the holder of a M.A. in Arabic Studies from the American University in Beirut who spent a number of years in the Middle East as the wife of a Foreign Service Officer.

18 See n. 8, above.

19 See Florence Groff, *Guide to Cairo and Environs: Catalogues to the Museums of Egyptian Antiquities at Gizeh and Arab Antiquities at the Mosque of El Hakim* (Cairo: Lavados, 1893), esp. 36–37.

20 The tomb is now located in the Northern Cemetery; see Richard Parker, Robin Sabin, and Caroline Williams, *Islamic Monuments in Cairo: A Practical Guide*, 3rd ed. (Cairo: The American University in Cairo Press, 1985), 257–58.

21 John Gardner Wilkinson, *Hand-book for Travellers in Egypt* (London: John Murray, 1847), 134.

22 Groff, *Guide to Cairo*, 79–82.

23 See Creswell, *Muslim Architecture of Egypt*, 1:68. See also M. Edmond Pauty, "La défense de l'ancienne ville du Caire et de ses monuments: Urbanisme et archéologie," *Bulletin de l'Institut Français d'archéologie orientale du Caire* 31 (1931): 135–76, where the tomb is identified as "T. Badr al-Gamali."

24 The tomb's current location is in the Northern Cemetery, next to the tomb of Ganibak (1427). It is listed monument No. 170. See Parker, Sabin, and Williams, *Islamic Monuments in Cairo*, 257–58 and Map 11, p. 332.

25 *Al-Ahram*, 10 November 1980, p. 6; *The Egyptian Gazette*, 25 November 1980.

26 Creswell, *Muslim Architecture of Egypt*, 1:276–88.

27 On the decoration of al-Hakim and al-Aqmar mosques, see Irene Bierman, *Writing Signs: The Fatimid Public Text* (Berkeley: University of California Press, 1998); Samuel Flury, *Die Ornamente der Hakim- und Ashar-Moschee: Materialien zur Geschichte der älteren Kunst des Islam* (Heidelberg: Carl Winters, 1912); Caroline Williams, "The Cult of 'Alid Saints in the Fatimid Monuments of Cairo," *Muqarnas* 1 (1983): 37–52; 3 (1985): 39–60.

28 See Paula Sanders, "Bohra Architecture and the Restoration of Fatimid Culture," in Marianne Barrucand, ed., *L'Égypte fatimide: Son art et son*

histoire. Actes du colloque organisé à Paris, le 28–30 mai 1998 (Paris: Presses de l'Université de Paris-Sorbonne, 1999), 159–65. The relationship between textual authority and architecture is explored fully in David Simonowitz, "On the Cutting Edges of *Dhu'l-Fiqar*: Authority and the Discourse of Architecture in the Musta'li-Tayyibi and Nizari Communities" (PhD diss., University of California, Los Angeles, 2004).

29 "The main feature of the elevation of the Masjid is the use of 'Fatemi' arches the use of which has a modular repitative *[sic]* character. These repeated arches on all four sides and the Masjid along with concret *[sic]* mushroom type columns give the Masjid elevation a unique character. The arches are kept very simple and plain in design." The section is entitled "Heritage of Fatemi Architecture," in *Masjid Dubai* (n.p., n.d.), unpaginated. There are many other examples of the arch as the defining element of neo-Fatimid architecture, whether as a feature of the structure of a building otherwise part of a different tradition (as in the case of the Bohra University in Surat, Jameatu-Sayfiyah) or as part of decorative elements, such as the ornamental chandeliers at the new mosque in Dubai: "The chandeliers were carefully chosen and designed to strike the visitors with its Fatemi features. They were so designed incorporating [the] Fatemi arch and the main chandellier which is 3.5m diameter by 5.5m height located in the center to be appropriate to look at from any angle or levels of the Masjid. All chandelliers were manufactured in Italy and have their frame work made out of prue *[sic]* brass, gold plated in 24K gold and crystals used are 'strauss' Australian made, machine cut and machine polished." *Masjid Dubai.*

30 Creswell, *Muslim Architecture of Egypt*, 1:86.

31 See Bierman, *Writing Signs*, 93 and 178, and additional references cited there.

32 *A Historic Dedication: Fulfillment of Spiritual and Religious Aspirations* (Bombay: Department of Satistics and Information, 1993).

33 I have seen the following pamphlets, all published by the Department of Statistics and Information, Dawat-E-Hadiyah in Bombay: *A Golden Chapter in Islamic Economy* (December 1985); *From Strength to Strength* (June 1986); *The Fatimi Tradition* (March 1988); *In The Footsteps of a Glorious Tradition* (November 1990); *Day of Thanksgiving* (January 1992); *Heir to a Great Spiritual Heritage* (January 1992); *A Historic Visit to Bangladesh* (June 1992); *Historic Visit to the Republic of Madagascar* (August, 1992); *Faith of the Dawoodi Bohras* (October 1992); *A Historic Dedication: Fulfillment of Spiritual and Religious Aspirations* (June 1993); *The Mombasa Experience: 1993 A.D.* (September 1993); *Iftitah at Shaam* (October 1993); *Compendium of Unalloyed Reverence and Devotion* (January 1994); *A Chronicle of the Mausoleum, the Heritage, and the Dedication* (June 1994); *Karbala* (March 1995); *Edifice of Faith* (December 1995). I am very grateful to Shaykh Nooreddin Yamani, formerly of Houston, Texas, who so generously made these and other printed matrials available to me. See also the books written by Ja'far us Sadiq M. Saifuddin, grandson of the

52nd *da'i* Syedna Muhammad Burhanuddin: *al-Aqmar: A Living Testimony to the Fatemiyeen* (London: Graphico, 2000) and *al-Juyushi: A Vision of the Fatemiyeen* (London: Graphico, 2002).

34 Zoyab A. Kadi, *Sidhpur and its Dawoodi Bohra Houses* (New Delhi: Minerva Press, 2000), xiii. Kadi is a Dawoodi Bohra and an architect who wrote his volume in order to draw attention to the complex tradition of vernacular architecture in his hometown of Sidhpur and to demonstrate the complex fusion of indigenous Gujerati, Islamic, and other 'foreign' styles in the construction of a distinctive architectural tradition. Most of this section relies heavily on his visual material and his architectural analysis. While the Dawoodi Bohra hierarchy expounds in print on its religious architecture, it has not (to my knowledge) discussed the community's domestic architecture.

35 Kadi, *Sidhpur*, *passim*.

36 Ibid., 25.

37 Ibid., 35.

38 Indeed, Kadi accounts for much of the character of the Bohra community, its city plans, and its domestic architecture, by pointing to the community's extensive commercial contacts with the 'outside' world owing to its long history of trade: see ibid., 71ff.

39 Ibid., 69–71ff.

40 Ibid., 76.

41 Ibid., 76.

42 Ibid., 100.

43 Ibid., 195.

44 SPARE, Newsletter 3, 1981.

45 See "A Celebration of Piety," http://archive.mumineen.org/essays/piety.html (accessed 14 March 2007).

46 See William Lyster, "The Battle for Restoration," *Cairo Today*, June 1988, 78–80.

47 Donald Preziosi, "Containing the Orient: Museology and Urbanism in Nineteenth Century Cairo" (paper delivered at the Annual Conference of the Universities Art History Association of Canada, Vancouver, British Columbia, 8 November 1997).

48 See Nelson Goodman, *How Classification Works: Nelson Goodman among the Social Sciences*, Mary Douglas and David Hull, eds. (Edinburgh: Edinburgh University Press, 1992).

49 Antoniou, *Conservation of the Old City of Cairo*, 56.

50 *The Egyptian Gazette*, 25 November 1980; see also Lyster, "Battle for Restoration."

51 UNESCO, *United Nations Educational, Scientific and Cultural Organization Convention Concerning the Protection of the World Cultural and Natural Heritage, World Heritage Committee, Third Session, Cairo and Luxor, 22–26 October 1979. Report of the Rapporteur on the Third Session of the World*

Heritage Committee, November 1979, paragraph 35.iv. 79/CONF.003/13. Full text available online at http://www.unesco.org/whc/archive/rep-com79.htm (accessed 14 March 2007).

52 UNESCO, *Operational Guidelines for the Implementation of the World Heritage Convention* (Revision adopted by the World Heritage Committee at its 22th Session, December 1998), paragraph 24. WHC.99/2, March 1999. This is echoed in paragraph 29. Full text available online at http://whc.unesco.org/archive/opguide99.pdf (accessed 14 March 2007). Paragraph 24 (b) (i) further states that the World Heritage Committee deems "that reconstruction is only acceptable if it is carried out on the basis of complete and detailed documentation on the original and to no extent on conjecture." Full documentation of the history of the operational guidelines is available through links at http://whc.unesco.org/en/guidelineshistorical (accessed 14 March 2007). The full texts of charters and international standards for historic preservation are available at http://www.international.icomos.org/e_charte.htm (accessed 14 March 2007).

53 See, for example, paragraph I.A.9 of the *Operational Guidelines*. "The fundamental principle stipulated in the Convention is that properties nominated must be of outstanding universal value and the properties nominated therefore should be carefully selected. The criteria and conditions of authenticity or integrity against which the Committee will evaluate properties are set out in paragraphs 24 and 44 below." For a discussion of universal value and authenticity in modern conservation usage, see Jokilehto, *History of Architectural Conservation*, esp. chapter 10. For a discussion of the tension between the ideas of universal value and cultural heritage, see Henry Cleere, "The Uneasy Bedfellows: Universality and Cultural Heritage," in Robert Layton et al., *Destruction and Conservation of Cultural Property* (London: Routledge, 2001), 22–29.

54 UNESCO, *World Heritage Committee, Third Session, Cairo and Luxor, 22–26 October 1979*, 35.v.

55 The different versions of the cultural heritage criteria are available in a comparative table, "Changes to the World Heritage Cultural Heritage Criteria as presented in the *Operational Guidelines for the Implementation of the World Heritage Convention, 1978–1998*," on the World Heritage Convention website at http://whc.unesco.org/c-criteria-changes.htm (accessed 14 March 2007).

56 UNESCO, *Operational Guidelines* (1999), General Principles I.A.6.ii.

57 See *The Athens Charter for the Restoration of Historic Monuments, Adopted at the First International Congress of Architects and Technicians of Historic Monuments, Athens 1931*. The Athens Charter, a core text for the World Heritage Convention, is available online at http://www.icomos.org/docs/athens_charter.html (accessed 14 March 2007).

58 The relation of the conservation of Cairo to Egyptian state nationalism, challenges to Egyptian state authority, and debates among Egyptian

communities over such matters, is an important question that still needs to be addressed.

59 See full text at http://www.international.icomos.org/naradoc_eng.htm (accessed 14 March 2007). For a full discussion of the different meanings of authenticity among conservationists historically, see Jokilehto, *History of Architectural Conservation*, *passim.*

60 See his "Past and Present: Towards an Aesthetics of Colonialism," in G.H.R. Tillotson, ed., *Paradigms of Indian Architecture: Space and Time in Representation and Design* (Surrey: Curzon Press, 1998).

61 It should be noted that these are two different Muhammad 'Alis. On clock-towers in nineteenth-century Ottoman architecture elsewhere as markers of modernity, see Selim Deringil, *The Well-Protected Domains: Ideology and the Legitimation of Power in the Ottoman Empire, 1876–1909* (London: I.B. Tauris, 1999), 14ff. and 31.

Select Bibliography

'Abd el-Hady, Mohamed. "Re-restoration of the Ancient Restorations to Historical Buildings in Cairo." In *Restauration, dé-restauration, re-restauration . . . Paris, 5, 6, 7 octobre 1995*, 55–60. Paris: Association des restaurateurs d'art et d'archéologie de formation universitaire, 1995.

'Abduh, Muhammad. *The Theology of Unity*. Translated by Ishaq Musa'ad and Kenneth Cragg. London: George Allen Unwin Ltd, 1966.

Abdul Husain, Mian Bhai Mulla. *Gulzare Daudi for the Bohras of India: A Short Note on the Bohras of India, their 21 Imams & 51 Dais, with their Customs and Tenets*. Surat: Progressive Publication, 1977 [1920].

Abu al-'Amayim, Muhammad and Ekmeleddin Ihsanoglu. *Athar al-Qahira al-islamiya fi-l-'asr al-'uthmani*. Vol. 1. Istanbul: Markaz al-Abhath li-l-Tarikh wa-l-Funun wa-l-Thaqafa al-Islamiya bi-Istanbul, 2003.

Abu Lughod, Janet. *Cairo: 1001 Years of the City Victorious*. Princeton: Princeton University Press, 1971.

Abu-Zahra, Nadia. *The Pure and the Powerful: Studies in Contemporary Muslim Society*. Reading, UK: Ithaca Press, 1997.

Adams, Charles C. *Islam and Modernism in Egypt: A Study of the Modern Reform Movement Inaugurated by Muhammad 'Abduh*. Oxford: Oxford University Press, 1933.

Ahmad, Mahmud. *Dalil mujiz li-ashhar al-athar al-'arabiya bi-l-Qahira*. Cairo: al-Matba'a al-Amiriya bi-Bulaq, 1938.

Ahmed, Jamal Mohammed. *The Intellectual Origins of Egyptian Nationalism*. London: Oxford University Press, 1968.

Alleaume, Ghislaine. "Politiques urbaines et contrôle de l'entreprise: une loi inédite de 'Ali Mubarak sur les corporations du bâtiment." *Annales Islamologiques* 21 (1985): 147–88.

AlSayyad, Nezar, Irene A. Bierman, and Nasser Rabbat, eds. *Making Cairo Medieval*. Lanham, MD: Lexington Books, 2005.

Amin, Ahmad. *Zu'ama' al-islah fi-l-'asr al-hadith*. Cairo: Maktabat al-Nahda al-'Asriya, 1949.

Amin, Muhammad Muhammad. *al-Awqaf wa-l-hayat al-ijtima'iya fi-Misr, 648–923 A.H./1250–1517 A.D.* Cairo: Dar al-Nahda al-'Arabiya, 1980.

Antoniou, Jim. *The Conservation of the Old City of Cairo*. London: UNESCO, 1979–80.

'Arif, Muhammad. *al-Juz' al-rabi' min khulasat al-afkar fi fann al-mi'mar*. Bulaq: al-Matba'a al-Kubra al-Amiriya, 1902.

al-Asad, Mohammad. "The Mosque of Muhammad 'Ali in Cairo." *Muqarnas* 9 (1992): 39–55.

———. "The Mosque of al-Rifa'i in Cairo." *Muqarnas* 10 (1993): 108–24.

Ayalon, Ami. *The Press in the Arab Middle East: A History*. New York: Oxford University Press, 1995.

Bacharach, Jere L., ed. *The Restoration and Conservation of Islamic Monuments in Cairo*. Cairo: The American University in Cairo Press, 1995.

Baedeker, Karl, ed. *Egypt, Handbook for Travellers, Part 1. Lower Egypt, with the Fayûm and the Peninsula of Sinai [Baedeker's Lower Egypt]*. Leipsic: Karl Baedeker, 1878.

———. *Egypt, Handbook for Travellers, Part 1. Lower Egypt, with the Fayûm and the Peninsula of Sinai [Baedeker's Lower Egypt]*. 2nd ed. Leipsic: Karl Baedeker, 1885.

———. *Egypt, Handbook for Travellers, Part 1. Lower Egypt and the Peninsula of Sinai [Baedeker's Lower Egypt]*. 3rd ed. Leipsic: Karl Baedeker, 1895.

———. *Egypt, Handbook for Travellers [Baedeker's Egypt]*. 4th ed. Leipsic: Karl Baedeker, 1898.

———. *Egypt, Handbook for Travellers [Baedeker's Egypt]*. 5th ed. Leipsic: Karl Baedeker, 1902.

———. *Egypt and the Sudan, Handbook for Travellers [Baedeker's Egypt]*. 6th ed. Leipzig: Karl Baedeker, 1908.

———. *Egypt and the Sudan, Handbook for Travellers [Baedeker's Egypt]*. 7th ed. Leipzig: Karl Baedeker, 1914.

———. *Egypt and the Sudan, Handbook for Travellers [Baedeker's Egypt]*. 8th ed. Leipzig: Karl Baedeker, 1929.

Baer, Gabriel. "Egyptian Attitudes towards Turks and Ottomans in the 17th and 18th centuries," *Prilozi za orijentalnu filologiju = Revue de philologie orientale* 30 (1980): 25–34.

———. "Waqf Reform." In *Studies in the Social History of Modern Egypt*, 79–62. Chicago and London: University of Chicago Press, 1969.

Behrens-Abouseif, Doris. *Egypt's Adjustment to Ottoman Rule: Institutions, Waqf and Architecture in Cairo, 16th and 17th centuries*. Leiden: E.J. Brill, 1994.

———. *Islamic Architecture in Cairo: An Introduction*. Leiden: E.J. Brill, 1989.

———, ed. *The Cairo Heritage: Essays in Honor of Laila Ali Ibrahim*. Cairo: The American University in Cairo Press, 2000.

Bianca, Stefano and Philip Jodidio, eds. *Cairo: Revitalising a Historic Metropolis*. Turin: Umberto Allemandi and Co. and the Aga Khan Trust for Culture, 2004.

Biegman, Nicolaas H. *Egypt: Moulids, Saints, Sufis*. London: Kegan Paul International, 1990.

Bierman, Irene A. "Art and Architecture in the Medieval Period." In Petry, *Cambridge History of Egypt*, vol. 1, *Islamic Egypt*, 339–74.

———. "Disciplining the Eye: Perceiving Medieval Cairo." In AlSayyad et al., *Making Cairo Medieval*, 9–27.

———. "Urban Memory and the Preservation of Monuments." In Bacharach, *Restoration and Conservation*, 1–12.

———. *Writing Signs: The Fatimid Public Text*. Berkeley: University of California Press, 1998.

Bourgoin, Jules. *Les arts arabes*. Paris: Vve. A. Morel, 1873.

British Parliament. House of Commons. *Further Correspondence Respecting the Reorganization of Egypt*. 1883 [C.3696] LXXXIII.

———. *Report on the Finances, Administration, and Condition of Egypt, and the Progress of Reforms*. 1896 [C.7978] XCVII; 1897 [C.8332] CII; 1898 [C.8815] CVII; 1899 [C.9231] CXII; 1900 [Cd.95] CV; 1901 [Cd.441] XCI.

Bruant, Catherine, S. Leprun, and Mercedes Volait. "Figures de l'orientalisme en architecture." Special issue, *Révue du Monde Musulman et de la Méditeranée*, 73–74 (1996).

Burckhardt, John Lewis. *Arabic Proverbs, or, The manners and Customs of the Modern Egyptians: Illustrated from their Proverbial Sayings Current at Cairo*. London: John Murray, 1830.

Burt, N.C. *The Far East; or, Letters from Egypt, Palestine, and Other Lands of the Orient*. Cincinnati: R.W. Carroll and Company, 1868.

Çelik, Zeynep. *Displaying the Orient: Architecture of Islam at Nineteenth-Century World's Fairs*. Berkeley and Los Angeles: University of California Press, 1992.

———. *The Remaking of Istanbul: Portrait of an Ottoman City in the Nineteenth Century*. Seattle: University of Washington Press, 1986.

Chakrabarti, Dilip K. *A History of Indian Archaeology from the Beginning to 1947*. New Delhi: Munshiram Manoharial Publishers, 1988.

Chraïbi, Aboubakr. "Galland's 'Ali Baba' and other Arabic versions." *Marvels & Tales: Journal of Fairy-Tale Studies* 18, no. 2 (2004): 159–69.

Colston, R.E. "Modern Egypt and Its People," *Journal of the American Geographical Society of New York* 13 (1881): 133–64.

Comité de conservation des monuments de l'art arabe. *Exercice. Procès-verbaux des séance—rapports de la deuxième commission*. Cairo: Imprimerie Nationale, 1892–1911 [1882–1910].

Commins, David D. "*Al-Manar* and Popular Religion in Syria, 1898–1920." In Dudoignon et al., *Intellectuals in the Modern Islamic World*, 40–54.

Coote, Henry Charles. "Folk-Lore the Source of Some of M. Galland's Tales." *The Folk-Lore Record* 3, no. 2 (1880): 178–91.

Coste, Pascal. *Architecture arabe ou monuments du Kaire mesurés et dessinés de 1818 à 1826*. Paris: Firmin-Didot, 1837.

Crabbs, Jack. "Historiography and the Eighteenth-century Milieu." In *Eighteenth Century Egypt: The Arabic Manuscript Sources*, edited by Daniel Crecelius, 9–24. Claremont, CA: Regina Books, 1990.

Creswell, K.A.C. *The Muslim Architecture of Egypt*. 2 vols. Oxford: Clarendon Press, 1952–59.

Crinson, Mark. *Empire Building: Orientalism and Victorian Architecture*. London and New York: Routledge, 1996.

Cromer, Evelyn Baring, Earl of. *Modern Egypt*, 2 vols. London: Macmillan, 1908.

———. *Modern Egypt*, 2 vols. New York: Macmillan and Co., 1916.

———. *Abbas II*. London: Macmillan and Co., 1915.

Daftary, Farhad. *The Isma'ilis: Their History and Doctrines*. Cambridge: Cambridge University Press, 1990.

Daly, M.W., ed. *The Cambridge History of Egypt*. Vol. 2, *Modern Egypt, from 1517 to the End of the Twentieth Century*. Cambridge: Cambridge University Press, 1998.

Delanoue, Gilbert. *Moralistes et politiques musulmans dans l'Égypte du XIXe siècle (1798–1882)*. Vol. 2. Cairo: Institut Français d'Archéologie Orientale du Caire, 1982.

Deringil, Selim. "'They Live in a State of Nomadism and Savagery': The Late Ottoman Empire and the Post-colonial Debate." *Comparative Studies in Society and History* 45 (2003): 311–42.

———. *The Well-Protected Domains: Ideology and the Legitimation of Power in the Ottoman Empire, 1876–1909*. London: I.B. Tauris, 1999.

Di-Capua, Yoav. "The Thought and Practice of Modern Egyptian Historiography, 1890–1970." PhD diss., Princeton University, 2004.

Dudoignon, Stéphane A., Komatsu Hisao, and Kosugi Yasushi, eds. *Intellectuals in the Modern Islamic World: Transmission, Transformation, Communication*. London: Routledge, 2006.

Dykstra, Darrell. "A Biographical Study in Egyptian Modernization: 'Ali Mubarak (1823/4–1893)." 2 vols. PhD diss., University of Michigan, 1977.

Edmond, Charles. *L'Égypte à l'exposition universelle de 1867*. Paris: Dentu, 1867.

The Encyclopaedia of Islam, New Edition. Edited by H.A.R. Gibb et al. 12 vols. Leiden: E.J. Brill, 1960–2004.

Engineer, Ashgar Ali. *The Bohras*. New Delhi: Vikas Publishing House Pvt, 1980.

———. *The Muslim Communities of Gujarat*. Delhi: Ajanta Publications, 1989.

Ersoy, Ahmet. "On the Sources of the 'Ottoman Renaissance': Architectural Revival and its Discourse during the Abdulaziz Era (1861–1876)." PhD diss., Harvard University, 2000.

Evin, Ahmet, ed. *The Expanding Metropolis: Coping with the Urban Growth of Cairo*. Singapore: Concept Media and the Aga Khan Award for Architecture, 1985.

Farghali, Abu'l-Hamid Mahmud. *al-Dalil al-mujiz li-ahamm al-athar al-islamiya wa-l-qibtiya*. Cairo: al-Dar al-Misriya al-Lubnaniya, 1996.

Faroqhi, Suraiya. *Approaching Ottoman History: An Introduction to the Sources*. Cambridge: Cambridge University Press, 1999.

Flury, Samuel. *Die Ornamente der Hakim- und Ashar-Moschee: Materialien zur Geschichte der älteren Kunst des Islam*. Heidelberg: Carl Winters, 1912.

Gershoni, Israel and James P. Jankowski. *Commemorating the Nation: Collective Memory, Public Commemoration, and National Identity in Twentieth-century Egypt*. Chicago: Middle East Documentation Center [University of Chicago], 2004.

———. *Egypt, Islam, and the Arabs: The Search for Egyptian Nationhood, 1900–1930*. New York: Oxford University Press, 1987.

———. *Redefining the Egyptian Nation, 1930–1945*. Cambridge: Cambridge University Press, 1995.

Gesink, Indira Falk. "Beyond Modernisms: Opposition and Negotiation in the Azhar Reform Debate in Egypt, 1870–1911." PhD diss., Washington University, St. Louis, Missouri, 2000.

Gil, Moshe. *Documents of the Jewish Pious Foundations from the Cairo Geniza*. Leiden: E.J. Brill, 1976.

Goitein, S.D. *A Mediterranean Society: The Jewish Communities of the Arab World as Portrayed in the Documents of the Cairo Geniza*. 6

vols. Berkeley and Los Angeles: University of California Press, 1967–93.
———. "The Oldest Documentary Evidence for the Title *Alf laila wa-laila*." *Journal of the American Oriental Society* 78 (1958): 301–302.
Gregory, Derek. "Performing Cairo: Orientalism and the City of the Arabian Nights." In AlSayyad et al., *Making Cairo Medieval*, 69–93.
Groff, Florence. *Guide to Cairo and Environs: Catalogues to the Museums of Egyptian Antiquities at Gizeh and Arab Antiquities at the Mosque of el Hakim*. Cairo: Lavados, 1893.
Haarmann, Ulrich. "Arabic in Speech, Turkish in Lineage: Mamluks and their Sons in the Intellectual Life of Fourteenth-century Egypt and Syria." *Journal of Semitic Studies* 33 (1988): 81–114.
———. "Ideology and History, Identity and Alterity: The Arab image of the Turk from the Abbasids to Modern Egypt." *International Journal of Middle East Studies* 20, no. 2 (1988): 175–96.
———. "Joseph's Law—the Careers and Activities of Mamluk Descendants before the Ottoman Conquest of Egypt." In Philipp and Haarmann, *Mamluks in Egyptian Politics*, 55–84.
———. "Rather the Injustice of the Turks than the Righteousness of the Arabs—Changing *ulama* Attitudes towards Mamluk Rule in the Late Fifteenth Century." *Studia Islamica* 68 (1988): 61–77.
———. "The Sons of Mamluks as Fief-holders in Late Medieval Egypt." In *Land Tenure and Social Transformation in the Middle East*, edited by Tarif Khalidi, 141–68. Beirut: American University of Beirut, 1984.
El-Habashi, Alaa El-Din Elwi. "*Athar* to Monuments: the Intervention of the *Comité de conservation des monuments de l'art arabe*." PhD diss., University of Pennsylvania, 2001.
El-Habashi, Alaa and Nicholas Warner. "Recording the Monuments of Cairo: An Introduction and Overview." *Annales Islamologiques* 32 (1998): 81–99.
Hackford, Terry Reece. "Fantastic Visions: Illustration of the *Arabian Nights*." In *The Aesthetics of Fantasy Literature and Art*, edited by Roger C. Schlobin, 143–75. Notre Dame, IN: University of Notre Dame Press, 1982.

Haddawy, Husain, trans. *The Arabian Nights = Alf laylah wa-laylah.* New York: Norton, 1990.

Hanna, Nelly. "Administration in Egypt from Ottoman Times to the Present: An Introduction." In Hanna, *State and its Servants*, 1–16.

———. *Construction Work in Ottoman Cairo (1517–1798).* Cairo: Institut Français d'Archéologie Orientale du Caire, 1984.

———. *In Praise of Books: A Cultural History of Cairo's Middle Class, Sixteenth to the Eighteenth Century.* Syracuse: Syracuse University Press, 2003.

———., ed. *The State and its Servants: Administration in Egypt from Ottoman Times to the Present.* Cairo: The American University in Cairo Press, 1995.

Hampikian, Nairy Heraz Karkour. "Complex of al-Salihiyya: Transformations through Time and a Proposal for the Future." PhD diss., University of California, Los Angeles, 1997.

———. "Re-birth of 'Historical Cairo' and Birth of Heliopolis." Paper delivered at the Symposium "An 'Authentic' City for a Modern World: Cairo in the Nineteenth Century." Berkeley, California, 29 October 1999.

Harawi, 'Ali ibn Abi Bakr. *Guide des lieux de pèlerinage.* Translated by Janine Sourdel-Thomine. Damascus: Institut Français de Damas, 1957.

———. *A Lonely Wayfarer's Guide to Pilgrimage: 'Ali ibn Abi Bakr al-Harawi's kitab al-isharat ila ma'rifat al-ziyarat.* Translated by Josef Meri. Princeton: Darwin Press, 2004.

Hathaway, Jane. "Egypt in the Seventeenth Century." In Daly, *Cambridge History of Egypt*, vol. 2, *Modern Egypt*, 34–58.

———. "'Mamluk Households' and 'Mamluk Factions' in Ottoman Egypt: a Reconsideration." In Philipp and Haarmann, *Mamluks in Egyptian Politics*, 107–17.

———. *The Politics of Households in Ottoman Egypt: The Rise of the Qazdaglis.* Cambridge: Cambridge University Press, 1997.

Herz Bey, Max. *Catalogue of the National Museum of Arab Art*, ed. Stanley Lane-Poole. London: B. Quaritch, 1896. [Original edition in French, 1895].

———. *La mosquée el-Rifaï au Caire, paru à l'occasion de la consécration de la mosquée.* Milan: H. Allegretti, 1906.

———. *La mosquée de Sultan Hassan au Caire*. Cairo: Comité de conservation des monuments de l'art arabe, 1899.

Heyworth-Dunne, James. *An Introduction to the History of Education in Modern Egypt*. London: Luzac and Co., 1939.

Hourani, Albert. *Arabic Thought in the Liberal Age, 1798–1939*. London and New York: Oxford University Press, 1962.

Huth, Hans. "The Evolution of Preservationism in Europe." *Journal of the American Society of Architectural Historians* 1, nos. 3–4 (July–October 1941): 5–12.

Ibn Abi al-Surur. *al-Muqtadab fi-ma wafaqa lughat ahl Misr min lughat al-'Arab*, edited by Hisham 'Abd al-'Aziz, 'Adil 'Abd al-Hamid al-'Adawi, and Madkur Thabit. Cairo: Akadimiyat al-Funun, 2006.

Ihsanoglu, Ekmeleddin and Salih Sa'adawi Salih. *al-Thaqafa al-turkiya fi misr; jawanib min al-tafa'ul al-hadari bayna al-misriyin wa-l-atrak*. Istanbul: Markaz al-Abhath li-l-Tarikh wa-l-Funun wa-l-Thaqafa al-Islamiya bi-Istanbul, 2003.

Ilbert, Robert. *Héliopolis: le Caire, 1905–1922: genèse d'une ville*. Paris: Éditions du Centre National de la Recherche Scientifique, 1981.

Irwin, Robert. *The Arabian Nights: A Companion*. London: Allen Lane, 1994.

Johansen, Baber. "Urban Structures in the View of Muslim Jurists: The Case of Damascus in the Early Nineteenth Century." *Revue du Monde Musulman et de la Méditerranée* 55–56 (1990): 94–100.

Jokilehto, Jukka. *A History of Architectural Conservation*. Oxford: Butterworth-Heinemann, 1999.

Jones, Owen. *The Grammar of Ornament*. London: Day and Son, 1856.

Joshi, M.C. and B.M. Pande. "The Archaeological Survey of India." *Architecture + Design* 6, no. 1 (1989): 29–31.

Kaptein, N.J.G. *Muhammad's Birthday Festival: Early History in the Central Muslim Lands and Development in the Muslim West until the 10th/16th Century*. Leiden: E.J. Brill, 1993.

Kedourie, Elie. *Afghani and 'Abduh: An Essay on Religious Unbelief and Political Activism in Modern Islam*. London: Cass, 1966.

Kerr, Malcolm H. *Islamic Reform: The Political and Legal Theories of Muhammad 'Abduh and Rashid Rida*. Berkeley: University of California Press, 1966.

Lahiri, Nayanjot. "Destruction or Conservation? Some Aspects of Monument Policy in British India (1899–1905)." In Layton et al., *Destruction and Conservation*, 264–75.

Lane, Edward William. *An Account of the Manners and Customs of the Modern Egyptians: The Definitive 1860 Edition*, introduced by Jason Thompson. Cairo: The American University in Cairo Press, 2003 [1860].

———. *Cairo Fifty Years Ago*, edited by Stanley Lane-Poole. London: John Murray, 1896.

———. *Description of Egypt*, edited by Jason Thompson. Cairo: The American University in Cairo Press, 2000.

Lane-Poole, Stanley. *The Art of the Saracens in Egypt*. London: Published for the Committee of Council on Education by Chapman and Hill Limited, 1886.

———. *Cairo: Sketches of its History, Monuments, and Social Life*. London: J.S. Virtue and Co., 1892.

———. *The Story of Cairo*. London: J. M. Dent and Co., 1902 [1906].

———. *The Story of the Nations: Mediaeval India under Mohammedan Rule, 1712–1764*. New York: G.P. Putnam's Sons, 1903.

Larzul, Sylvette. "Further Considerations on Galland's *Mille et une Nuits*: A Study of the Tales Told by Hanna." *Marvels & Tales: Journal of Fairy-Tale Studies* 18, no. 2 (2004): 258–71.

Layton, Robert, Peter G. Stone, and Julian Thomas, eds. *Destruction and Conservation of Cultural Property*. London and New York: Routledge, 2001.

Levanoni, Amalia. "Rank-and-file Mamluks versus Amirs: New Norms in the Mamluk Military Institution." In Philipp and Haarmann, *Mamluks in Egyptian Politics*, 17–31.

Lockman, Zachary. *Contending Visions of the Middle East: The History and Politics of Orientalism*. Cambridge: Cambridge University Press, 2004.

Lokhandwalla, Sh. T. "The Bohras, a Muslim Community of Gujarat." *Studia Islamica* 3 (1955): 117–35.

Mahdi, Muhsin. *Kitab alf layla wa-layla min usuliha al-'arabiya al-ula*. 3 vols. Leiden: E.J. Brill, 1995.

———. *The Thousand and One Nights*. Leiden: E.J. Brill, 1995.

Mahdy, Hossam M. "Travellers, Colonisers and Conservationists." In Starkey and Starkey, *Travellers in Egypt*, 157–67.

al-Majlis al-A'la li-l-Athar. *al-Qahira al-tarikhiya*. [Arabic edition]. *Historic Cairo* [English edition] Cairo: al-Majlis al-A'la li-l-Athar, 2002.

Makdisi, Ussama. "Mapping the Orient: Non-western Modernization, Imperialism, and the End of Romanticism." In *Nineteenth Century Geographies: The Transformation of Space from the Victorian Age to the American Century*, edited by Helena Michie and Ronald R. Thomas, 40–54. New Brunswick, NJ: Rutgers University Press, 2003.

———. "Ottoman Orientalism." *The American Historical Review* 107 (2002): 768–96.

———. "The 'Rediscovery' of Baalbek: A Metaphor for Empire in the Nineteenth Century." In *Baalbek: Image and Monument, 1898–1998*, edited by Hélène Sader, Thomas Scheffler, and Angelka Neuwirth, 137–56. Beirut: In Kommission bei Franz Steiner Verlag, 1998.

Marzolph, Ulrich. "The *Arabian Nights* in Comparative Folk Narrative Research." In Yamanaka and Nishio, *Arabian Nights and Orientalism*, 3–24.

Marzolph, Ulrich and Richard van Leeuwen. *The Arabian Nights Encyclopedia*. 2 vols. Santa Barbara, CA: ABC-CLIO, 2004.

McLeod, Hugh. "Protestantism and British National Identity, 1815–1945." In *Nation and Religion: Perspectives on Europe and Asia*, edited by Peter van der Veer and Hartmut Lehmann, 44–70. Princeton: Princeton University Press, 1999.

McPherson, J.W. *The Moulids of Egypt (Egyptian Saints-Days)*. Cairo: Ptd. N.M. Press, 1941.

Meinecke, Michael. *Islamic Cairo: Architectural Conservation and Urban Development of the Historic Centre. Proceedings of a Seminar Organised by the Goethe Institute, Cairo, October 1–5, 1978*. London: Deutsches Archäologisches Institut Abteilung Kairo, 1980.

Meri, Josef. *The Cult of Saints among Muslims and Jews in Medieval Syria*. Oxford and New York: Oxford University Press, 2002.

Metcalf, Thomas R. *Ideologies of the Raj*. The New Cambridge History of India, edited by Gordon Johnson. Cambridge: Cambridge University Press, 1995.

———. *An Imperial Vision: Indian Architecture and Britain's Raj.* Berkeley and Los Angeles: University of California Press, 1989.

———. "Past and Present: Towards an Aesthetics of Colonialism." In *Paradigms of Indian Architecture, Space and Time in Representation and Design*, edited by G.H.R. Tillotson, 12–25. Surrey: Curzon Press, 1998.

Mitchell, Timothy. *Colonising Egypt.* Cambridge: Cambridge University Press, 1988.

Mubarak, 'Ali. *al-Khitat al-tawfiqiya al-jadida li-Misr al-Qahira wa-muduniha wa-biladiha al-qadima wa-l-shahira.* Bulaq: al-Matba'a al-Kubra al-Amiriya, 1886–89. 2nd ed., Cairo: Dar al-Kutub, 1969.

Muir, Percy. *Victorian Illustrated Books.* New York: Praeger Publishers, 1971.

Murphy, Kevin D. *Memory and Modernity: Viollet-le-Duc at Vézelay.* University Park, PA: Pennsylvania State University Press, 2000.

Murray, John. *A Handbook for Travellers in Lower and Upper Egypt; Including Descriptions of the Course of the Nile through Egypt and Nubia, Alexandria, Cairo, the Pyramids, Thebes, the Suez Canal, the Peninsula of Mount Sinai, the Oases, the Fayoom, &c* . . . London: John Murray, 1888.

Ormos, István. "The Correspondence of Ignaz Goldziher and Max Herz." In *Goldziher Memorial Conference, June 21-22, 2000, Budapest, Oriental Collection, Library of the Hungarian Academy of Sciences*, edited by Éva Apor and István Ormos, 159–201. Budapest: Library of the Hungarian Academy of Sciences, 2005.

———. "Preservation and Restoration: The Methods of Max Herz Pasha, Chief Architect of the Comité de Conservation des Monuments de l'Art Arabe, 1890–1914." In *Historians in Cairo: Essays in Honor of George Scanlon*, edited by Jill Edwards, 123–53. Cairo: The American University in Cairo Press, 2002.

Owen, Roger. "The Cairo Building Industry and the Building Boom of 1897–1907." In *Colloque international sur l'histoire du Caire, 25 mars–5 avril 1969*, 337–50. Cairo: General Egyptian Book Organization, 1969.

———. "The Influence of Lord Cromer's Indian Experience on British Policy in Egypt, 1883–1907." *St. Antony's Papers* 17 (1965): 109–39.

———. *Lord Cromer: Victorian Imperialist, Edwardian Proconsul.* Oxford: Oxford University Press, 2004.

Pangalo, George. "The Story of Some Old Friends." *The Cosmopolitan* 23 (1897): 277–88.

Parker, Richard and Robin Sabin. *A Practical Guide to Islamic Monuments in Cairo.* 1st ed. Cairo: The American University in Cairo Press, 1974.

———. *A Practical Guide to Islamic Monuments in Cairo.* 2nd ed. Cairo: The American University in Cairo Press, 1981.

Parker, Richard, Robin Sabin, and Caroline Williams. *Islamic Monuments in Cairo: A Practical Guide.* 3rd ed. Cairo: The American University in Cairo Press, 1985.

———. *Islamic Monuments in Cairo: A Practical Guide.* 4th ed. Cairo: The American University in Cairo Press, 1993.

Pelizzari, Maria Antonella, ed. *Traces of India: Photography, Architecture, and the Politics of Representation, 1850–1900.* Montreal: Canadian Centre for Architecture; New Haven and London: Yale Center for British Art [by] Yale University Press, 2003.

Petry, Carl F., ed. *The Cambridge History of Egypt.* Vol. 1, *Islamic Egypt, 640–1517.* Cambridge: Cambridge University Press, 1998.

Philipp, Thomas and Ulrich Haarmann, eds. *The Mamluks in Egyptian Politics and Society.* Cambridge: Cambridge University Press, 1998.

Philipp, Thomas and Moshe Perlmann, eds. *'Abd al-Rahman al-Jabarti's History of Egypt: 'Aja'ib al-athar fi'l-tarajim wa'l-akhbar.* Stuttgart: Franz Steiner Verlag, 1994.

Prisse d'Avennes. *L'art arabe d'après les monuments du Kaire.* Paris: Vve. A. Morel, 1869–77.

al-Qadi, Wadad. "East and West in 'Ali Mubarak's *Alamuddin.*" In *Intellectual Life in the Arab East, 1890–1939*, edited by Marwan R. Buheiry, 21–37. Beirut: American University of Beirut, 1981.

Rabbat, Nasser. "The Formation of the Neo-Mamluk Style in Modern Egypt." In *The Education of the Architect: Historiography, Urbanism, and the Growth of Architectural Knowledge. Essays Presented to Stanford Anderson on his Sixty-second Birthday*, edited by M. Pollak, 363–86. Cambridge, MA: MIT Press, 1997.

———. "Restoration Projects in Islamic Cairo Critiqued." *Medina* 13 (2000): 48–51.

———. *Thaqafat al-bina' wa-bina' al-thaqafa: buhuth wa-maqalat fi naqd wa-tarikh al-'imara, 1985–2000.* Beirut: Riad al-Rayyis, 2002.

Raymond, André. *Cairo.* Translated by Willard Wood. Cambridge, MA: Harvard University Press, 2000. Originally published as *Le Caire* (Paris: Fayard, 1993).

———. "Essai de géographie des quartiers de résidence aristocratique au Caire au XVIIIème siècle." *Journal of the Economic and Social History of the Orient* 6 (1963): 58–103.

———. "La population du Caire et de l'Egypte à l'époque ottomane et sous Muhammad 'Ali." In *Mémorial Ömer Lûtfi Barkan.* Paris: Librairie d'Amérique et d'Orient Adrien Maisonneuve, 1980.

Reardon, Bernard M.G. *Religious Thought in the Victorian Age: A Survey from Coleridge to Gore.* 2nd ed. London: Longman, 1995.

Reid, Donald M. "Cultural Imperialism and Nationalism: The Struggle to Define and Control the Heritage of Arab Art in Egypt." *International Journal of Middle East Studies* 24 (1992): 57–76.

———. "Indigenous Egyptology: The Decolonization of a Profession?" *Journal of the American Oriental Society* 105 (1985): 233–46.

———. *Whose Pharaohs? Archaeology, Museums, and Egyptian National Identity from Napoleon to World War I.* Berkeley: University of California Press, 2002.

Reimer, Michael J. "Contradiction and Consciousness in Ali Mubarak's Description of al-Azhar." *International Journal of Middle East Studies* 29 (1997): 53–69.

———. "Urban Government and Administration in Egypt, 1805–1914." *Die Welt des Islams*, New Series 39 (1999): 289–318.

Reynolds-Ball, Eustace. *City of the Caliphs: A Popular Study of Cairo and its Environs and the Nile and its Environs.* Boston: Estes and Lauriat, 1897.

Richards, Donald S. "Mamluk Amirs and their Families and Households." In Philipp and Haarmann, *Mamluks in Egyptian Politics*, 32–54.

Rida, Muhammad Rashid. *Tarikh al-ustadh al-imam al-shaykh Muhammad 'Abduh*. 3 vols. in 4. Cairo: Dar al-Fadila, 2003 [1906–31].

Rizk, Younan Labib. "The Development of the Ministerial System in Egypt, 1878–1923." In *The State and its Servants: Administration in Egypt from Ottoman Times to the Present*, edited by Nelly Hanna, 88–97. Cairo: The American University in Cairo Press, 1995.

Robinson, Ronald and John Gallagher. *Africa and the Victorians: The Climax of Imperialism in the Dark Continent*. New York: St. Martin's Press, 1961.

Ronen, Raz. "The Transparent Mirror: Arab Intellectuals and Orientalism, 1798–1950." PhD diss., Princeton University, 1997.

Said, Edward. *Orientalism*. New York: Pantheon Books, 1978.

Saifuddin, Ja'far us Sadiq M. *al-Aqmar, a Living Testimony to the Fatemiyeen*. London: Graphico Printing, 2000.

———. *al-Juyushi, a Vision of the Fatemiyeen*. London: Graphico Printing, 2002.

Sakr, Tarek Mohamed Refaat. *Early Twentieth-Century Islamic Architecture in Cairo*. Cairo: The American University in Cairo Press, 1993.

Sallis, Eva. *Sheherazade through the Looking Glass: The Metamorphosis of the "Thousand and One Nights."* Surrey: Curzon Press, 1999.

Sanders, Paula. "Bohra Architecture and the Restsoration of Fatimid Culture." In *L'Égypte fatimide: Son art et son histoire. Actes du colloque organisé à Paris, le 28–30 mai 1998*, edited by Marianne Barrucand, 159–65. Paris: Presses de l'Université de Paris-Sorbonne, 1999.

———. "The Contest over Context: Fatimid Cairo in the Twentieth Century. In *Text and Context in Islamic Societies: Sixteenth Girogio Levi Della Vida Conference Papers*, edited by Irene A. Bierman, 123–47. Reading, UK: Ithaca Press, 2004.

———. "The Victorian Invention of Medieval Egypt." *Bulletin of the Middle East Studies Association* 37 (2003): 179–98.

Sayyid-Marsot, Afaf Lutfi. *Egypt and Cromer: A Study in Anglo-Indian Relations*. New York: Praeger, 1969 [1968].

Schimmel, Annemarie. *Islam in the Indian Subcontinent.* Leiden and Köln: E.J. Brill, 1980.

Schölch, Alexander. *Egypt for the Egyptians! The Socio-political Crisis in Egypt 1878–1882.* London: Ithaca Press, 1981. Originally published as *Ägypten den Ägyptern: Die politische und gesellschaftliche Krise der Jahre 1878–1882 in Ägypten* (Zurich: Atlantis Verlag, 1972).

El-Shamy, Hasan. "Oral Traditional Tales and the *Thousand Nights and a Night*: The Demographic Factor." In *The Telling of Stories: Approaches to a Traditional Craft: A Symposium*, edited by Morten Nøjgaard et al. [Odense]: Odense University Press, 1990.

———. *A Motif Index of The Thousand and One Nights.* Bloomington, IN: Indiana University Press, 2006.

———. *Types of the Folktale in the Arab World: A Demographically Oriented Tale-type Index.* Bloomington and Indianapolis: Indiana University Press, 2004.

Shaykhuh, Mustafa 'Abd Allah. *al-Athar al-islamiya fi Misr min al-fath al-'arabi hatta nihayat al-'asr al-ayyubi.* Cairo: Maktabat al-Nahda al-Misriya, 1992.

Simonowitz, David. "On the Cutting Edges of Dhu'l-Fiqar: Authority and the Discourse of Architecture in the Musta'li-Tayyibi and Nizari Communities." PhD diss., University of California, Los Angeles, 2004.

Sladen, Douglas. *Oriental Cairo: The City of the "Arabian Nights."* London: Hurst and Blackett, 1911.

Speiser, Philipp. *Die Geschichte der Erhaltung arabischer Baudenkmäler in Ägypten. Die Restaurierung der Madrasa Tatar al Higaziya und des Sabil Kuttab Abde ar-Rahman Kathuda im Rahmen des Darb-al-Qirmiz-Projektes in Kairo.* Abhandlungen des Deutschen Archäologischen Instituts Kairo, Islamische Reihe, 8. Heidelberg: Heidelberger Orientverlag, 2001.

Starkey, Paul and Janet Starkey, eds. *Travellers in Egypt.* London and New York: I.B. Tauris, 1998.

Starrett, Gregory. *Putting Islam to Work: Education, Politics, and Religious Transformation in Egypt.* Berkeley: University of California Press, 1998.

Tahtawi, Rifa'a Rafi'. *An Imam in Paris: Account of a Stay in France by an Egyptian Cleric (1826–1831)*. Translated by Daniel L. Newman. London: Saqi Books, 2004.

Taylor, Christopher. *In the Vicinity of the Righteous: Ziyara and the Veneration of Muslim Saints in Late Medieval Egypt*. Leiden: E.J. Brill, 1998.

Thompson, Jason. "Edward William Lane's 'Description of Egypt.'" *International Journal of Middle East Studies* 28 (1996): 565–83.

———. "'Of the 'Osma'nlees, or Turks': An Unpublished Chapter from Edward William Lane's *Manners and Customs of the Modern Egyptians*." *Turkish Studies Association Bulletin* 19 (1995): 19–39.

Tignor, Robert L. "The 'Indianization' of the Egyptian Administration under British Rule." *The American Historical Review* 68, no. 3 (1963): 636–61.

———. "Lord Cromer on Islam." *The Muslim World* 52 (1962): 223–33.

———. *Modernization and British Colonial Rule in Egypt, 1882–1914*. Princeton: Princeton University Press, 1966.

van der Veer, Peter. *Imperial Encounters: Religion and Modernity in India and Britain*. Princeton: Princeton University Press, 2001.

Walker, Rev. F.A. *Nine Hundred Miles up the Nile*. London: West, Newman and Co., 1884.

Warner, Nicholas. *The Monuments of Historic Cairo: A Map and Descriptive Catalogue*. Cairo: The American University in Cairo Press, 2005.

Watenpaugh, Keith. *Being Modern in the Middle East: Nationalism, Colonialism, and the Arab Middle Class*. Princeton: Princeton University Press, 2006.

Wilkinson, Sir John Gardner. *Hand-book for Travellers in Egypt: Including Descriptions of the Course of the Nile to the Second Cataract, Alexandria, Cairo, the Pyramids, and Thebes, the Overland Transit to India, the Peninsula of Mount Sinai, the Oases etc.* London: John Murray, 1847.

———. *A Handbook for Travellers in Egypt: Including Descriptions of the Course of the Nile to the Second Cataract, Alexandria, Cairo, the Pyramids, and Thebes, the Overland Transit to India, the Peninsula of Mount Sinai, the Oases, &c. Condensed from 'Modern Egypt and Thebes.'* London: John Murray, 1867.

Williams, Caroline. "The Cult of 'Alid Saints in the Fatimid Monuments of Cairo." *Muqarnas* 1 (1983): 37–52, 3 (1985): 39–60.

———. *Islamic Monuments in Cairo: The Practical Guide*. 5th ed. Cairo and New York: The American University in Cairo Press, 2002.

Winter, Michael. "Attitudes Toward the Ottomans in Egyptian Historiography during Ottoman Rule." In *The Historiography of Islamic Egypt (c. 950–1800)*, edited by Hugh Kennedy, 195–210. Leiden: E.J. Brill, 2001.

———. *Egyptian Society under Ottoman Rule, 1517–1798*. London and New York: Routledge, 1992.

———. "The Re-emergence of the Mamluks following the Ottoman Conquest of Egypt." In Philipp and Haarmann, *Mamluks in Egyptian Politics*, 87–106.

———. *Society and Religion in Early Ottoman Egypt: Studies in the Writings of 'Abd al-Wahhab al-Sha'rani*. New Brunswick, NJ: Transaction Books, 1982.

———. "Turks, Arabs, and Mamluks in the Army of Ottoman Egypt." *Wiener Zeitschrift für die Kunde des Morgenlandes* 72 (1980): 97–122.

Wizarat al-Thaqafa, Hay'at al-Athar al-Misriya. *al-Qahira al-islamiya: jami' 'Amru ibn al-'As*. Cairo: Matba'at Hay'at al-Athar al-Misriya, 1986.

———. *al-Qahira al-islamiya: masajid maydan Salah al-Din*. Cairo: Matba'at Hay'at al-Athar al-Misriya, 1986.

———. *al-Qahira al-islamiya: al-mashhad al-husayni*. Cairo: Matba'at Hay'at al-Athar al-Misriya, 1985.

———. n.d. *al-Qahira al-islamiya: qasr al-amir Bashtak, sabil wa-kuttab 'Abd al-Rahman Katkhuda*. Cairo: Matba'at Hay'at al-Athar al-Misriya.

Yamanaka, Yuriko and Tetsuo Nishio, eds. *The Arabian Nights and Orientalism: Perspectives from East and West*. London: I.B. Tauris, 2006.

Yasushi, Kosugi. "*Al-Manar Revisited: the 'Lighthouse' of the Islamic Revival*." In Dudoignon et al., *Intellectuals in the Modern Islamic World*, 3–39.

Zack, Elisabeth. "Yusuf al-Maghribi's Egyptian-Arabic Word List. A Unique Manuscript in the St. Petersburg State University Library." *Manuscripta Orientalia: International Journal for Oriental Manuscript Research* 7, no. 3 (2001): 46–49.

Zaki, 'Abd al-Rahman. *al-Qahira: tarikhuha wa-atharuha*. Cairo: al-Dar al-Misriya li-l-Ta'lif wa-l-Tarjama, 1966.

Index